RESTAURANT
REVIEW JOURNAL

Copyright © Maureen Willis
All Rights Reserved.
No part of this publication can be used or reproduced in any manner whatsoever without written permission except in the case of brief quotations embodied in critical articles and reviews.
First Edition: 2021

This Belongs To:

Restaurant Name:

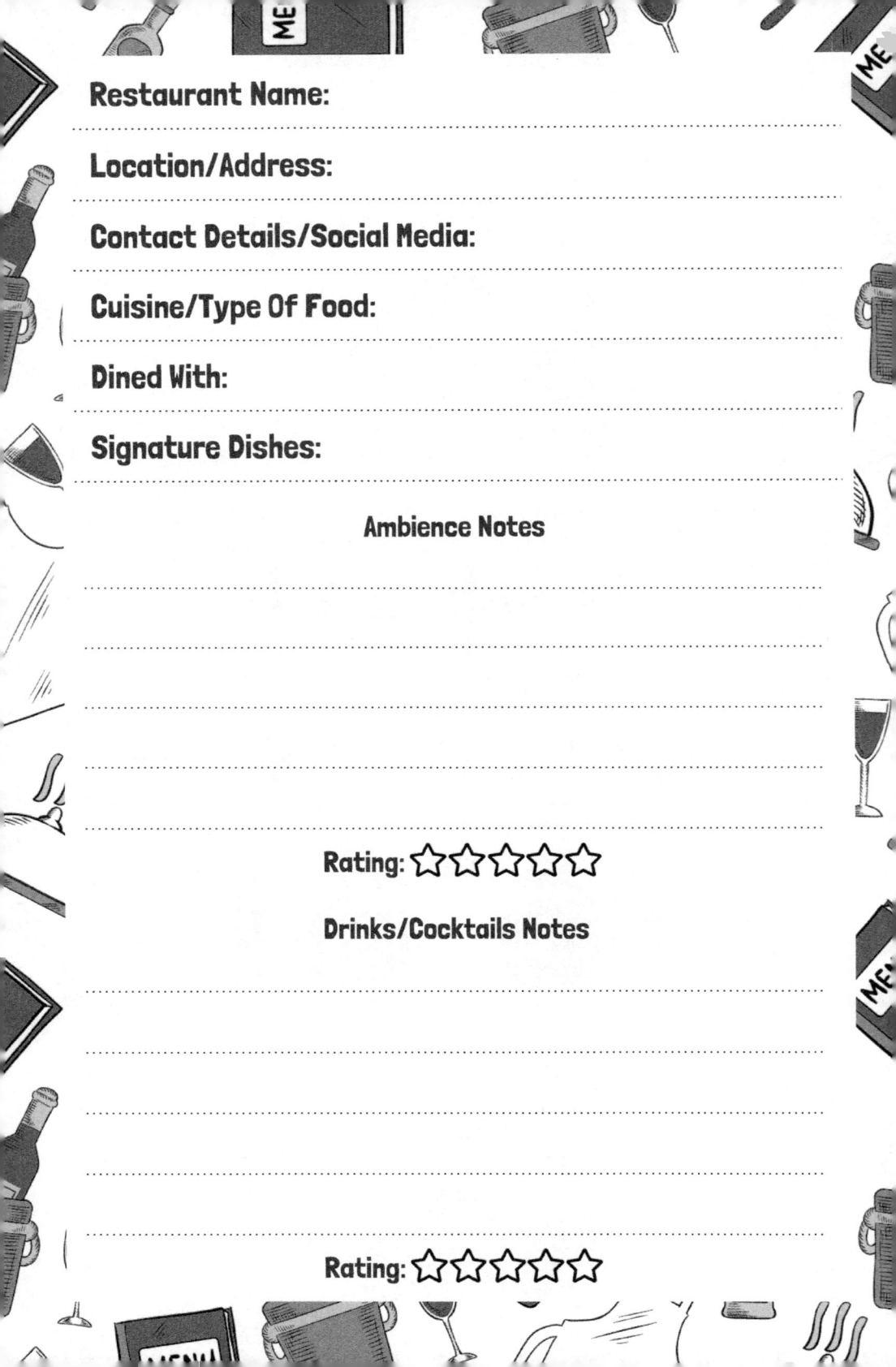

Location/Address:

Contact Details/Social Media:

Cuisine/Type Of Food:

Dined With:

Signature Dishes:

Ambience Notes

Rating: ☆☆☆☆☆

Drinks/Cocktails Notes

Rating: ☆☆☆☆☆

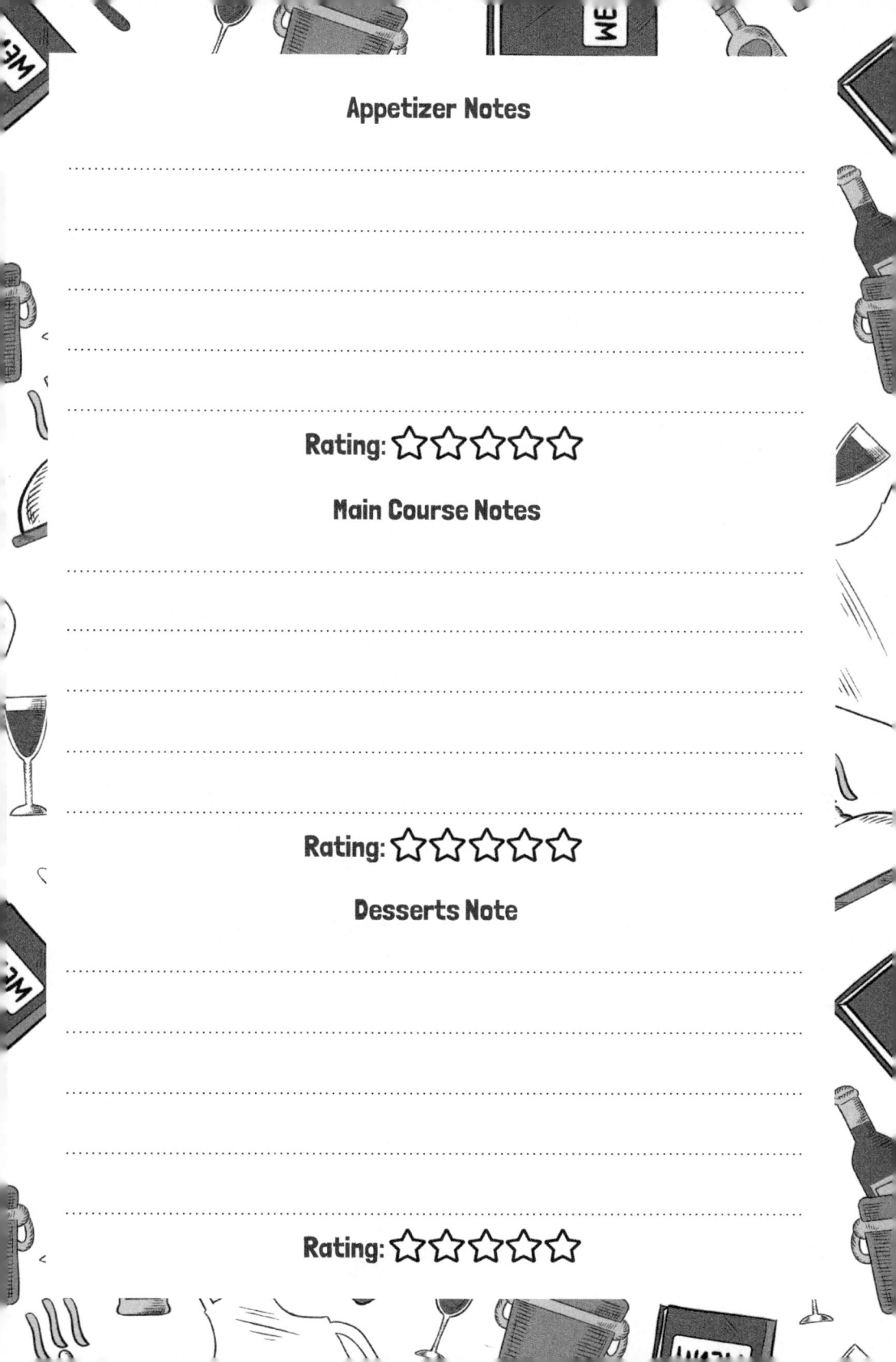

Appetizer Notes

....
....
....
....

Rating: ☆☆☆☆☆

Main Course Notes

....
....
....
....

Rating: ☆☆☆☆☆

Desserts Note

....
....
....
....

Rating: ☆☆☆☆☆

Restaurant Name:

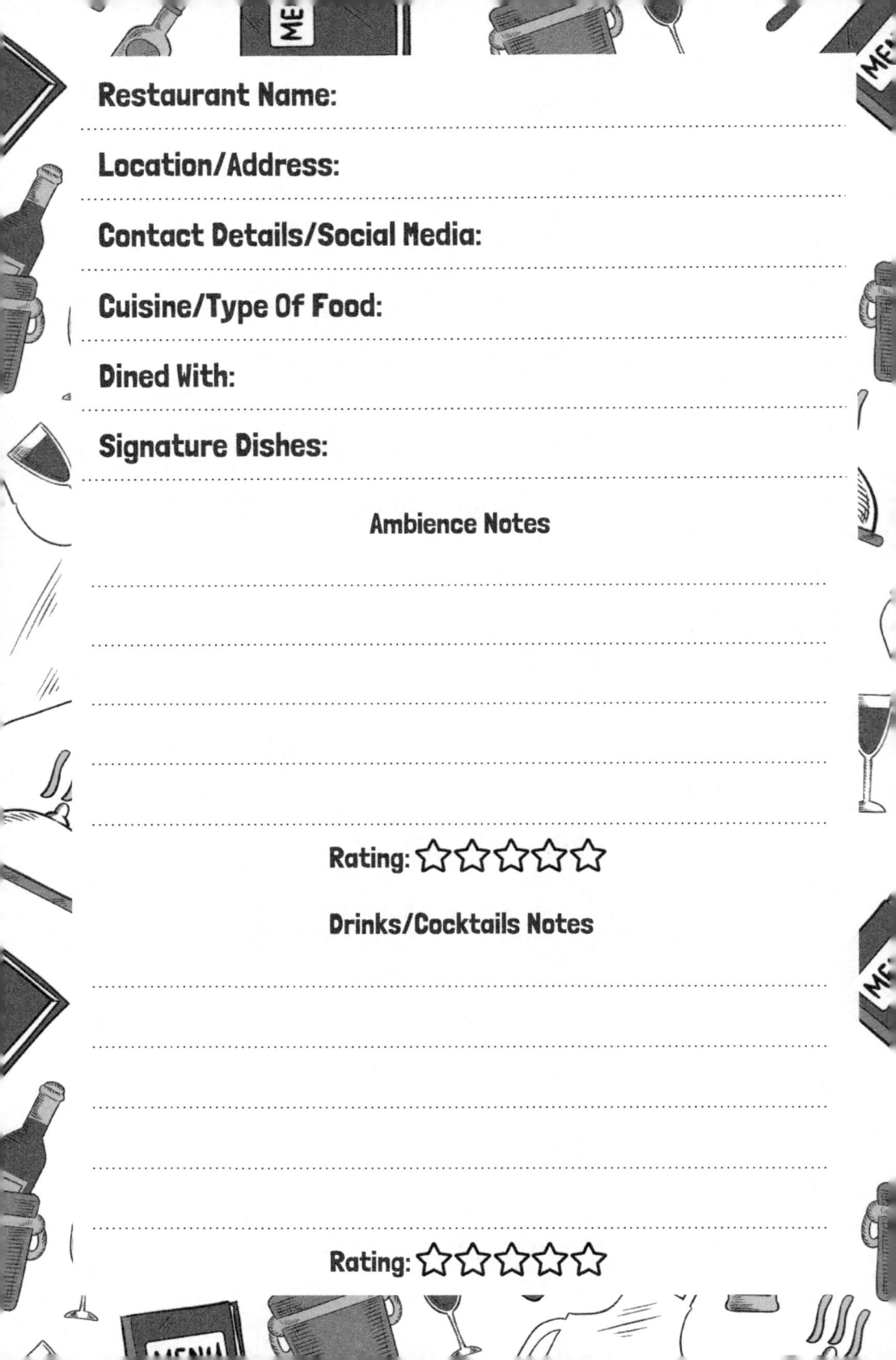

Location/Address:

Contact Details/Social Media:

Cuisine/Type Of Food:

Dined With:

Signature Dishes:

Ambience Notes

Rating: ☆☆☆☆☆

Drinks/Cocktails Notes

Rating: ☆☆☆☆☆

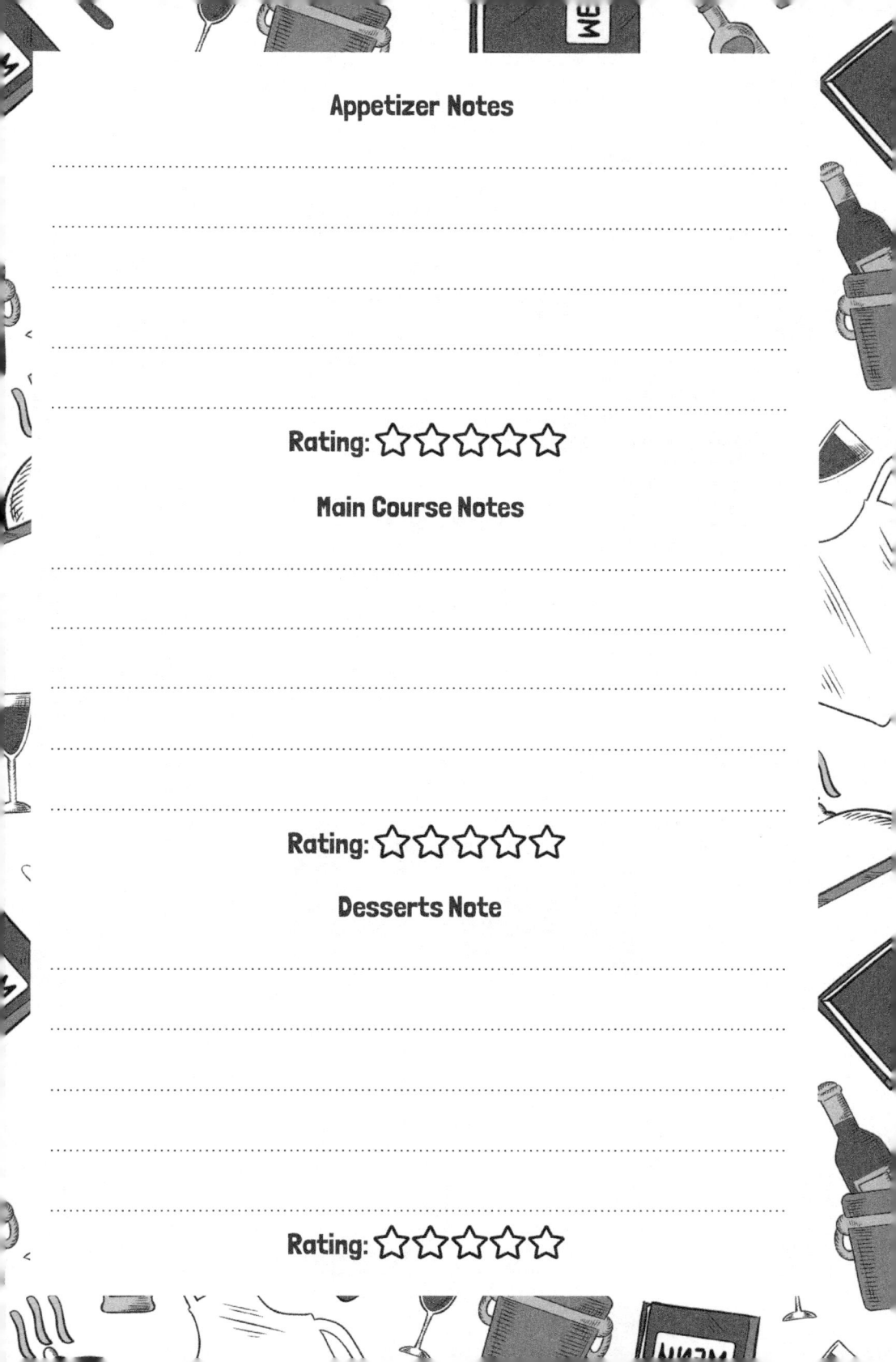

Appetizer Notes

....

....

....

....

....

Rating: ☆☆☆☆☆

Main Course Notes

....

....

....

....

....

Rating: ☆☆☆☆☆

Desserts Note

....

....

....

....

....

Rating: ☆☆☆☆☆

Restaurant Name:

Location/Address:

Contact Details/Social Media:

Cuisine/Type Of Food:

Dined With:

Signature Dishes:

Ambience Notes

Rating: ☆☆☆☆☆

Drinks/Cocktails Notes

Rating: ☆☆☆☆☆

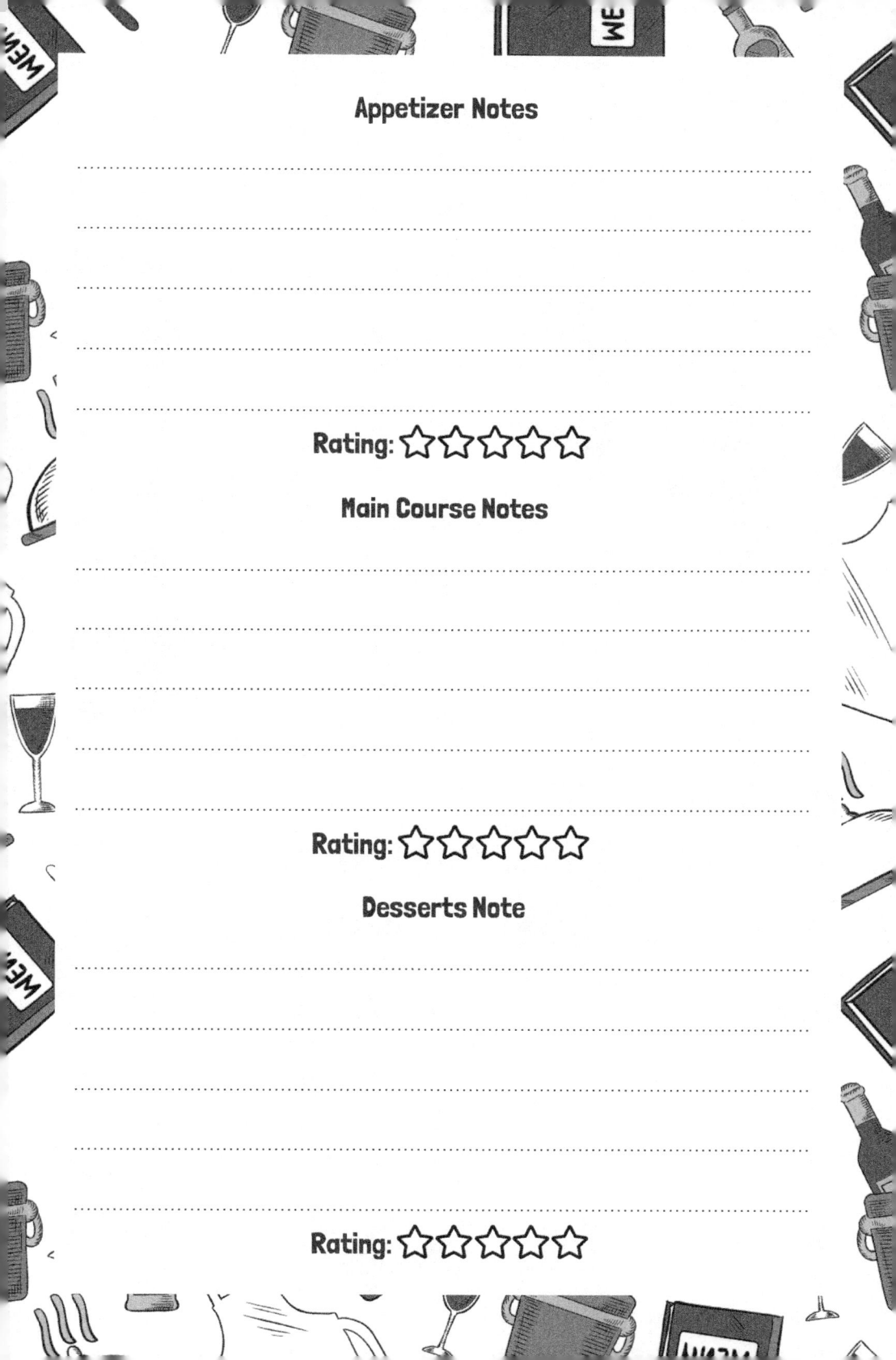

Appetizer Notes

....

....

....

....

Rating: ☆☆☆☆☆

Main Course Notes

....

....

....

....

Rating: ☆☆☆☆☆

Desserts Note

....

....

....

....

Rating: ☆☆☆☆☆

Restaurant Name:

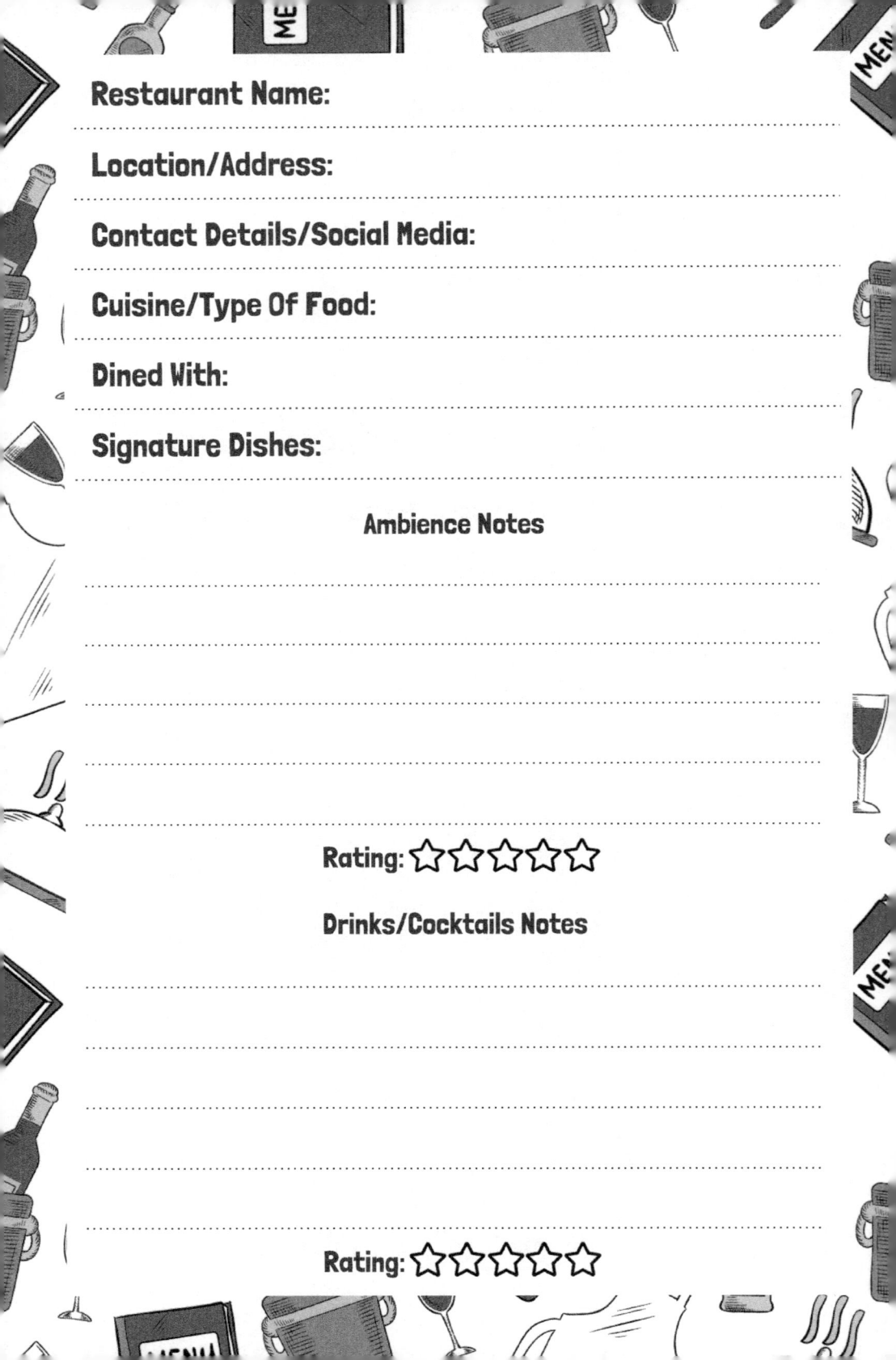

Location/Address:

Contact Details/Social Media:

Cuisine/Type Of Food:

Dined With:

Signature Dishes:

Ambience Notes

Rating: ☆☆☆☆☆

Drinks/Cocktails Notes

Rating: ☆☆☆☆☆

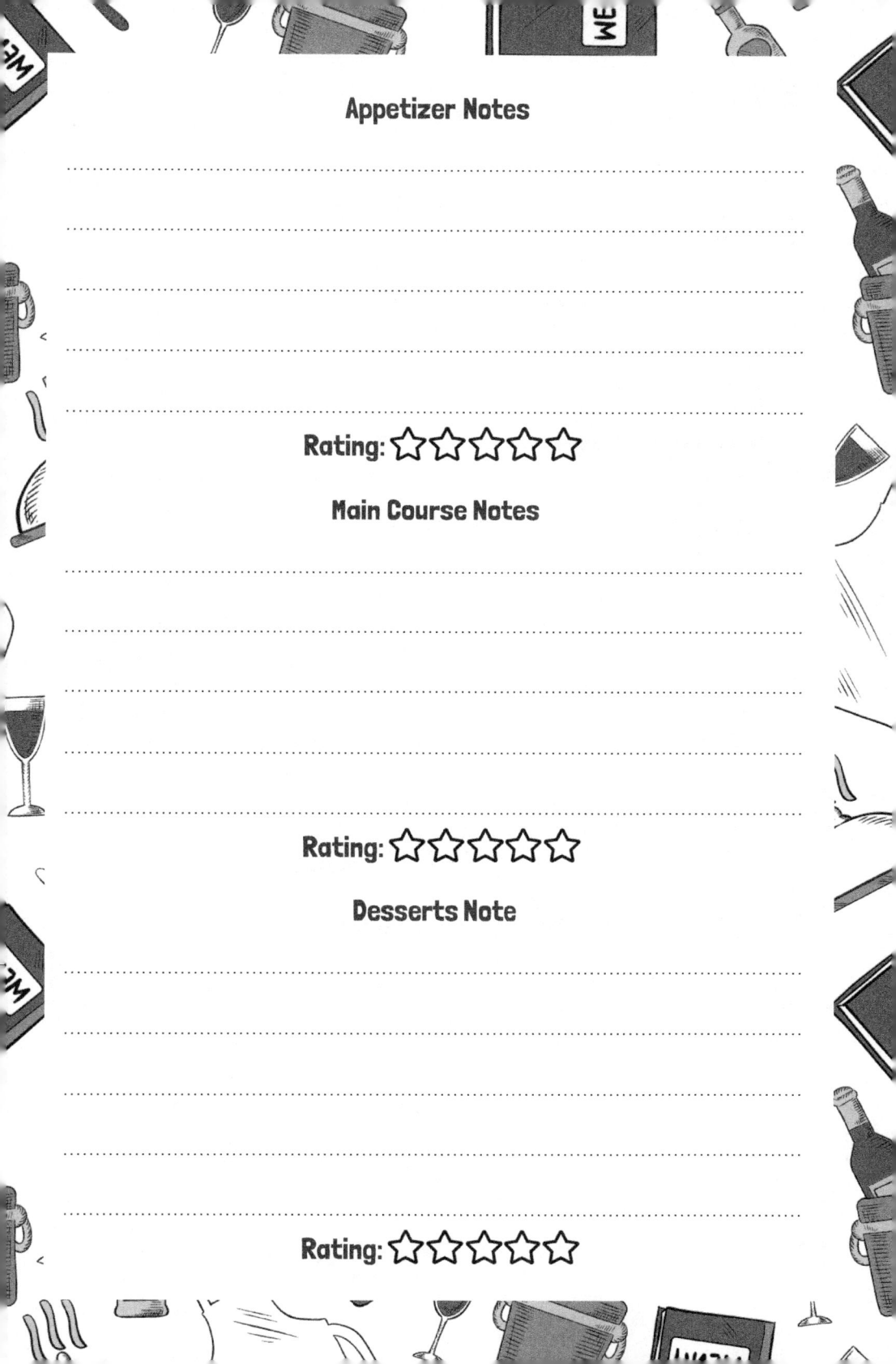

Appetizer Notes

....

....

....

....

....

Rating: ☆☆☆☆☆

Main Course Notes

....

....

....

....

....

Rating: ☆☆☆☆☆

Desserts Note

....

....

....

....

....

Rating: ☆☆☆☆☆

Restaurant Name:

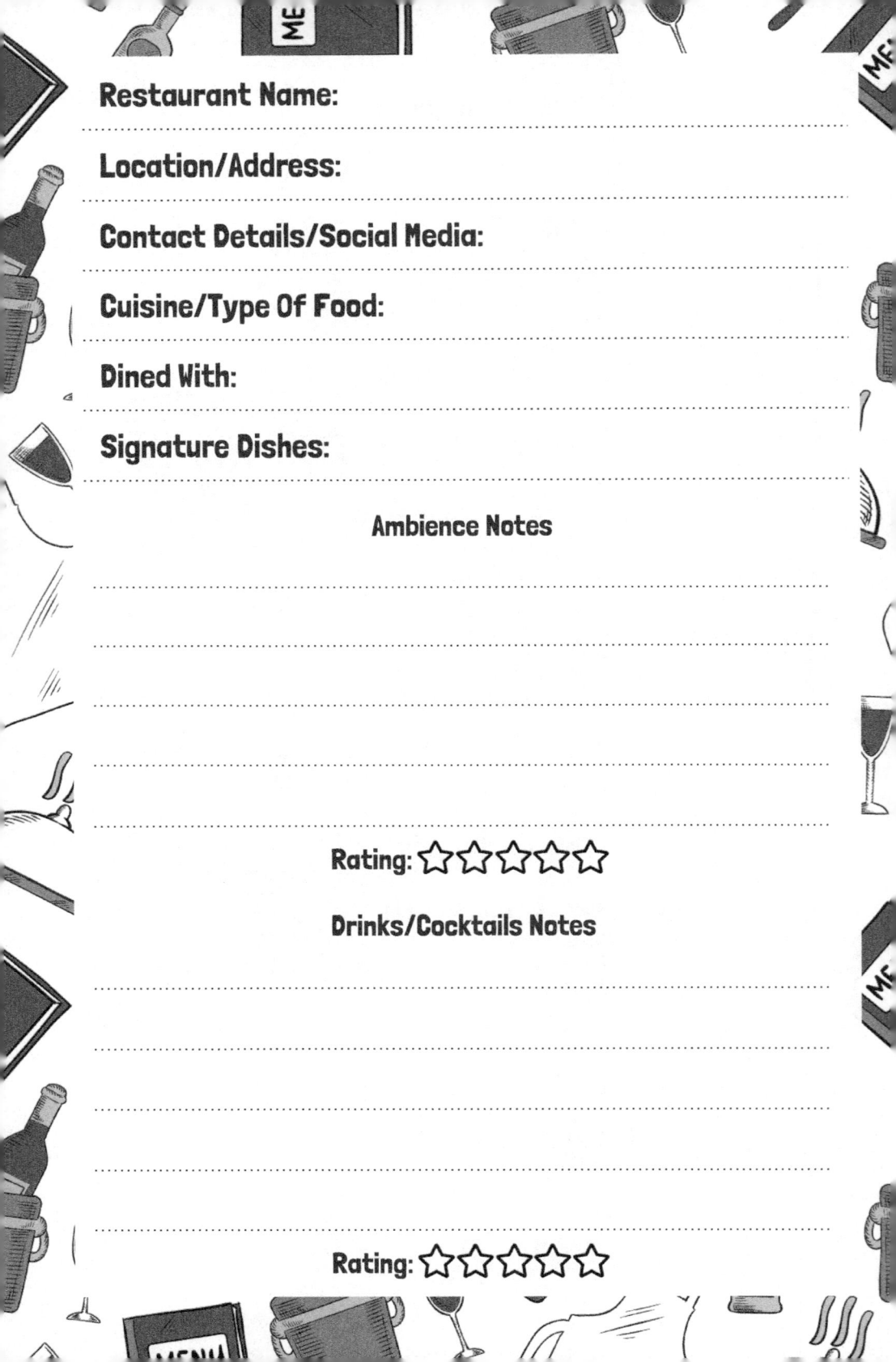

Location/Address:

Contact Details/Social Media:

Cuisine/Type Of Food:

Dined With:

Signature Dishes:

Ambience Notes

Rating: ☆☆☆☆☆

Drinks/Cocktails Notes

Rating: ☆☆☆☆☆

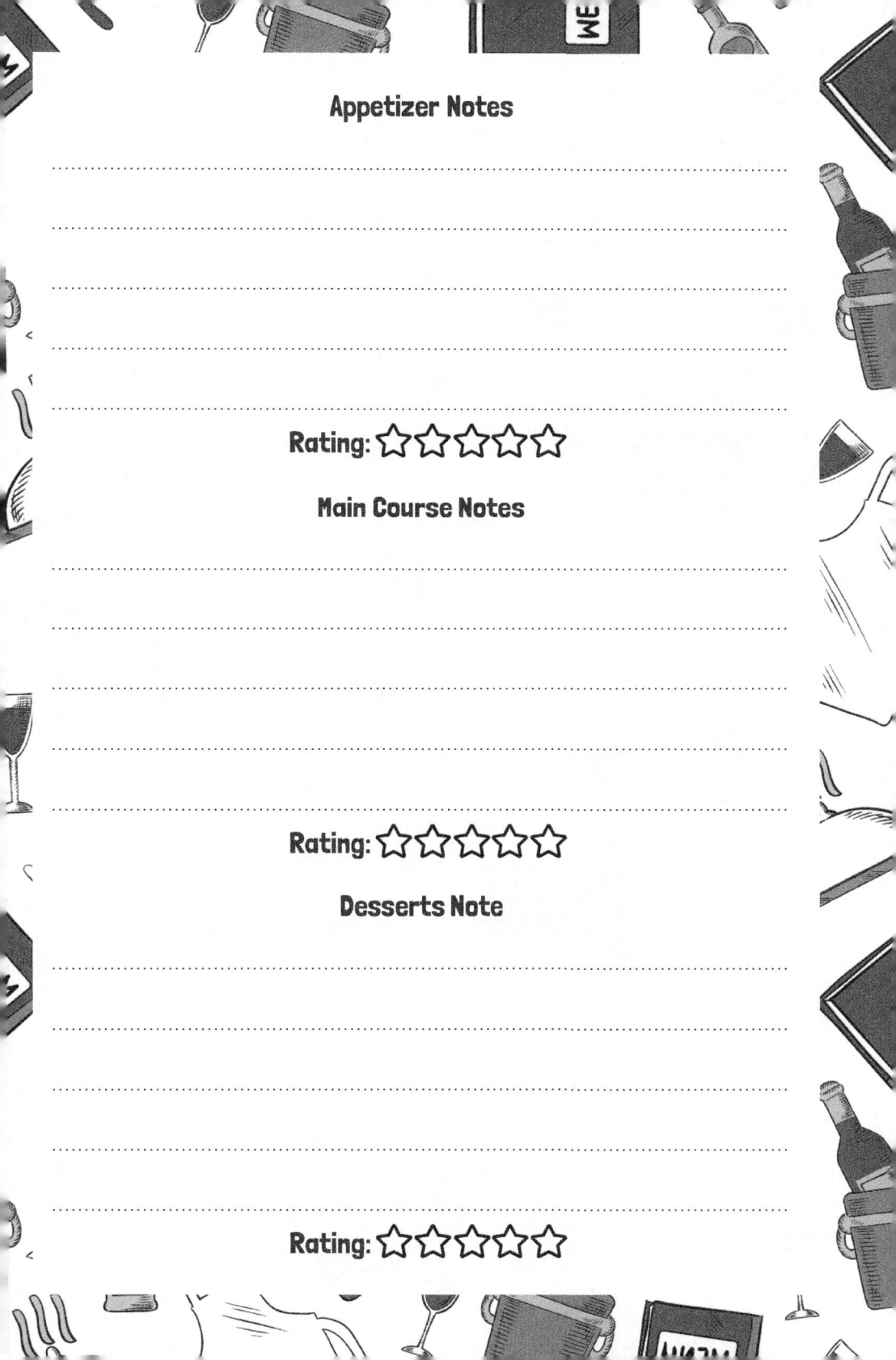

Appetizer Notes

....

....

....

....

Rating: ☆☆☆☆☆

Main Course Notes

....

....

....

....

Rating: ☆☆☆☆☆

Desserts Note

....

....

....

....

Rating: ☆☆☆☆☆

Restaurant Name:

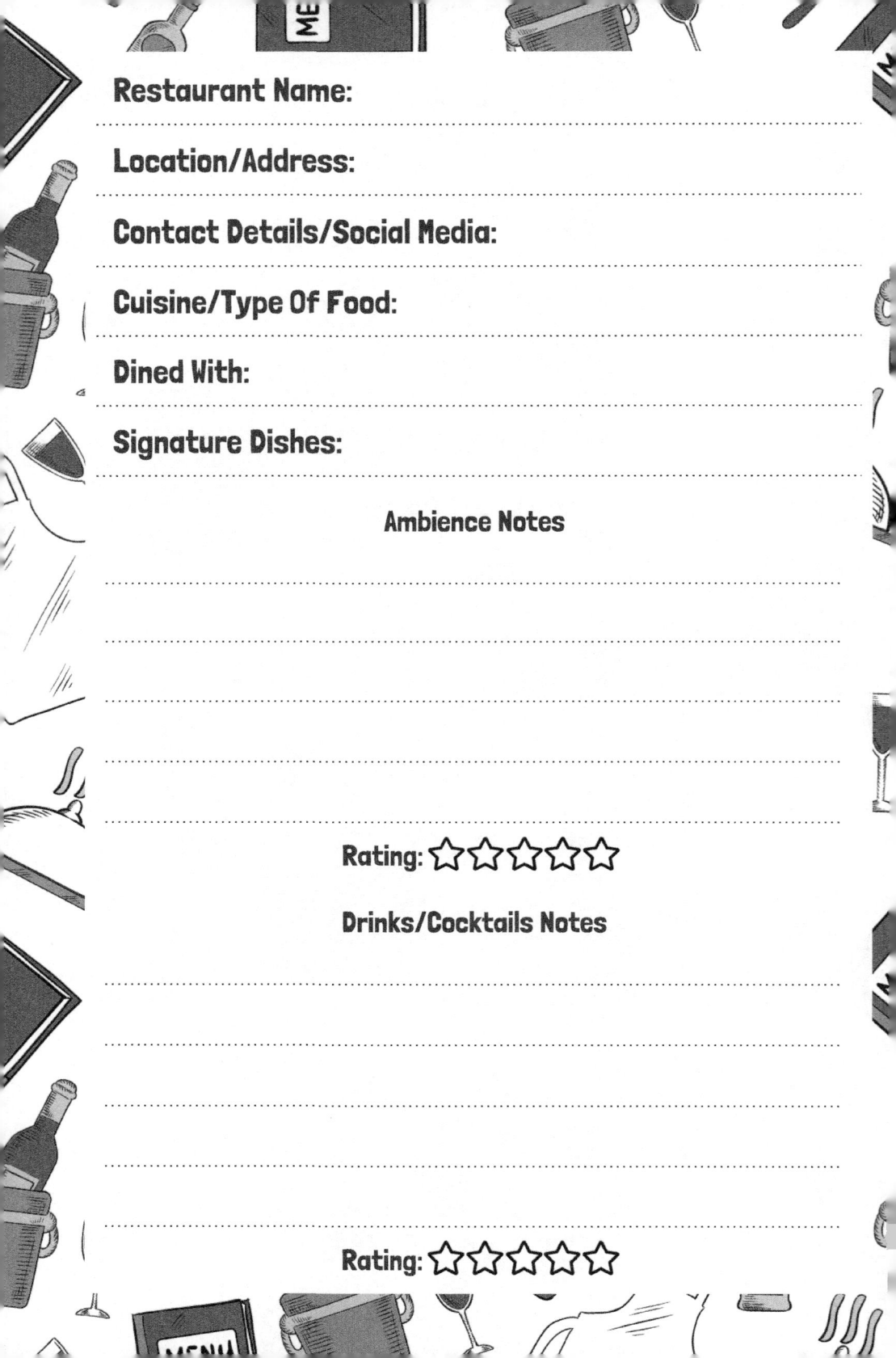

Location/Address:

Contact Details/Social Media:

Cuisine/Type Of Food:

Dined With:

Signature Dishes:

Ambience Notes

Rating: ☆☆☆☆☆

Drinks/Cocktails Notes

Rating: ☆☆☆☆☆

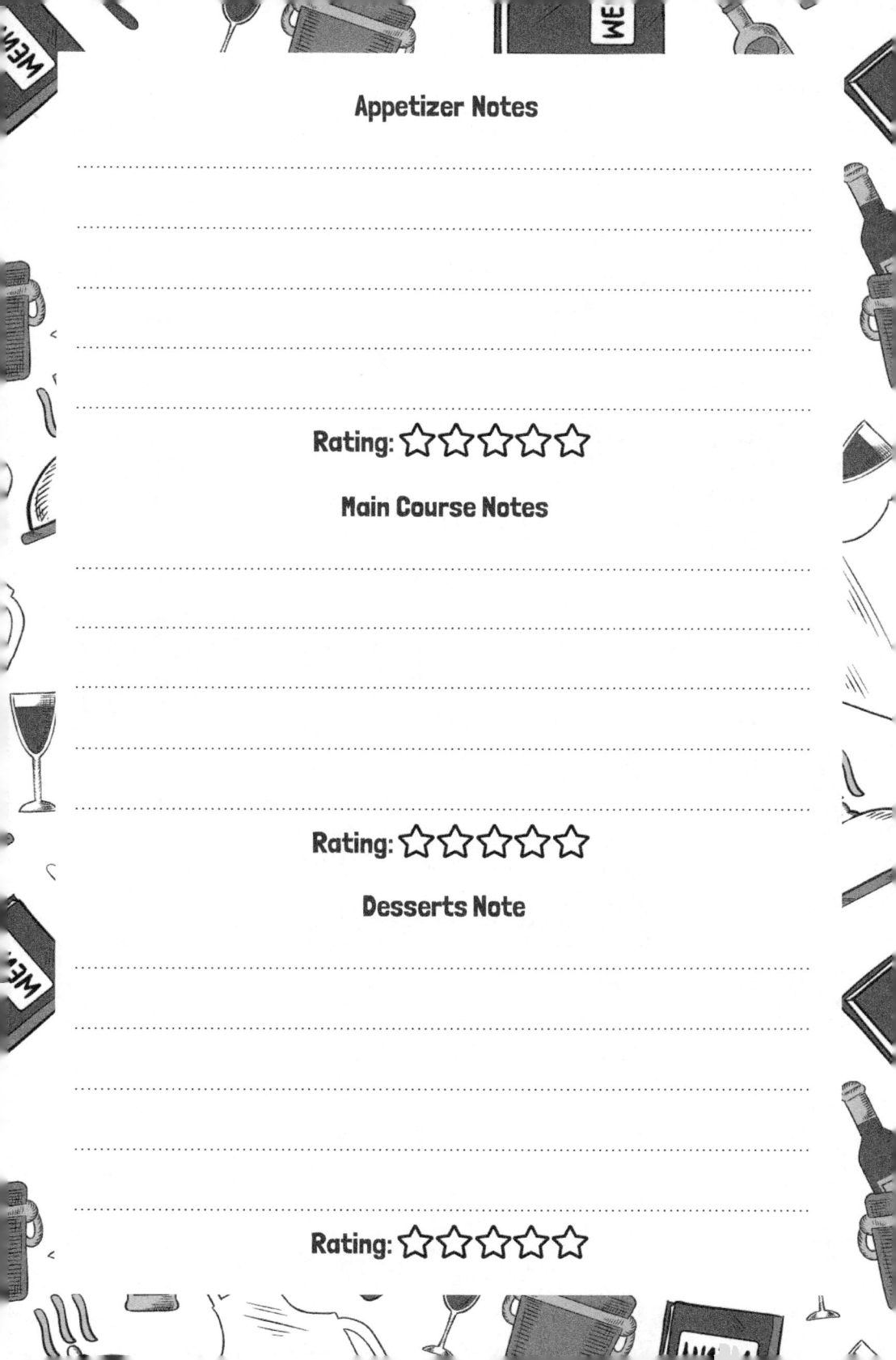

Appetizer Notes

....

....

....

....

Rating: ☆☆☆☆☆

Main Course Notes

....

....

....

....

Rating: ☆☆☆☆☆

Desserts Note

....

....

....

....

Rating: ☆☆☆☆☆

Restaurant Name:

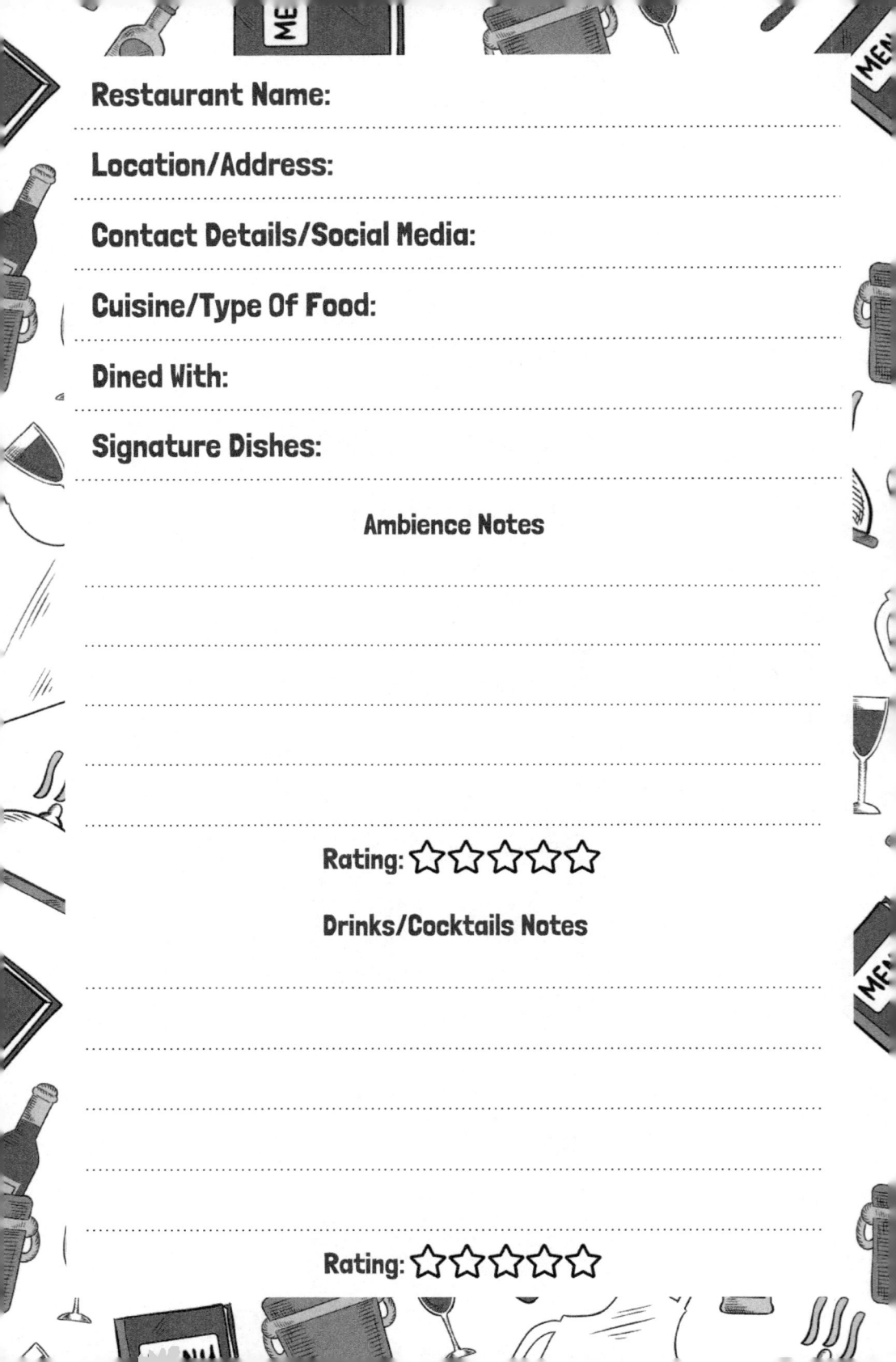

Location/Address:

Contact Details/Social Media:

Cuisine/Type Of Food:

Dined With:

Signature Dishes:

Ambience Notes

Rating: ☆☆☆☆☆

Drinks/Cocktails Notes

Rating: ☆☆☆☆☆

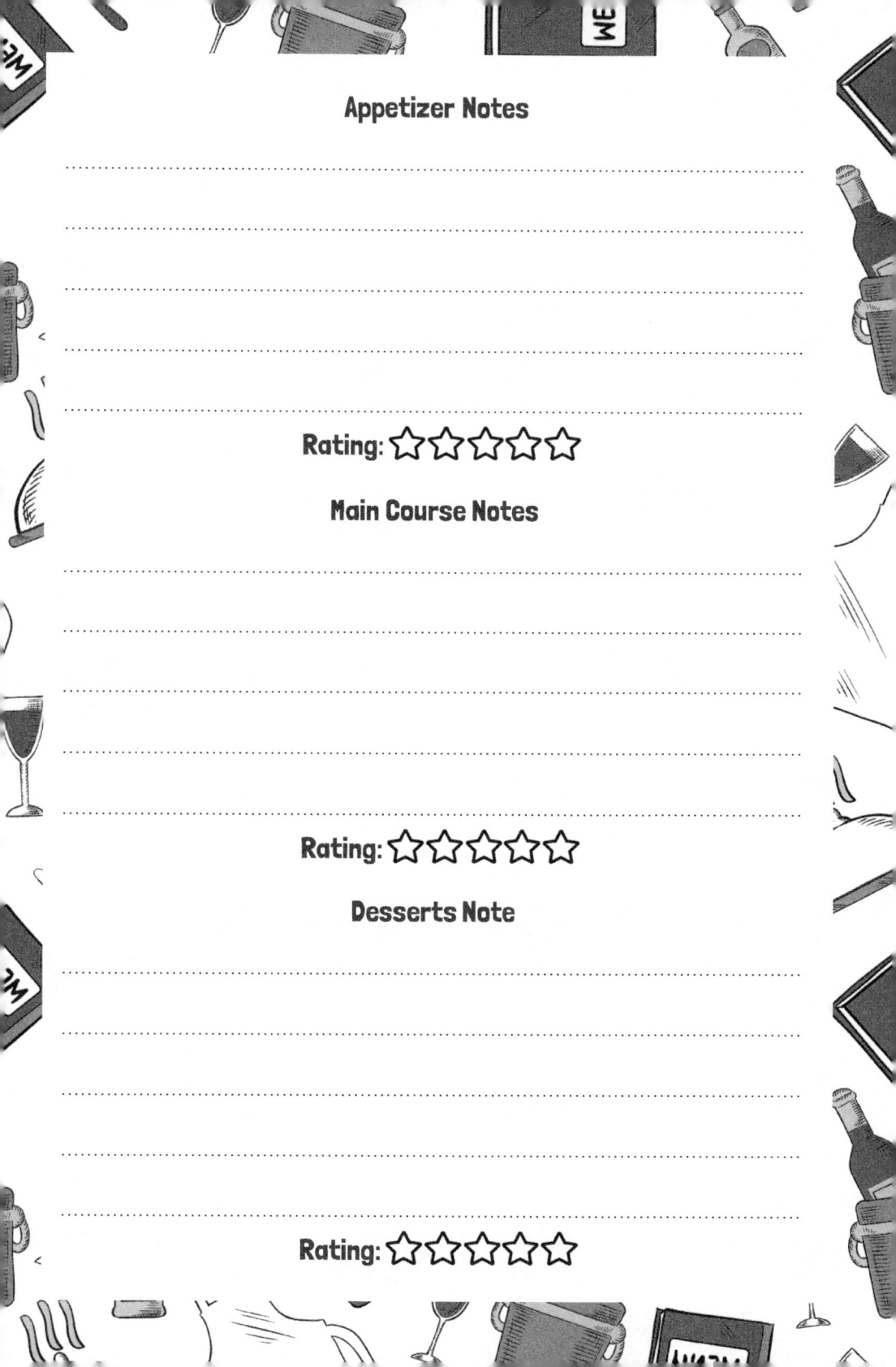

Appetizer Notes

....

....

....

....

Rating: ☆☆☆☆☆

Main Course Notes

....

....

....

....

Rating: ☆☆☆☆☆

Desserts Note

....

....

....

....

Rating: ☆☆☆☆☆

Restaurant Name:

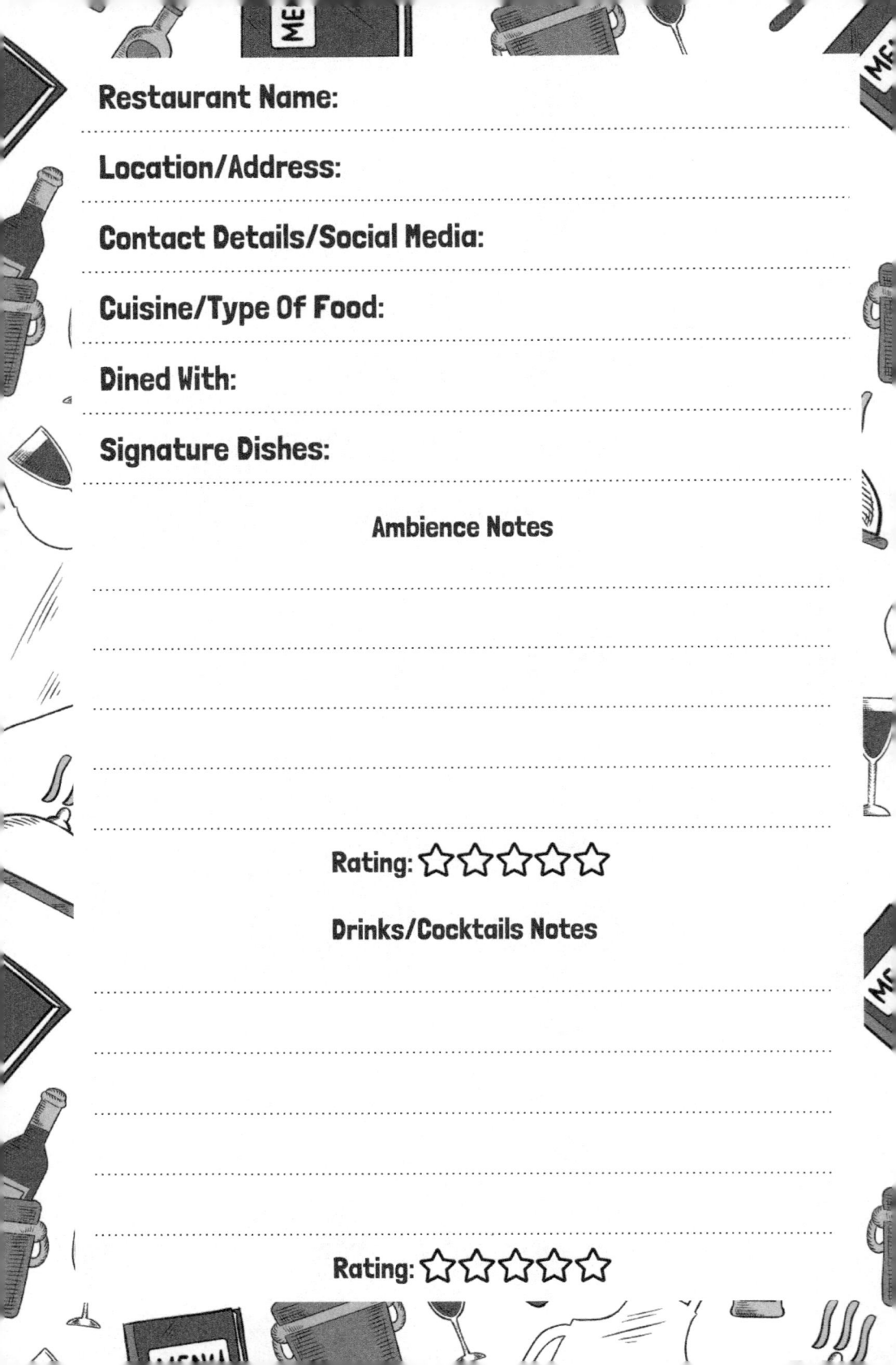

Location/Address:

Contact Details/Social Media:

Cuisine/Type Of Food:

Dined With:

Signature Dishes:

Ambience Notes

Rating: ☆☆☆☆☆

Drinks/Cocktails Notes

Rating: ☆☆☆☆☆

Appetizer Notes

....

....

....

....

Rating: ☆☆☆☆☆

Main Course Notes

....

....

....

....

Rating: ☆☆☆☆☆

Desserts Note

....

....

....

....

Rating: ☆☆☆☆☆

Restaurant Name:

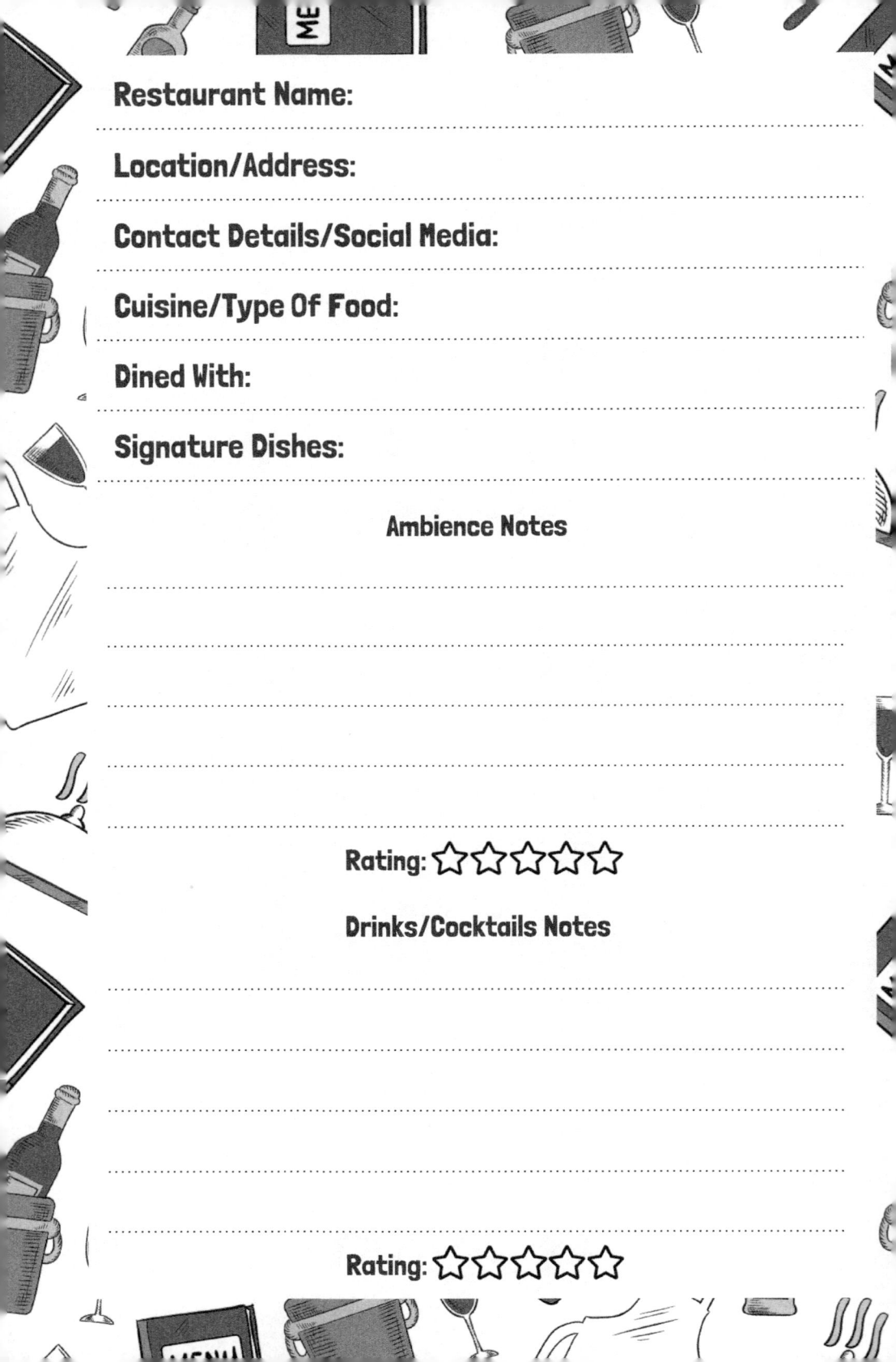

Location/Address:

Contact Details/Social Media:

Cuisine/Type Of Food:

Dined With:

Signature Dishes:

Ambience Notes

Rating: ☆☆☆☆☆

Drinks/Cocktails Notes

Rating: ☆☆☆☆☆

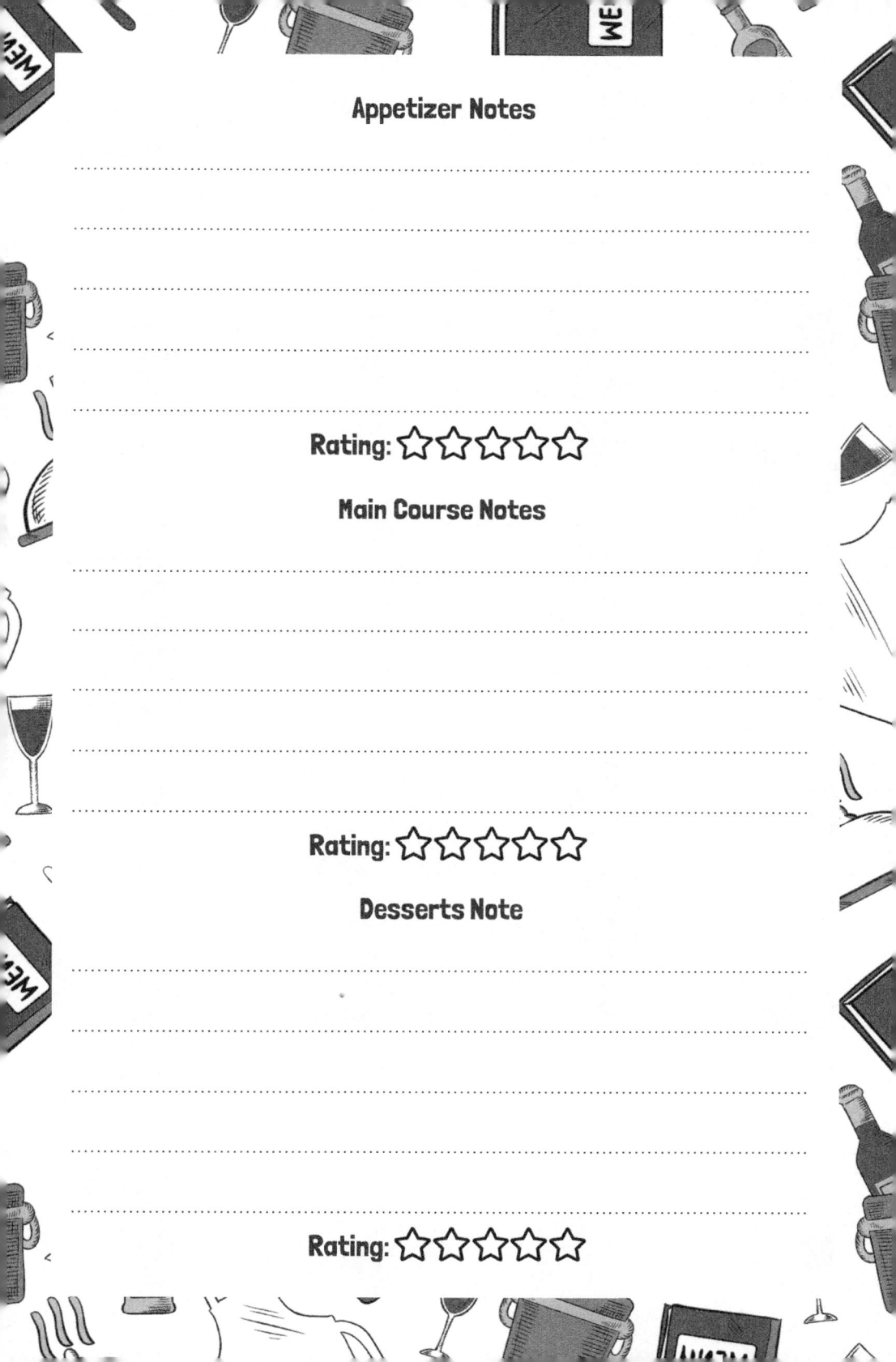

Appetizer Notes

....
....
....
....

Rating: ☆☆☆☆☆

Main Course Notes

....
....
....
....

Rating: ☆☆☆☆☆

Desserts Note

....
....
....
....

Rating: ☆☆☆☆☆

Restaurant Name:

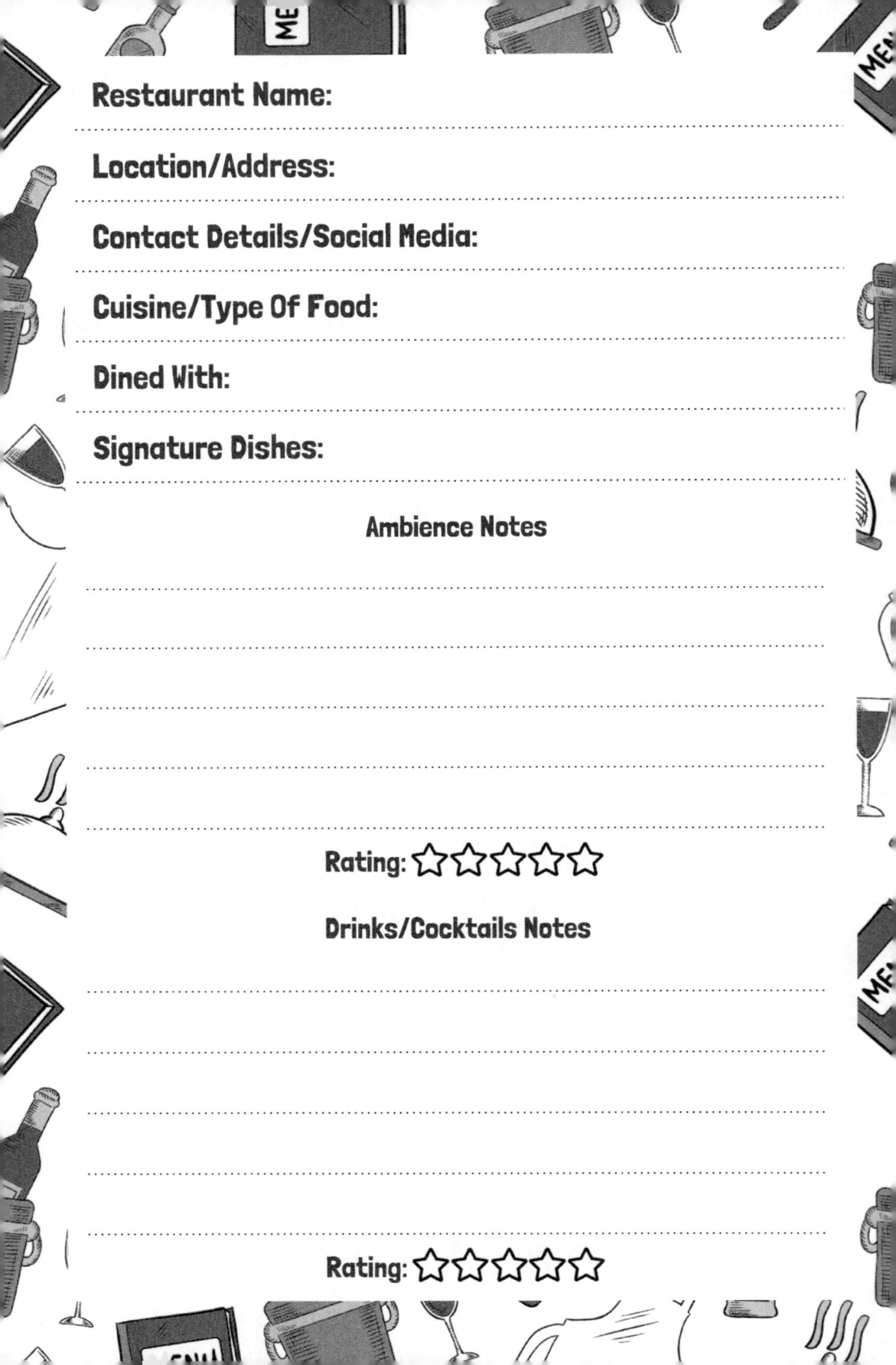

Location/Address:

Contact Details/Social Media:

Cuisine/Type Of Food:

Dined With:

Signature Dishes:

Ambience Notes

Rating: ☆☆☆☆☆

Drinks/Cocktails Notes

Rating: ☆☆☆☆☆

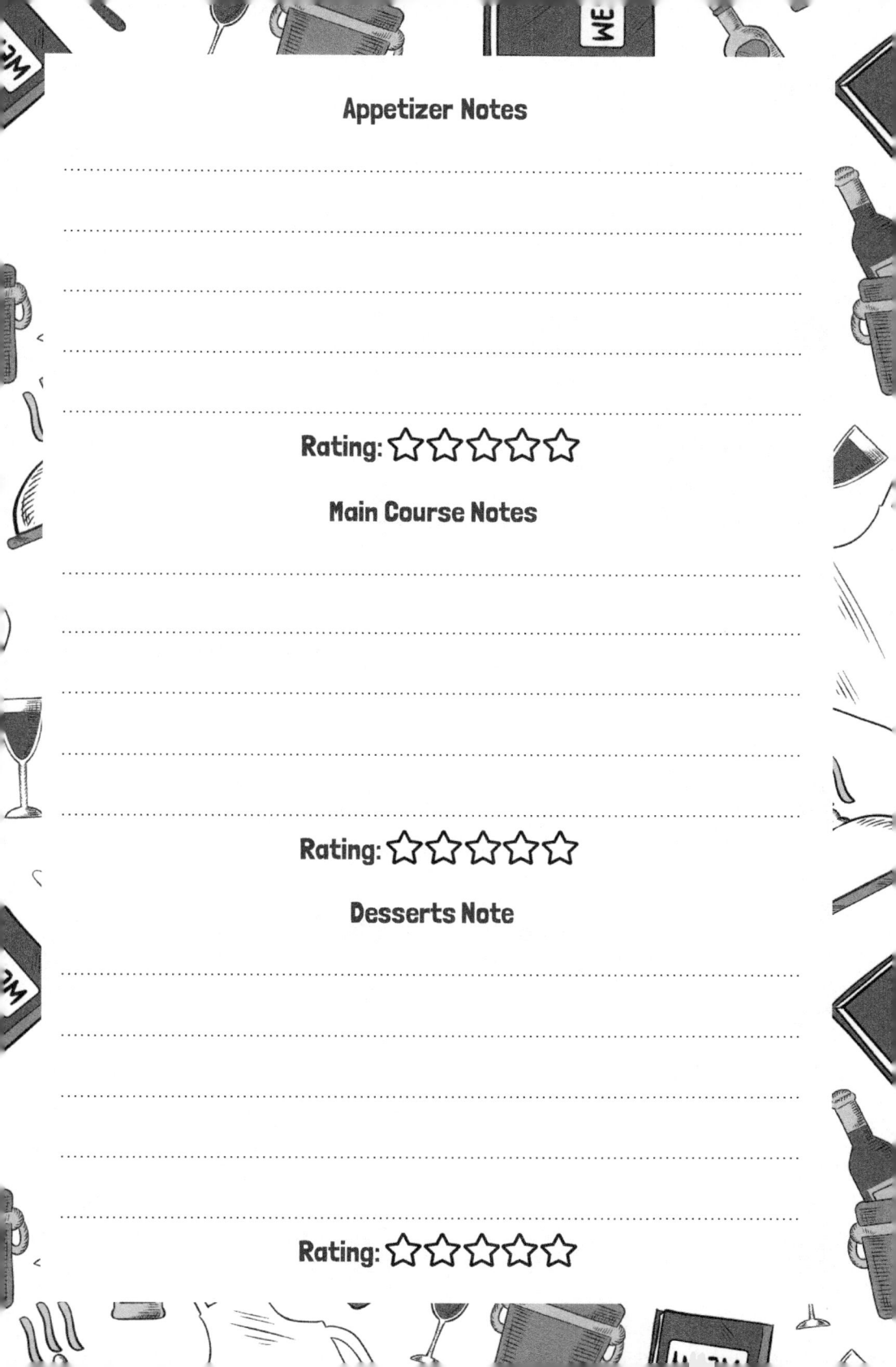

Appetizer Notes

....

....

....

....

Rating: ☆☆☆☆☆

Main Course Notes

....

....

....

....

Rating: ☆☆☆☆☆

Desserts Note

....

....

....

....

Rating: ☆☆☆☆☆

Restaurant Name:

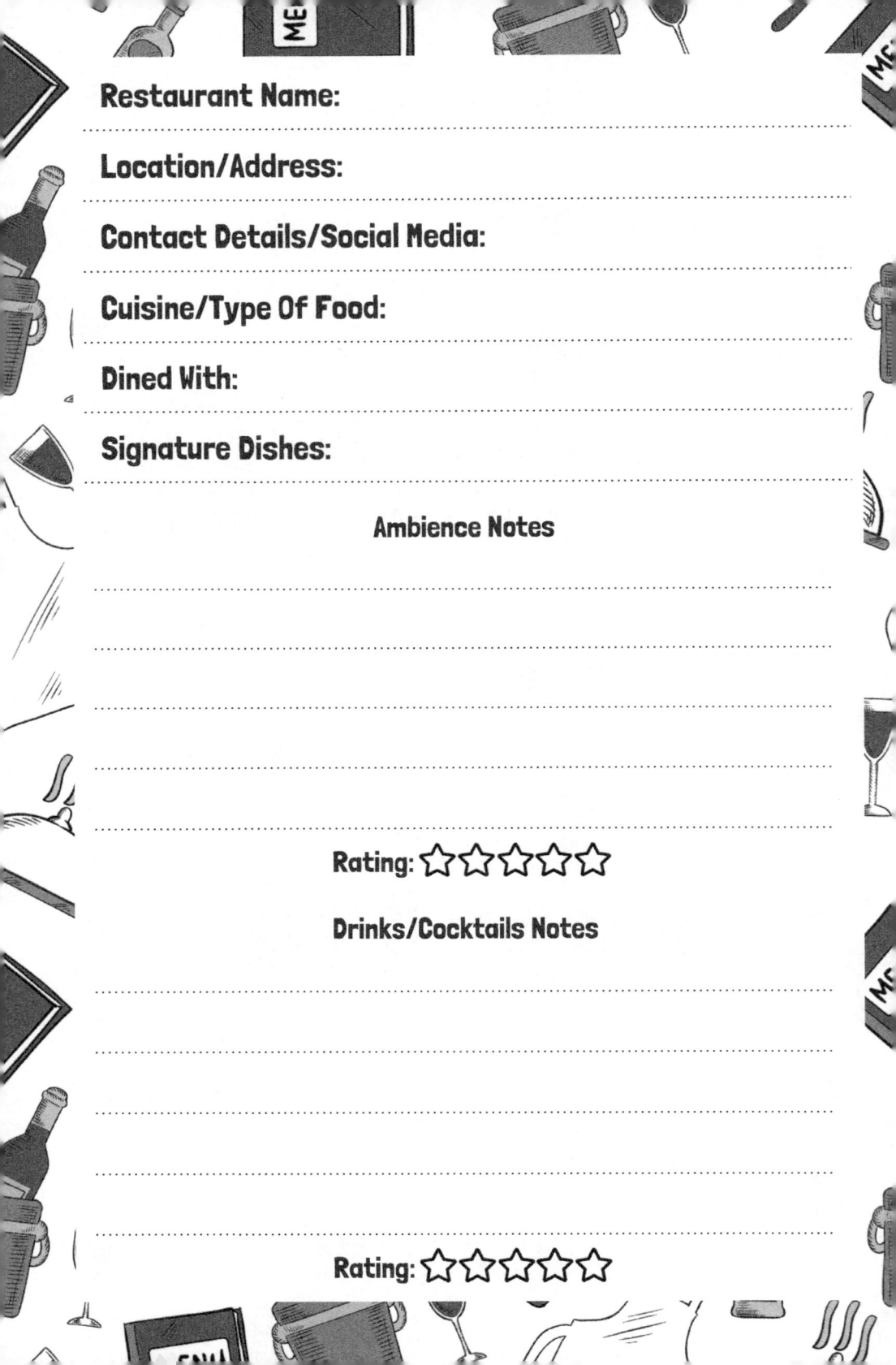

Location/Address:

Contact Details/Social Media:

Cuisine/Type Of Food:

Dined With:

Signature Dishes:

Ambience Notes

Rating: ☆☆☆☆☆

Drinks/Cocktails Notes

Rating: ☆☆☆☆☆

Appetizer Notes

....

....

....

....

Rating: ☆☆☆☆☆

Main Course Notes

....

....

....

....

Rating: ☆☆☆☆☆

Desserts Note

....

....

....

....

Rating: ☆☆☆☆☆

Restaurant Name:

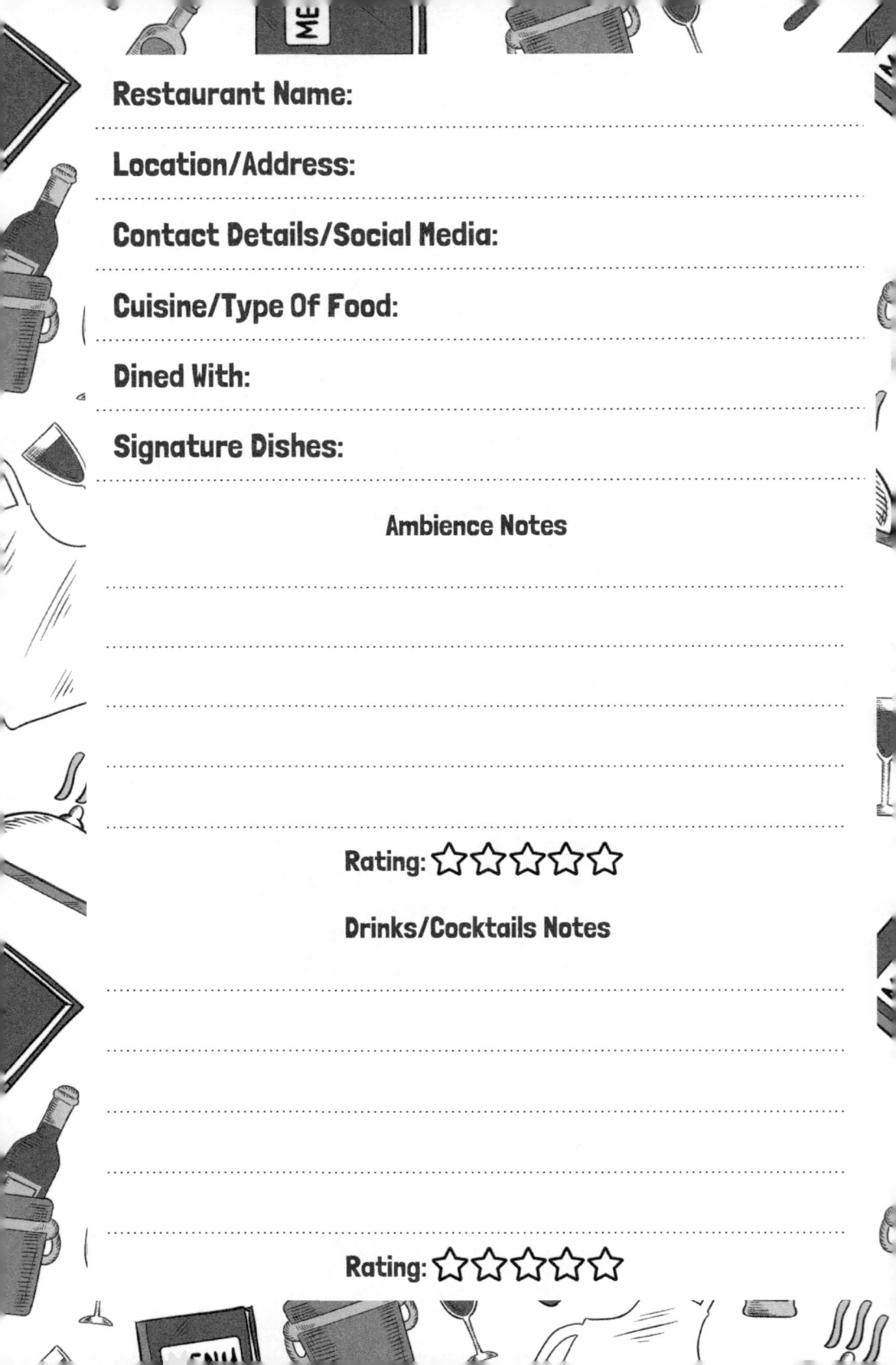

Location/Address:

Contact Details/Social Media:

Cuisine/Type Of Food:

Dined With:

Signature Dishes:

Ambience Notes

Rating: ☆☆☆☆☆

Drinks/Cocktails Notes

Rating: ☆☆☆☆☆

Appetizer Notes

....

....

....

....

....

Rating: ☆☆☆☆☆

Main Course Notes

....

....

....

....

....

Rating: ☆☆☆☆☆

Desserts Note

....

....

....

....

....

Rating: ☆☆☆☆☆

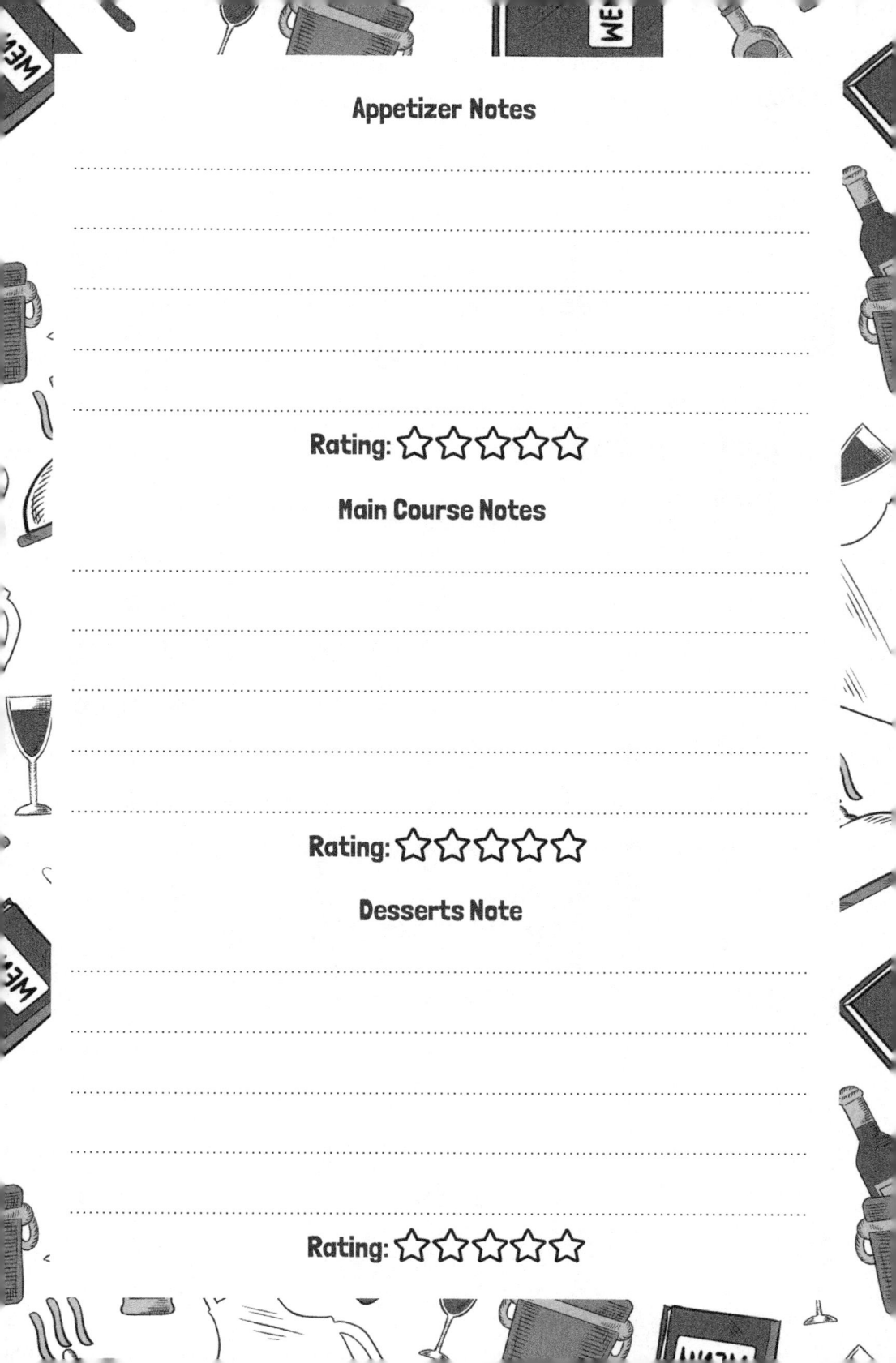

Restaurant Name:

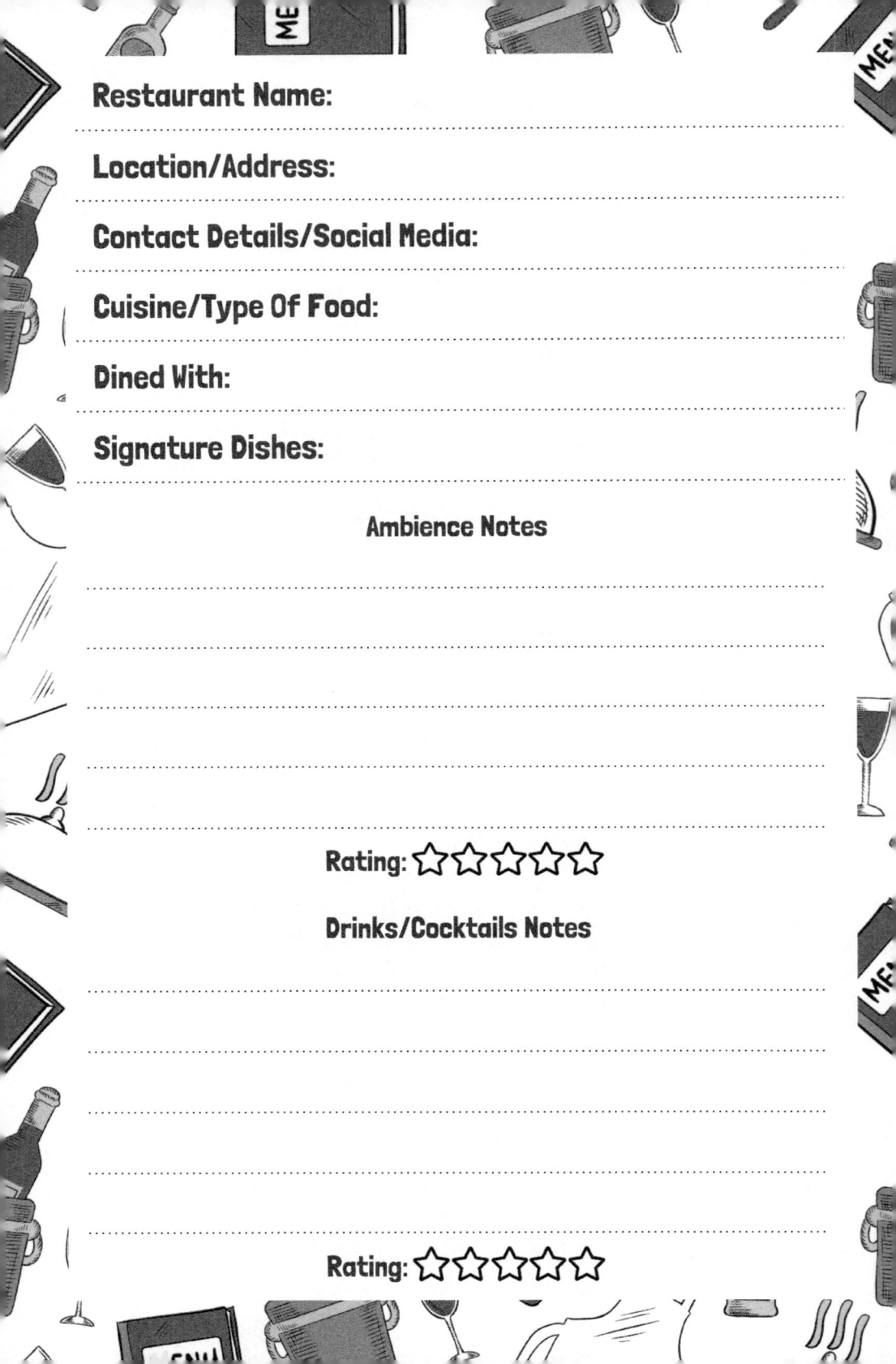

Location/Address:

Contact Details/Social Media:

Cuisine/Type Of Food:

Dined With:

Signature Dishes:

Ambience Notes

Rating: ☆☆☆☆☆

Drinks/Cocktails Notes

Rating: ☆☆☆☆☆

Appetizer Notes

....

....

....

....

Rating: ☆☆☆☆☆

Main Course Notes

....

....

....

....

Rating: ☆☆☆☆☆

Desserts Note

....

....

....

....

Rating: ☆☆☆☆☆

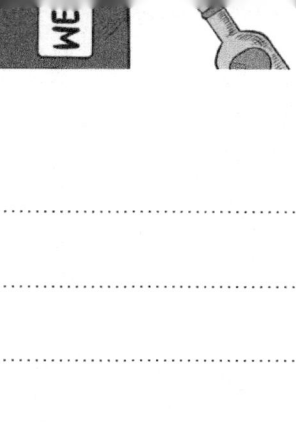

Restaurant Name:

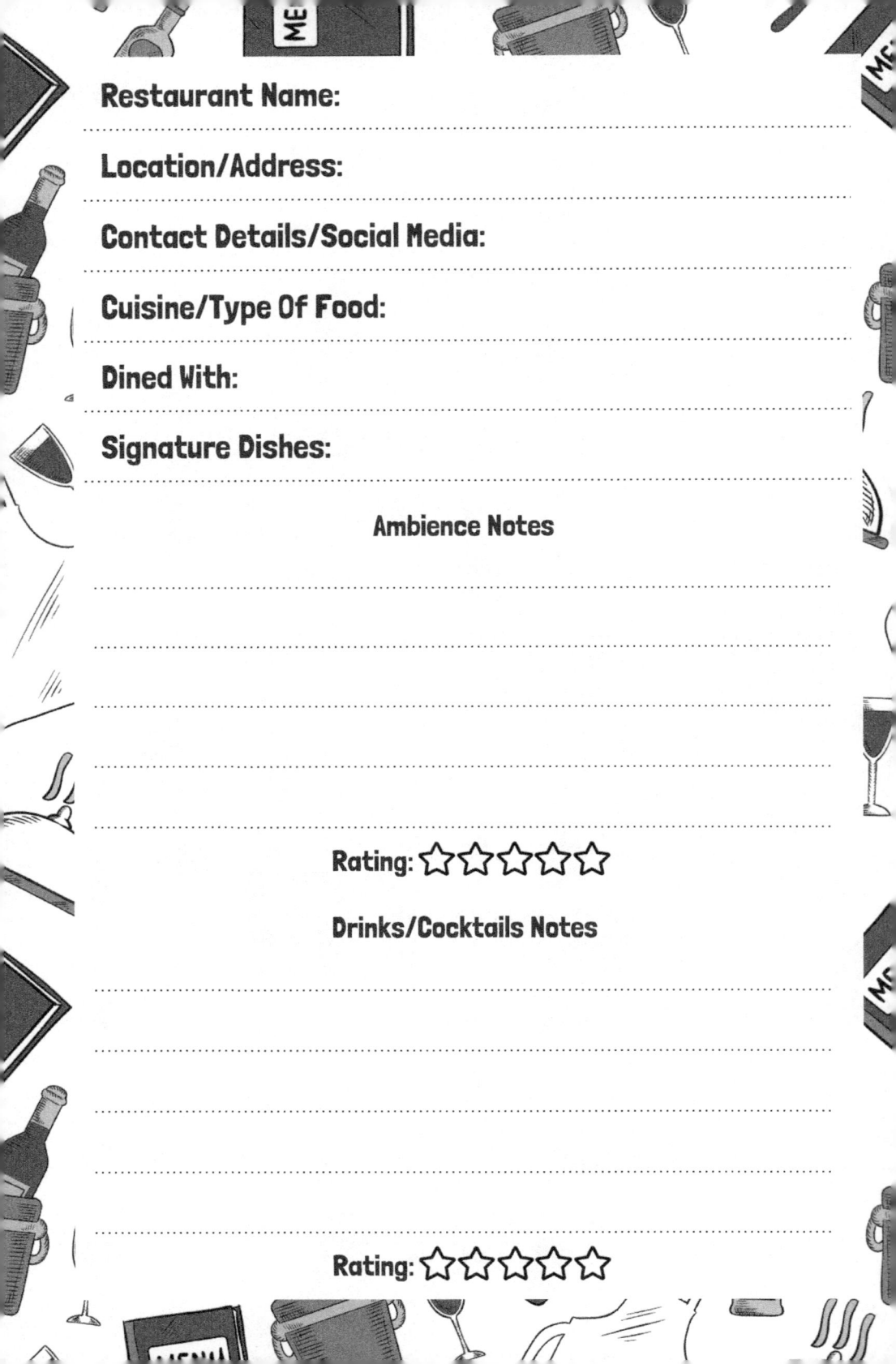

Location/Address:

Contact Details/Social Media:

Cuisine/Type Of Food:

Dined With:

Signature Dishes:

Ambience Notes

Rating: ☆☆☆☆☆

Drinks/Cocktails Notes

Rating: ☆☆☆☆☆

Appetizer Notes

....
....
....
....

Rating: ☆☆☆☆☆

Main Course Notes

....
....
....
....

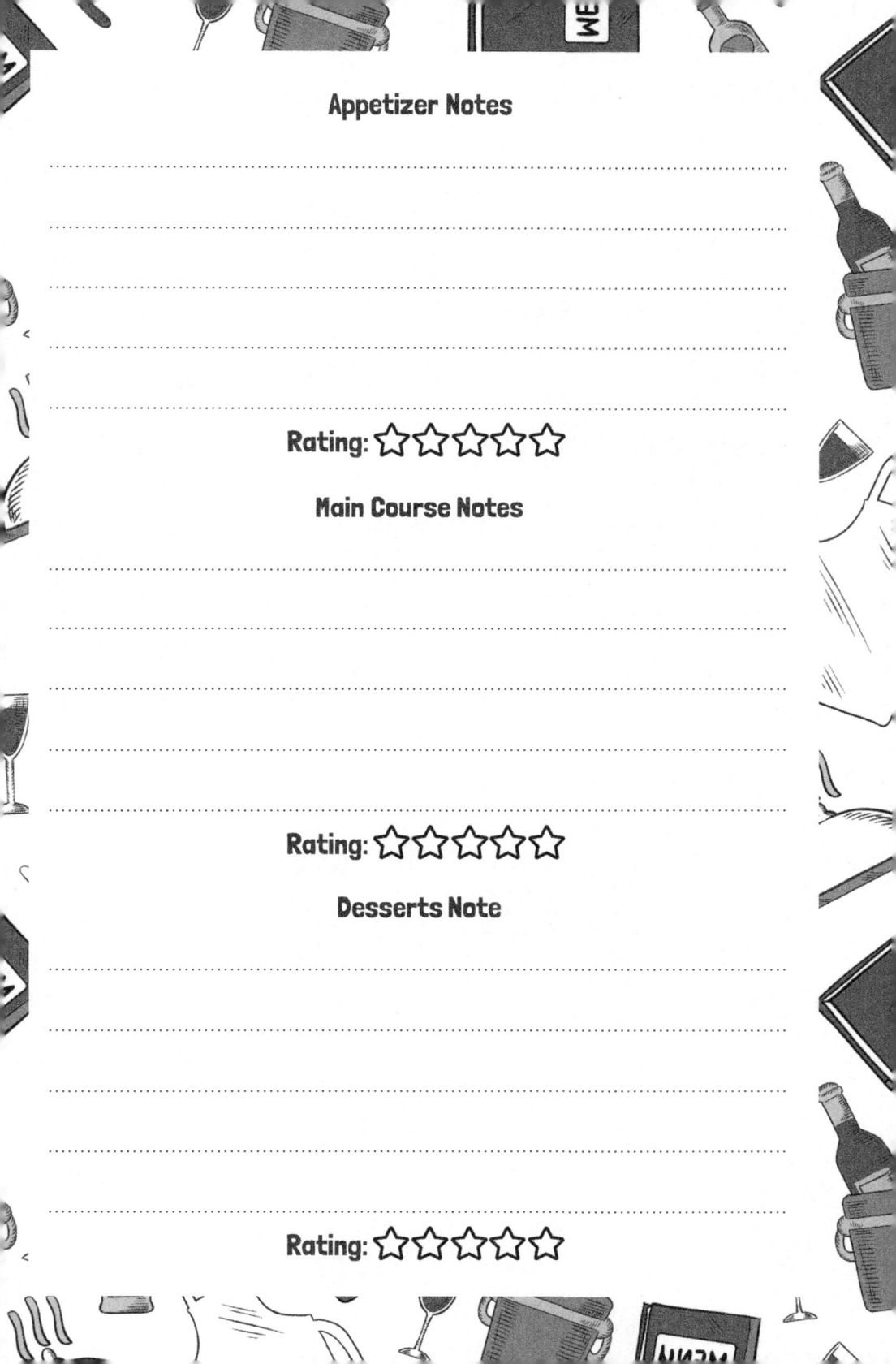

Rating: ☆☆☆☆☆

Desserts Note

....
....
....
....

Rating: ☆☆☆☆☆

Restaurant Name:

Location/Address:

Contact Details/Social Media:

Cuisine/Type Of Food:

Dined With:

Signature Dishes:

Ambience Notes

Rating: ☆☆☆☆☆

Drinks/Cocktails Notes

Rating: ☆☆☆☆☆

Appetizer Notes

....
....
....
....
....

Rating: ☆☆☆☆☆

Main Course Notes

....
....
....
....
....

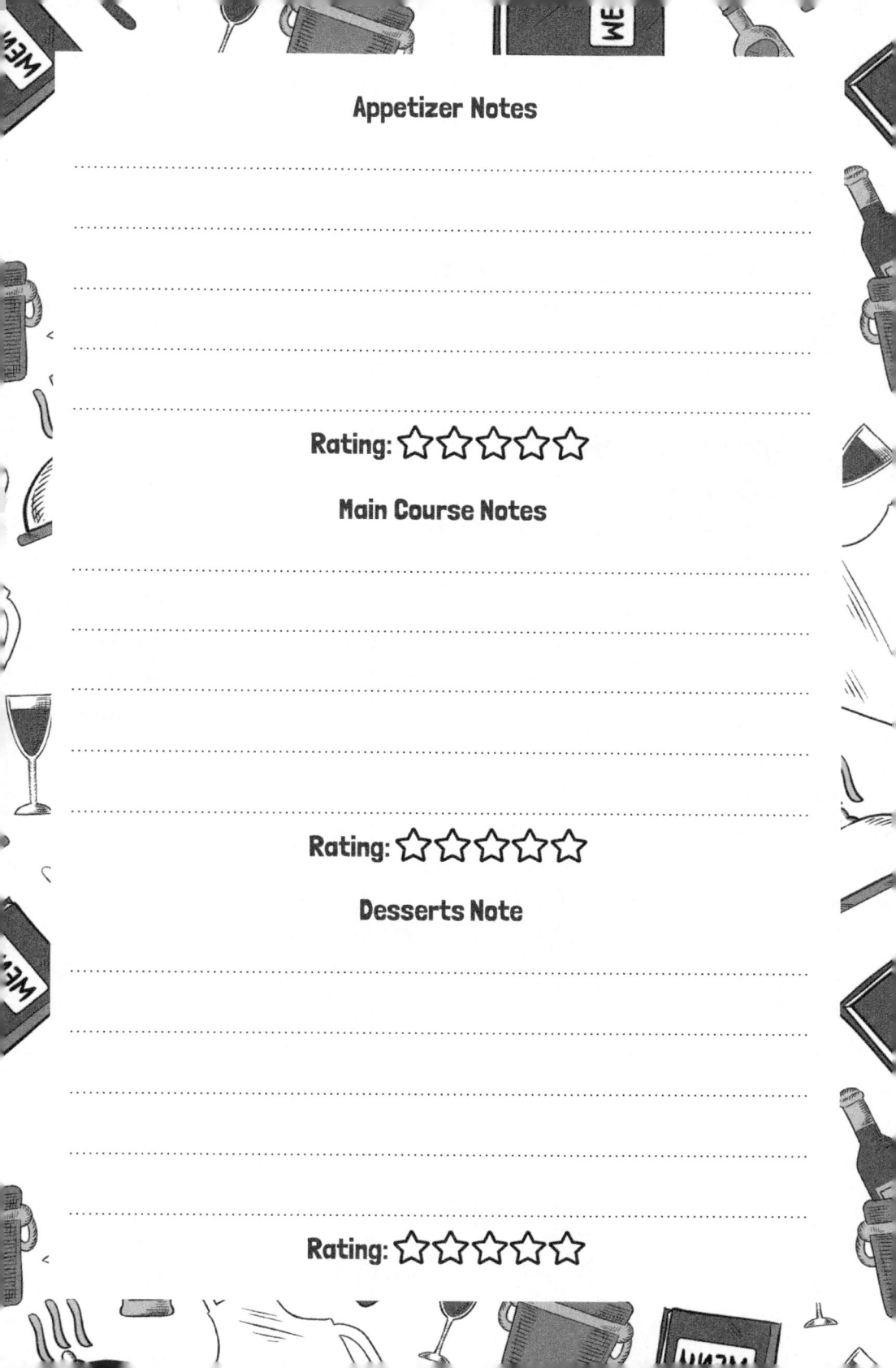

Rating: ☆☆☆☆☆

Desserts Note

....
....
....
....
....

Rating: ☆☆☆☆☆

Restaurant Name:

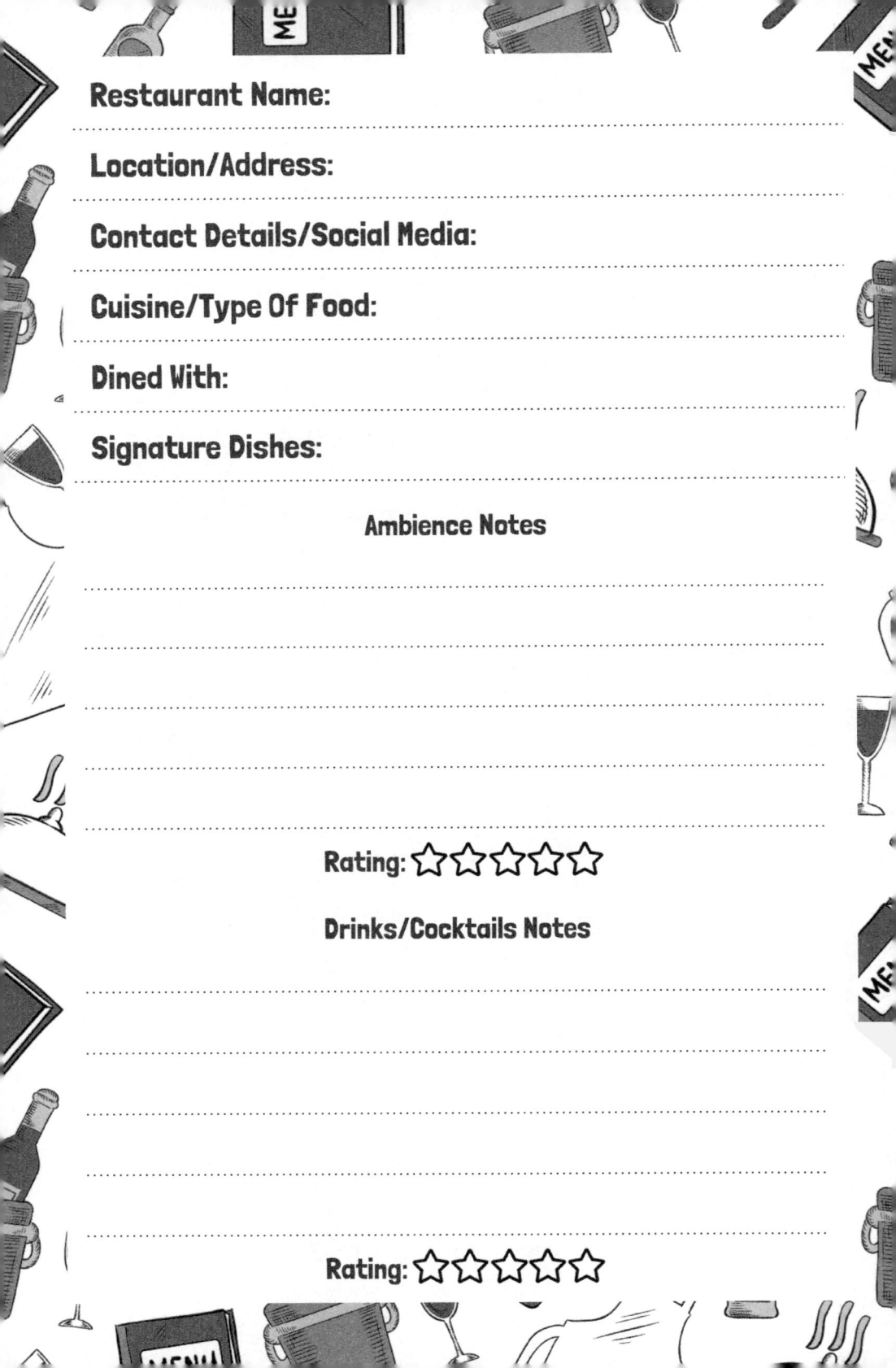

Location/Address:

Contact Details/Social Media:

Cuisine/Type Of Food:

Dined With:

Signature Dishes:

Ambience Notes

Rating: ☆☆☆☆☆

Drinks/Cocktails Notes

Rating: ☆☆☆☆☆

Appetizer Notes

....

....

....

....

Rating: ☆☆☆☆☆

Main Course Notes

....

....

....

....

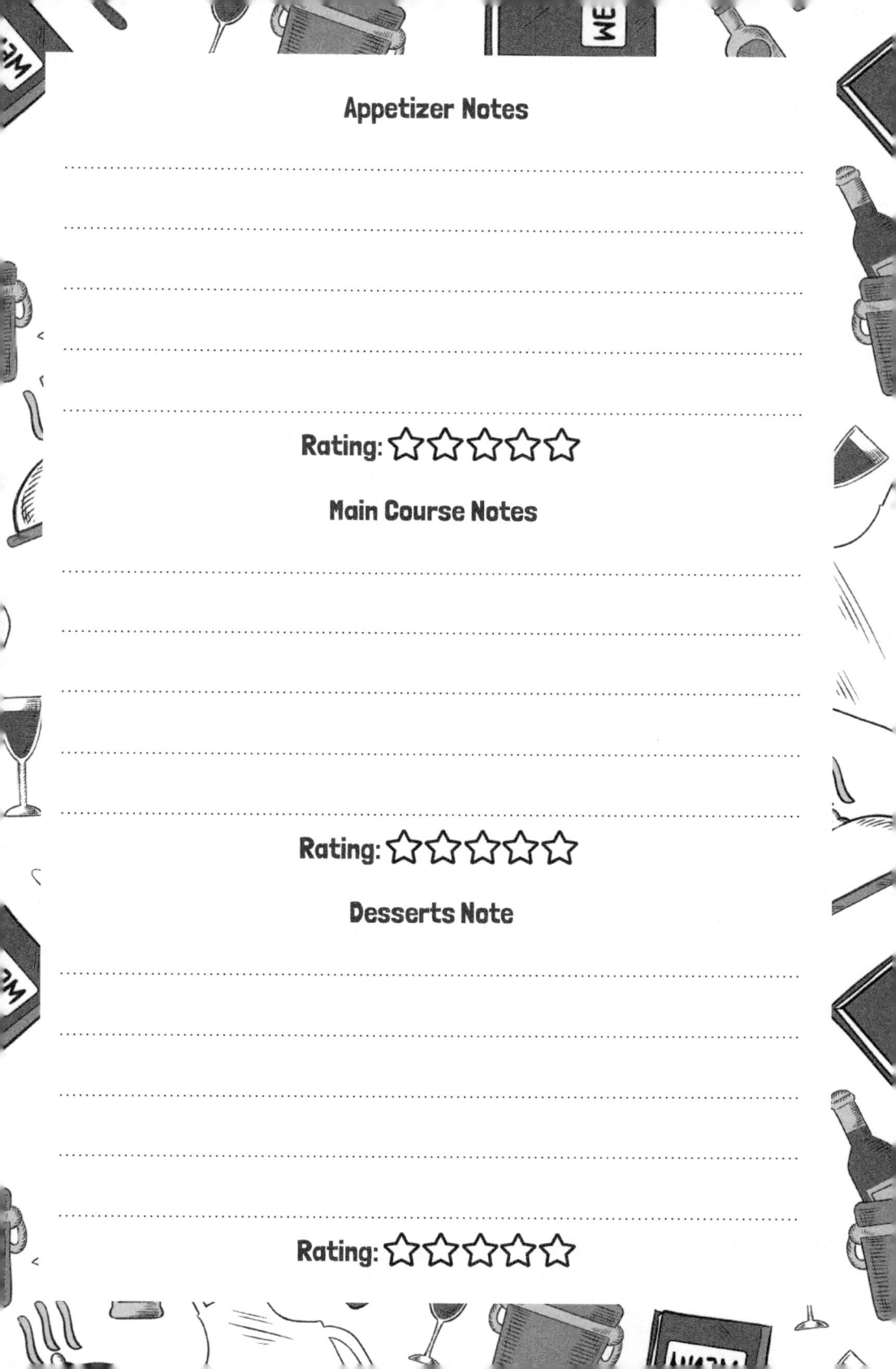

Rating: ☆☆☆☆☆

Desserts Note

....

....

....

....

Rating: ☆☆☆☆☆

Restaurant Name:

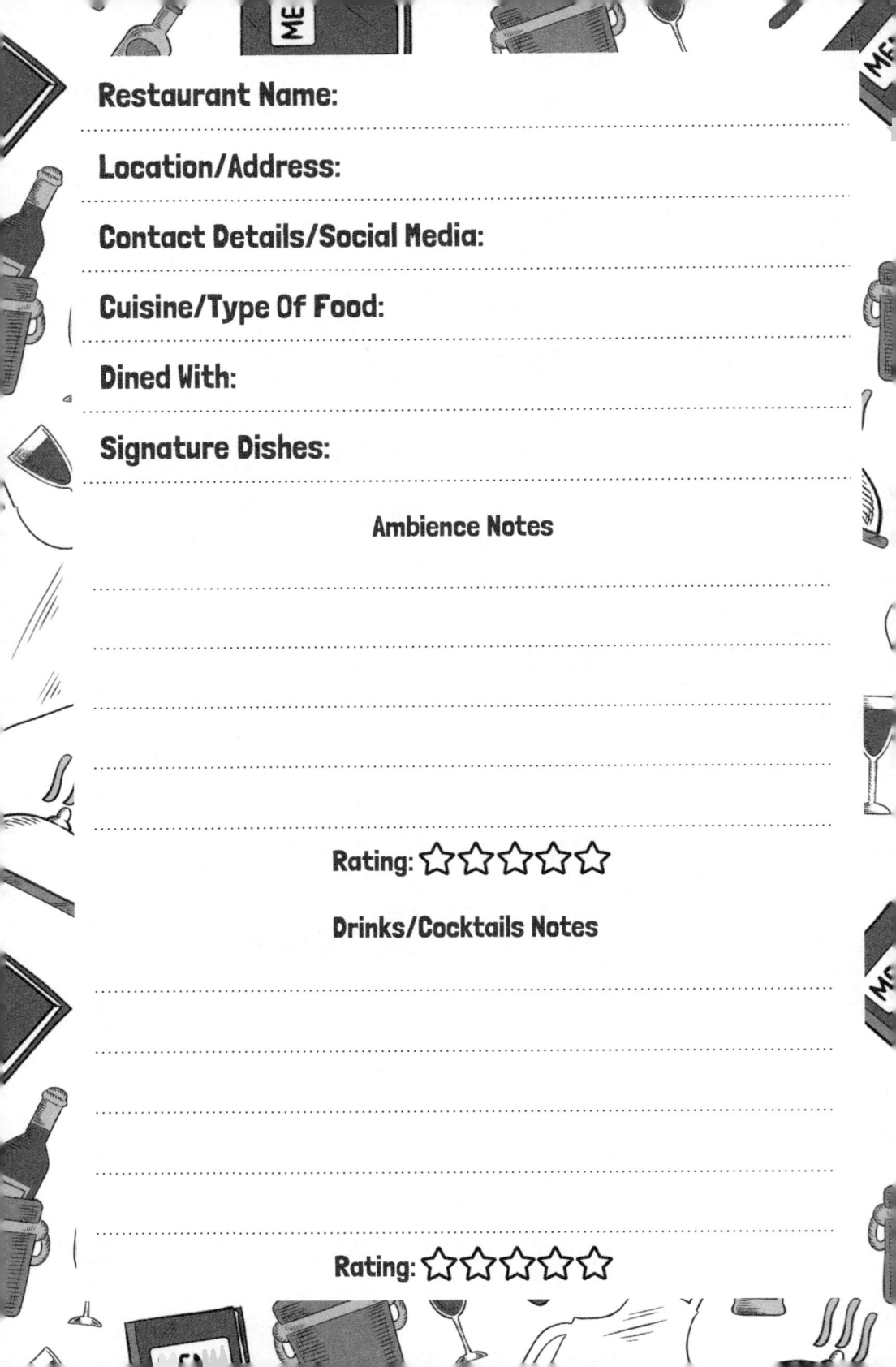

Location/Address:

Contact Details/Social Media:

Cuisine/Type Of Food:

Dined With:

Signature Dishes:

Ambience Notes

Rating: ☆☆☆☆☆

Drinks/Cocktails Notes

Rating: ☆☆☆☆☆

Appetizer Notes

....

....

....

....

Rating: ☆☆☆☆☆

Main Course Notes

....

....

....

....

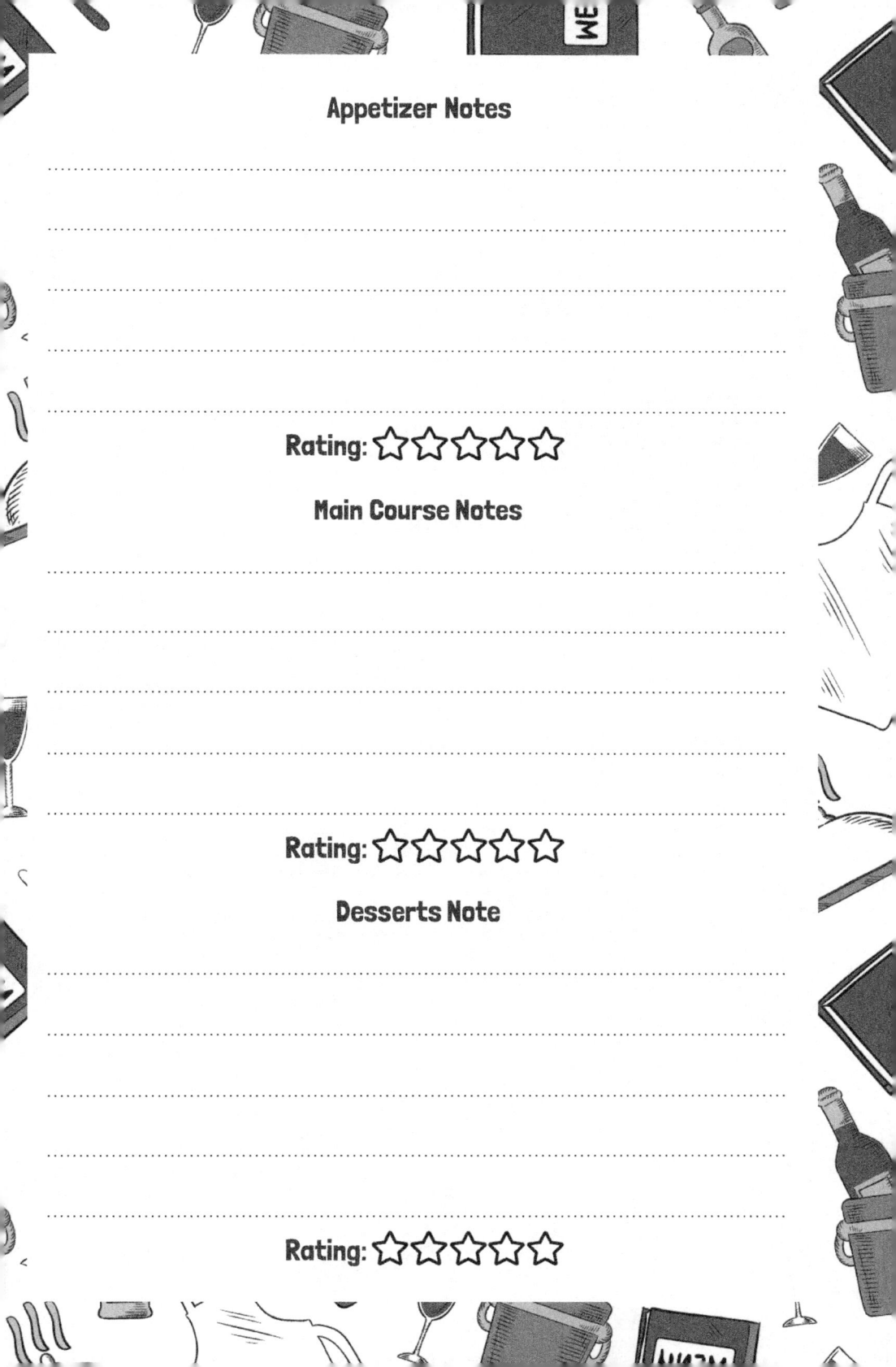

Rating: ☆☆☆☆☆

Desserts Note

....

....

....

....

Rating: ☆☆☆☆☆

Restaurant Name:

Location/Address:

Contact Details/Social Media:

Cuisine/Type Of Food:

Dined With:

Signature Dishes:

Ambience Notes

Rating: ☆☆☆☆☆

Drinks/Cocktails Notes

Rating: ☆☆☆☆☆

Appetizer Notes

....
....
....
....
....

Rating: ☆☆☆☆☆

Main Course Notes

....
....
....
....

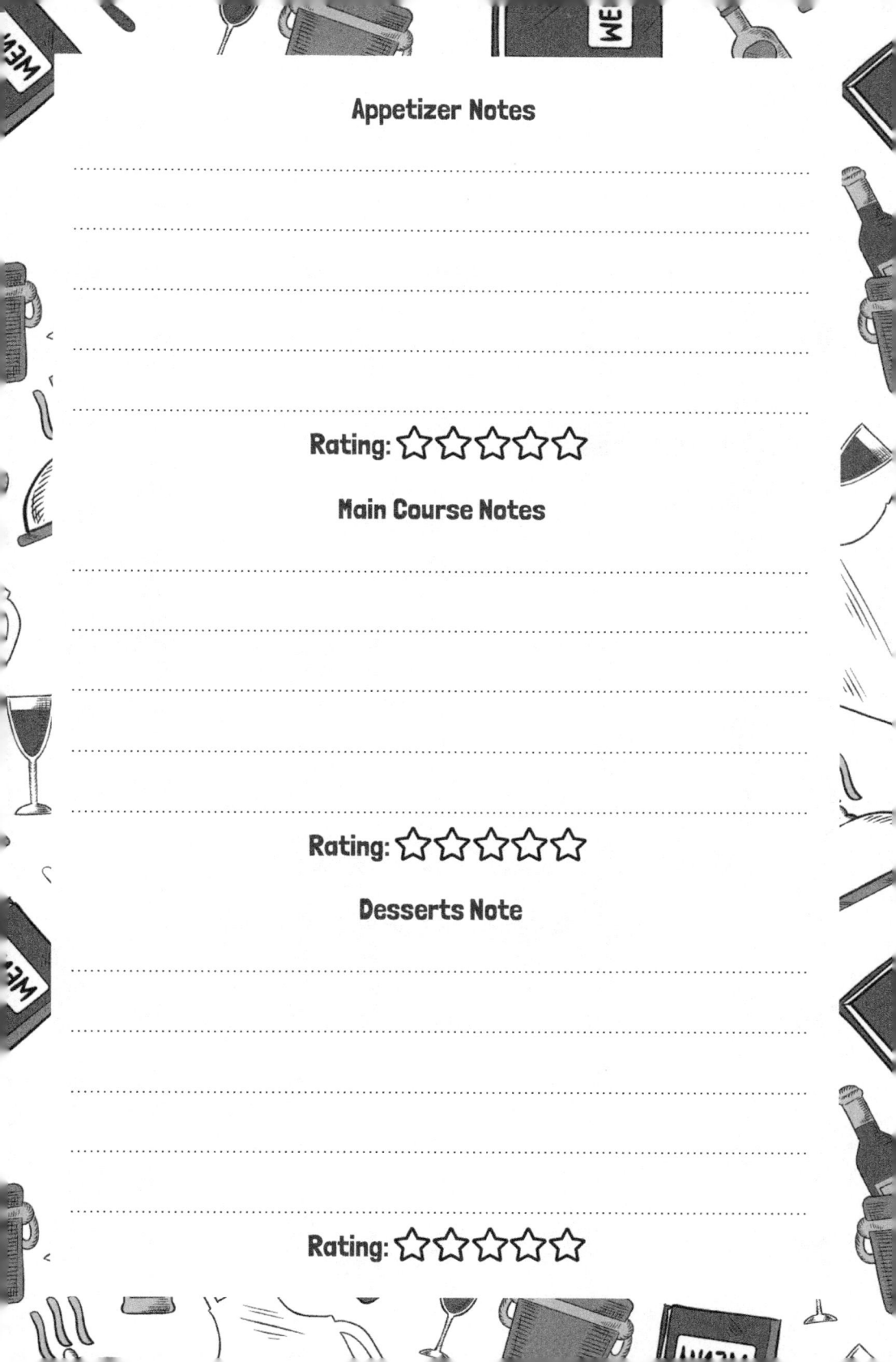

Rating: ☆☆☆☆☆

Desserts Note

....
....
....
....

Rating: ☆☆☆☆☆

Restaurant Name:

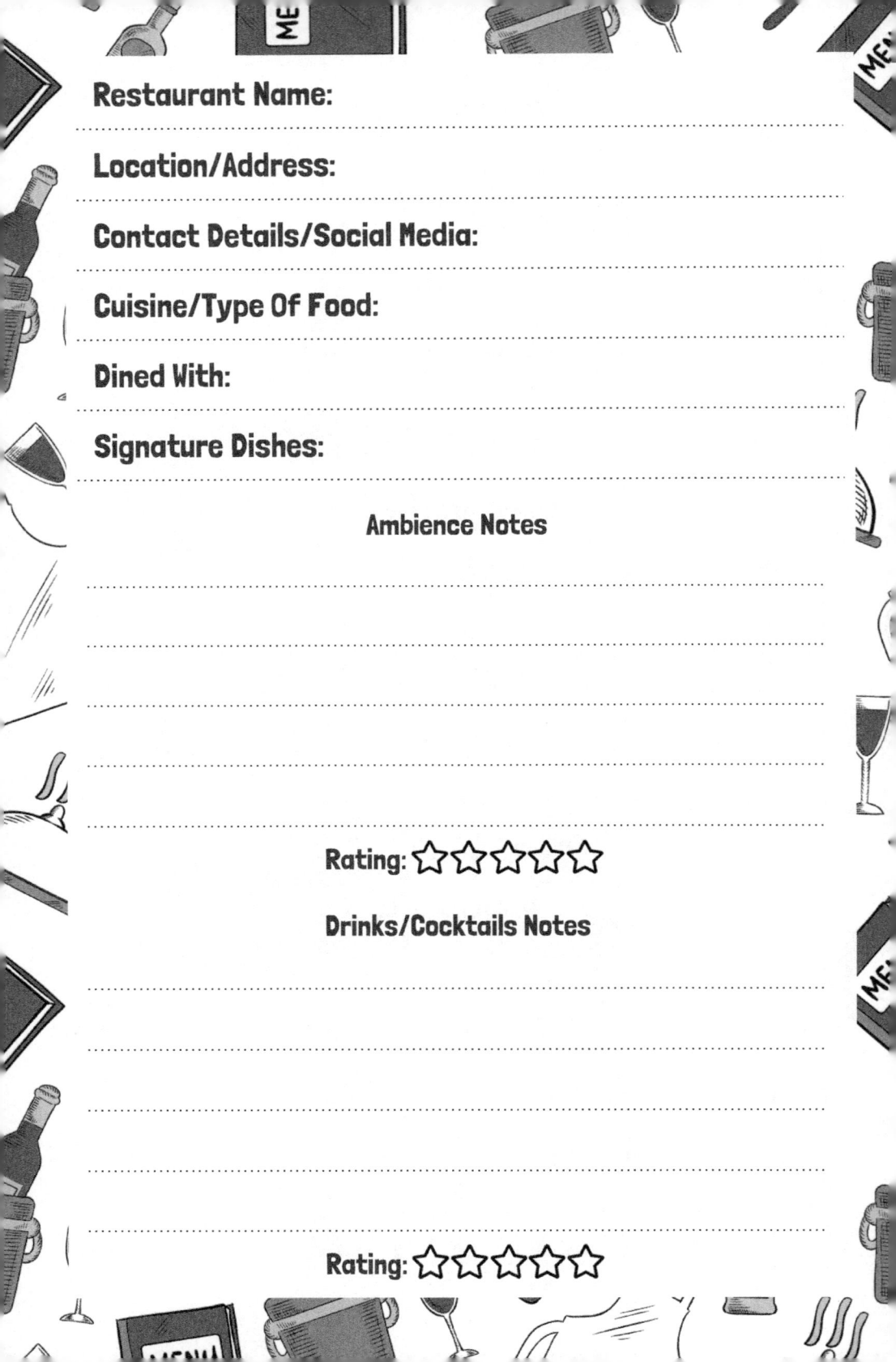

Location/Address:

Contact Details/Social Media:

Cuisine/Type Of Food:

Dined With:

Signature Dishes:

Ambience Notes

Rating: ☆☆☆☆☆

Drinks/Cocktails Notes

Rating: ☆☆☆☆☆

Appetizer Notes

....

....

....

....

Rating: ☆☆☆☆☆

Main Course Notes

....

....

....

....

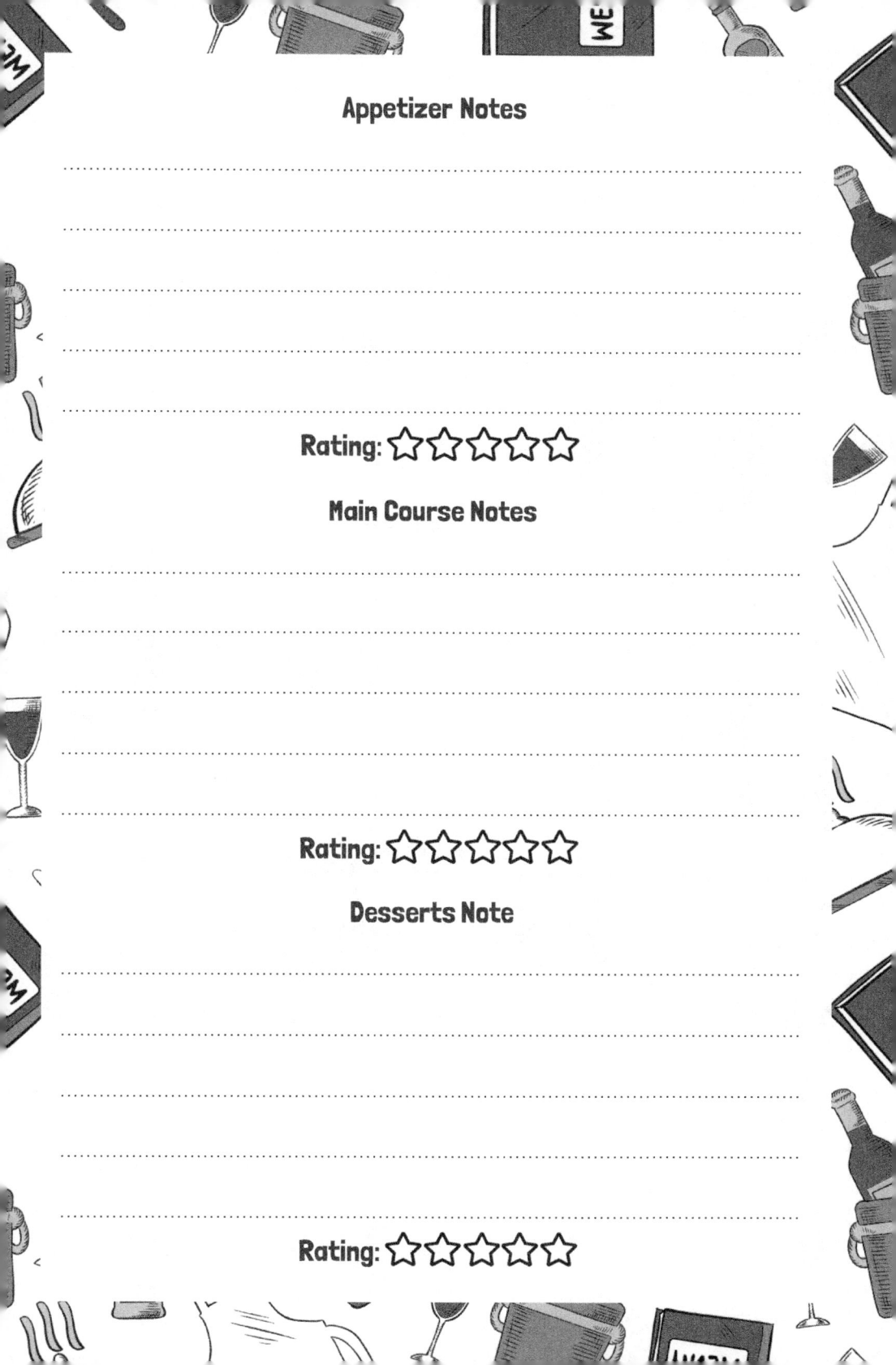

Rating: ☆☆☆☆☆

Desserts Note

....

....

....

....

Rating: ☆☆☆☆☆

Restaurant Name:

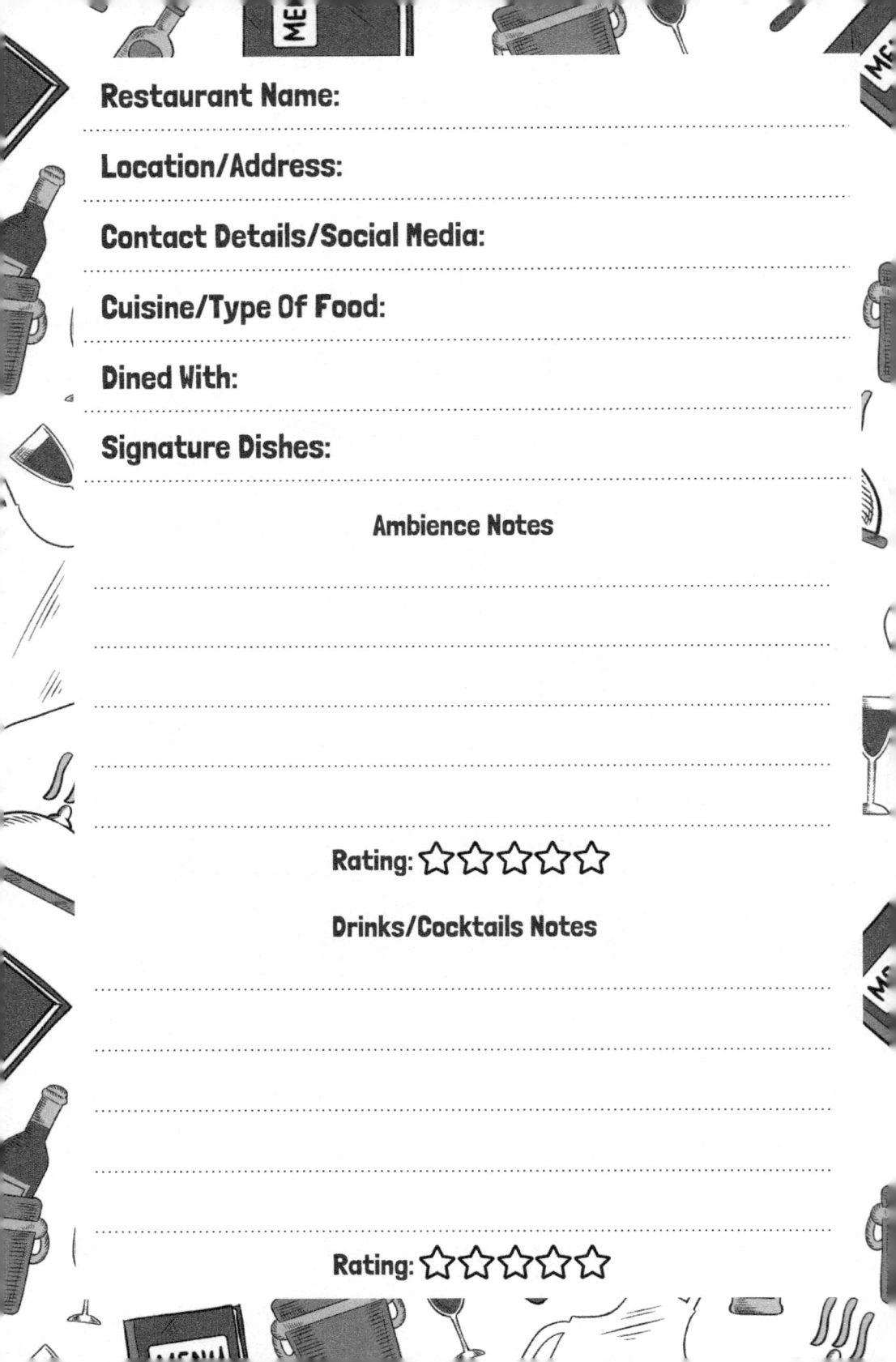

Location/Address:

Contact Details/Social Media:

Cuisine/Type Of Food:

Dined With:

Signature Dishes:

Ambience Notes

Rating: ☆☆☆☆☆

Drinks/Cocktails Notes

Rating: ☆☆☆☆☆

Appetizer Notes

....

....

....

....

Rating: ☆☆☆☆☆

Main Course Notes

....

....

....

....

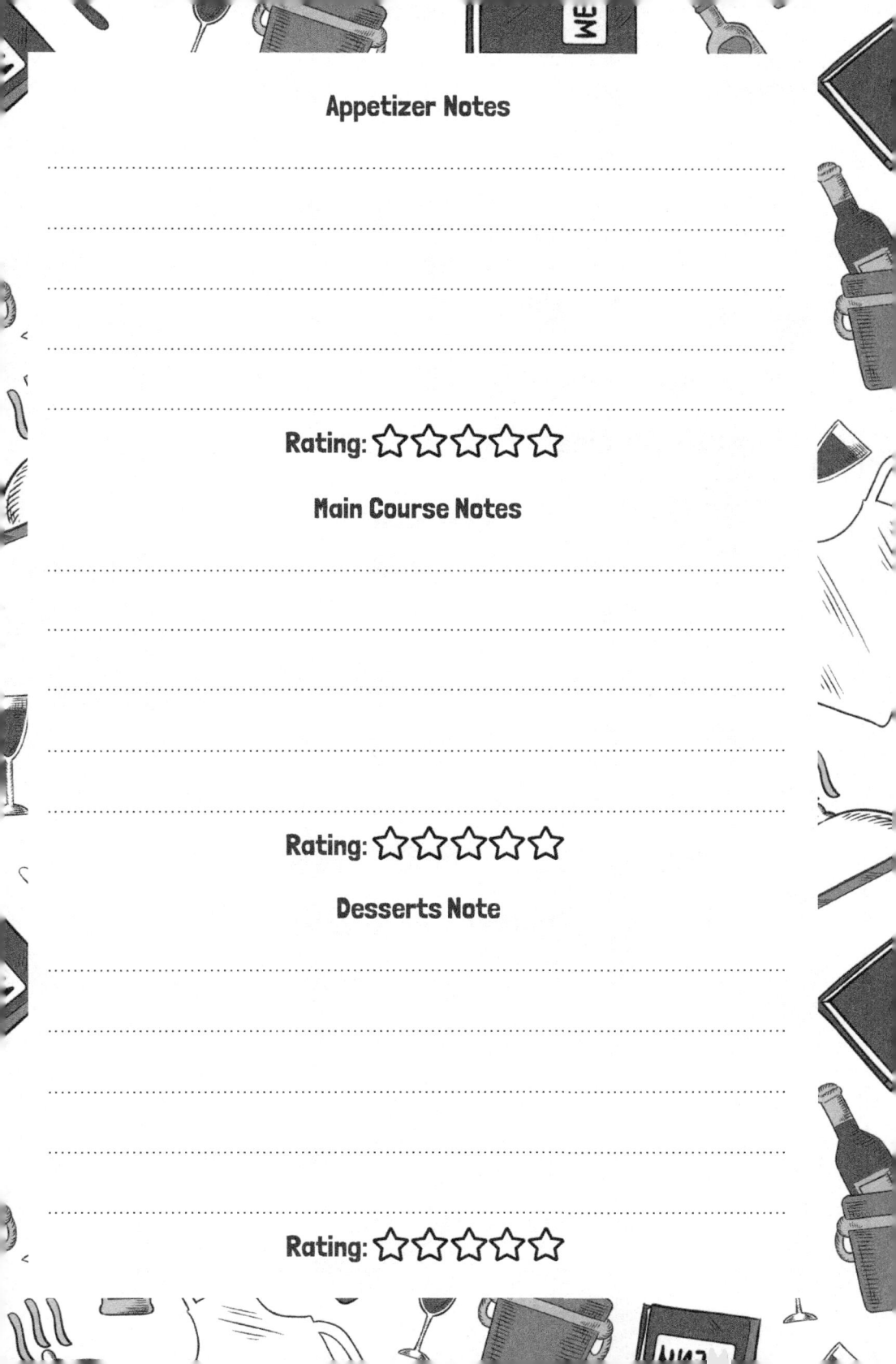

Rating: ☆☆☆☆☆

Desserts Note

....

....

....

....

Rating: ☆☆☆☆☆

Restaurant Name:

Location/Address:

Contact Details/Social Media:

Cuisine/Type Of Food:

Dined With:

Signature Dishes:

Ambience Notes

Rating: ☆☆☆☆☆

Drinks/Cocktails Notes

Rating: ☆☆☆☆☆

Appetizer Notes

....

....

....

....

Rating: ☆☆☆☆☆

Main Course Notes

....

....

....

....

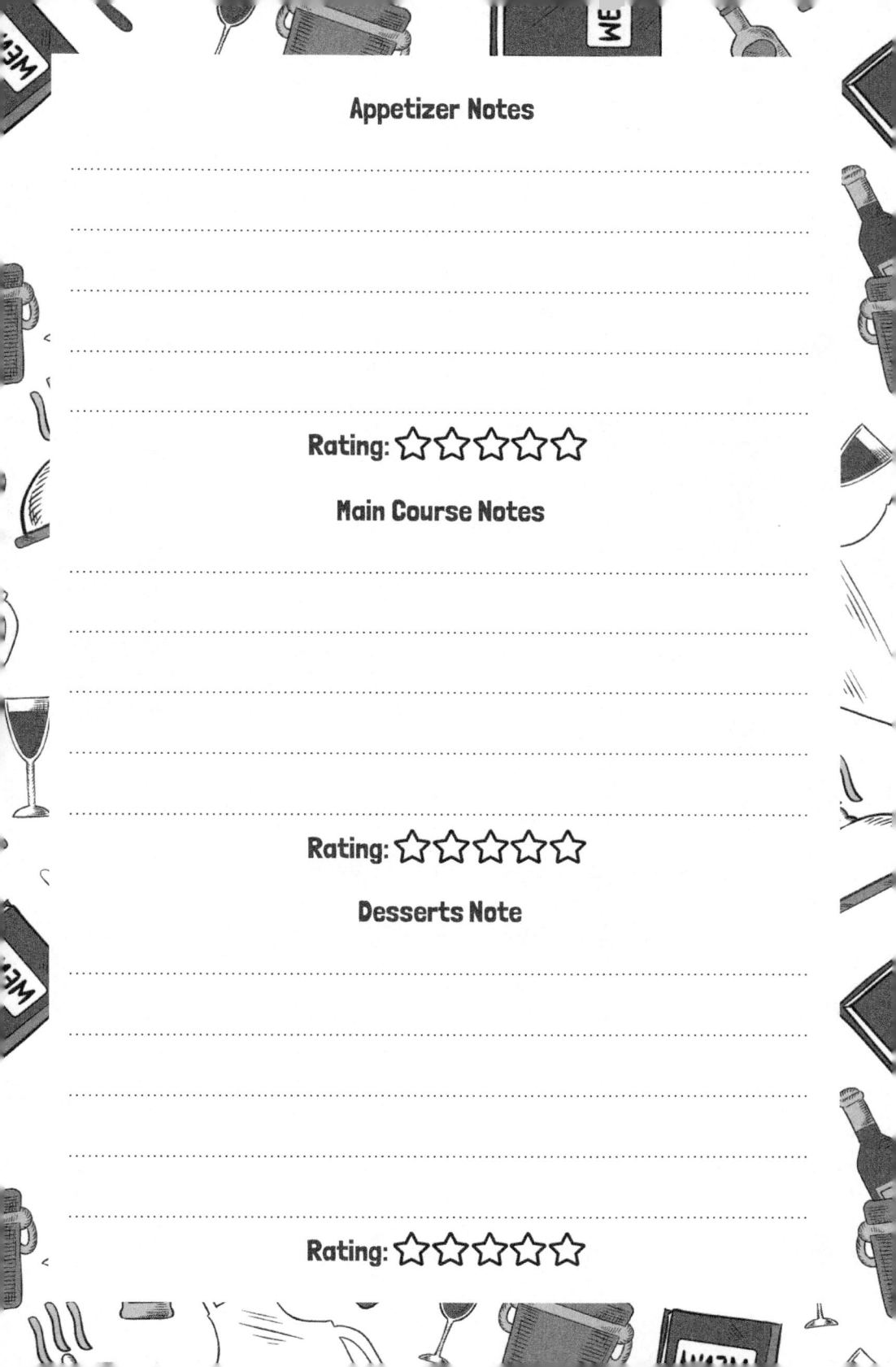

Rating: ☆☆☆☆☆

Desserts Note

....

....

....

....

Rating: ☆☆☆☆☆

Restaurant Name:

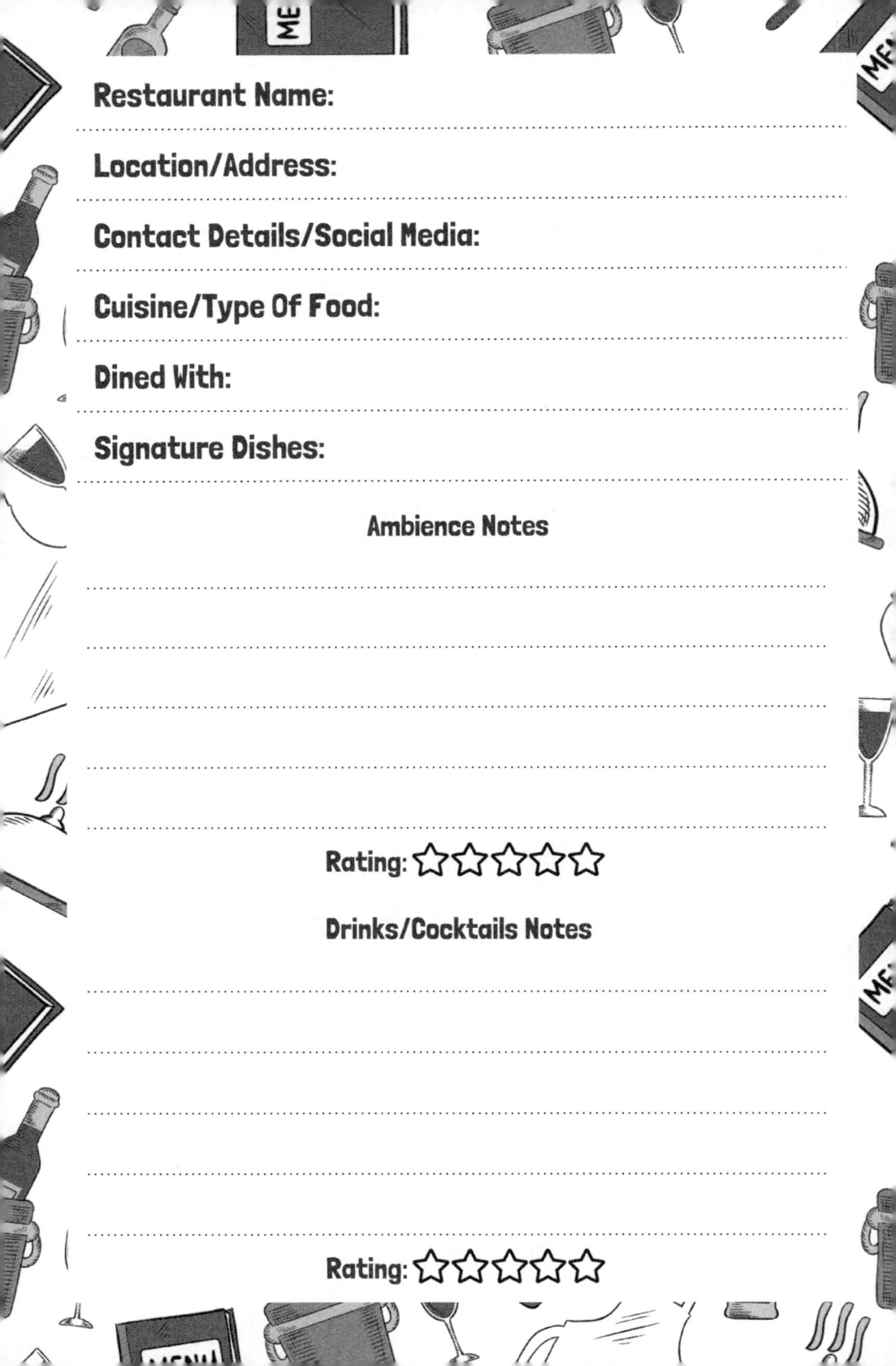

Location/Address:

Contact Details/Social Media:

Cuisine/Type Of Food:

Dined With:

Signature Dishes:

Ambience Notes

Rating: ☆☆☆☆☆

Drinks/Cocktails Notes

Rating: ☆☆☆☆☆

Appetizer Notes

....

....

....

....

Rating: ☆☆☆☆☆

Main Course Notes

....

....

....

....

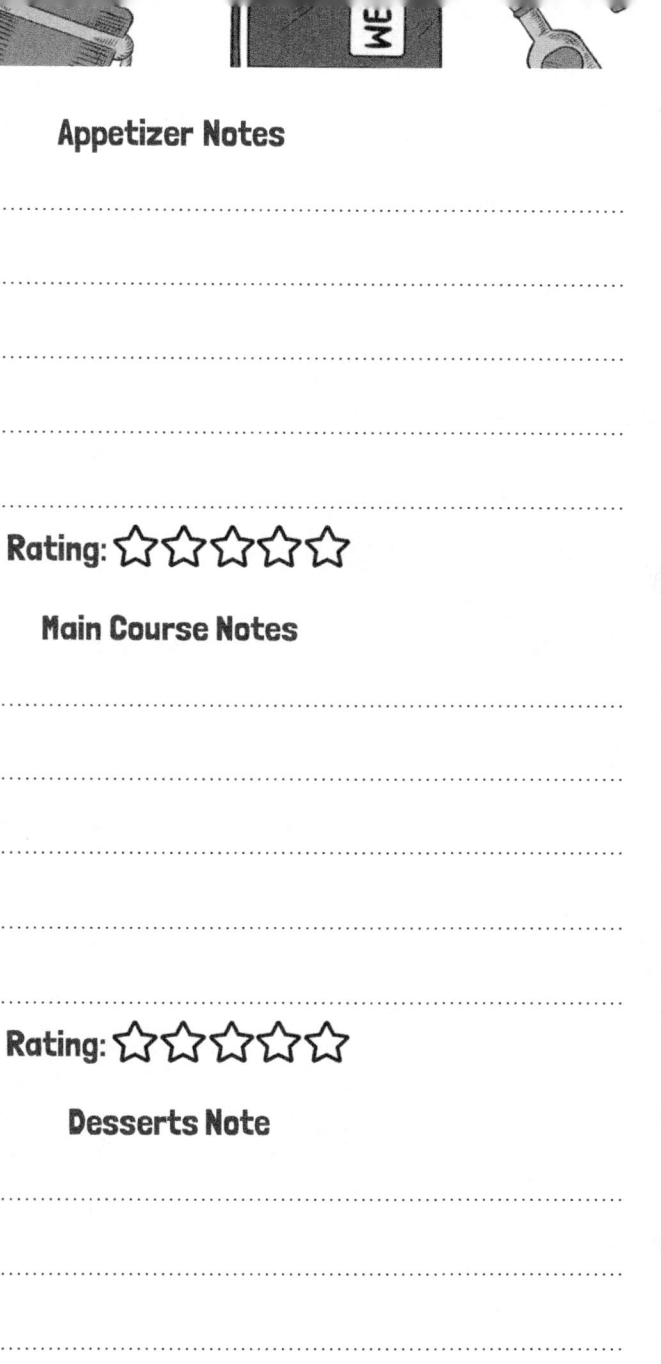

Rating: ☆☆☆☆☆

Desserts Note

....

....

....

....

Rating: ☆☆☆☆☆

Restaurant Name:

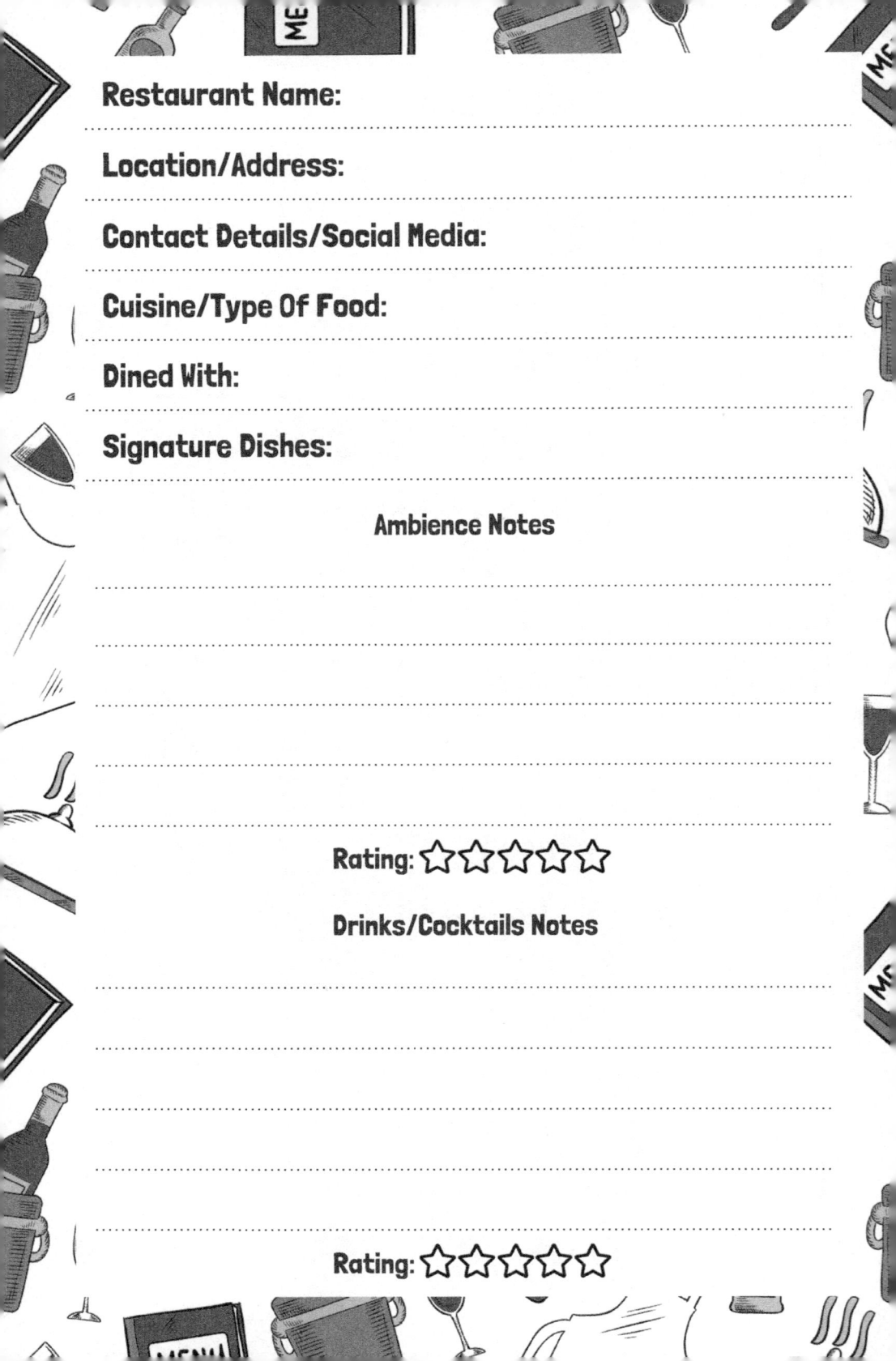

Location/Address:

Contact Details/Social Media:

Cuisine/Type Of Food:

Dined With:

Signature Dishes:

Ambience Notes

Rating: ☆☆☆☆☆

Drinks/Cocktails Notes

Rating: ☆☆☆☆☆

Appetizer Notes

....

....

....

....

Rating: ☆☆☆☆☆

Main Course Notes

....

....

....

....

Rating: ☆☆☆☆☆

Desserts Note

....

....

....

....

Rating: ☆☆☆☆☆

Restaurant Name:

Location/Address:

Contact Details/Social Media:

Cuisine/Type Of Food:

Dined With:

Signature Dishes:

Ambience Notes

Rating: ☆☆☆☆☆

Drinks/Cocktails Notes

Rating: ☆☆☆☆☆

Appetizer Notes

....

....

....

....

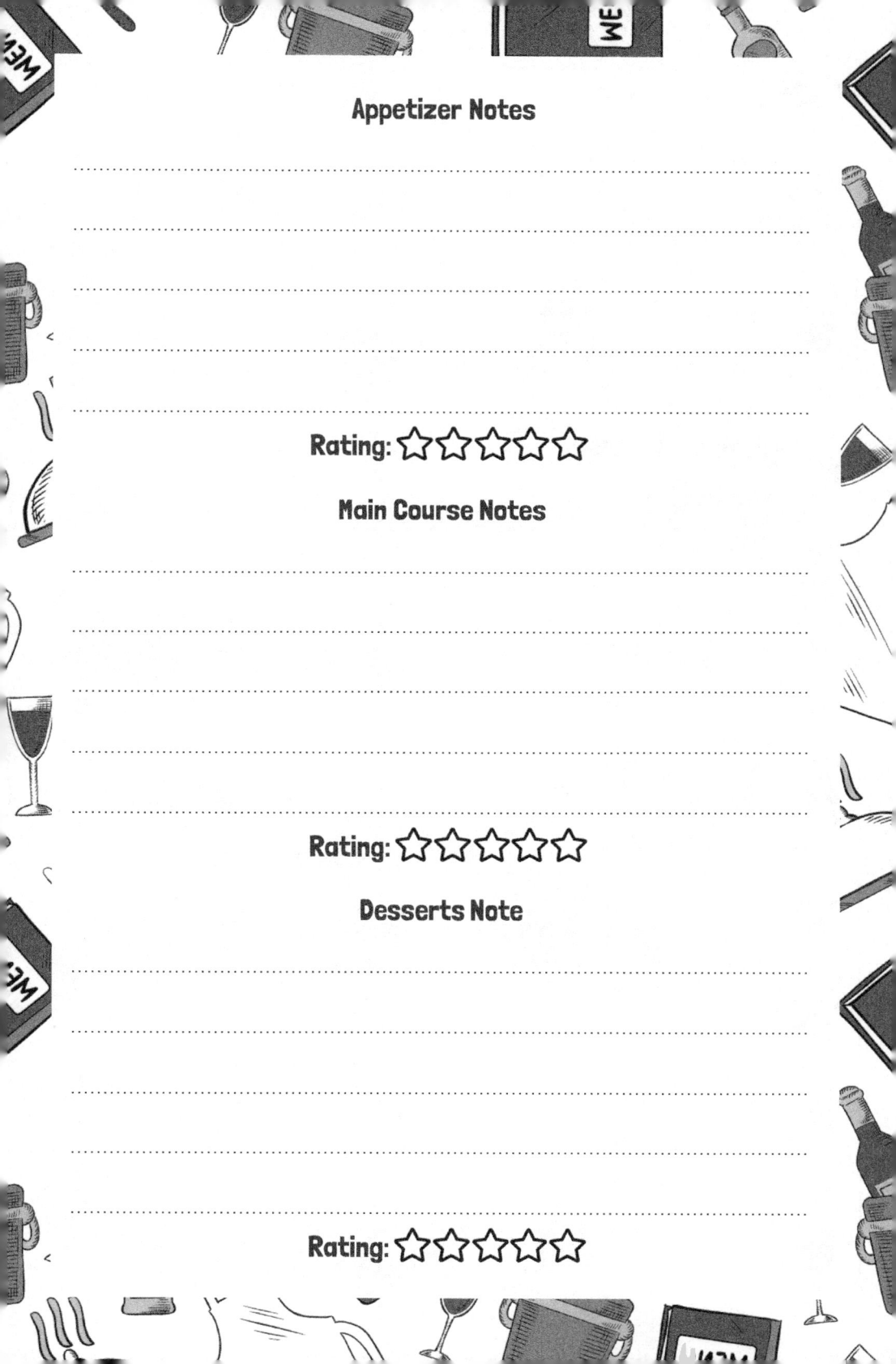

Rating: ☆☆☆☆☆

Main Course Notes

....

....

....

....

Rating: ☆☆☆☆☆

Desserts Note

....

....

....

....

Rating: ☆☆☆☆☆

Restaurant Name:

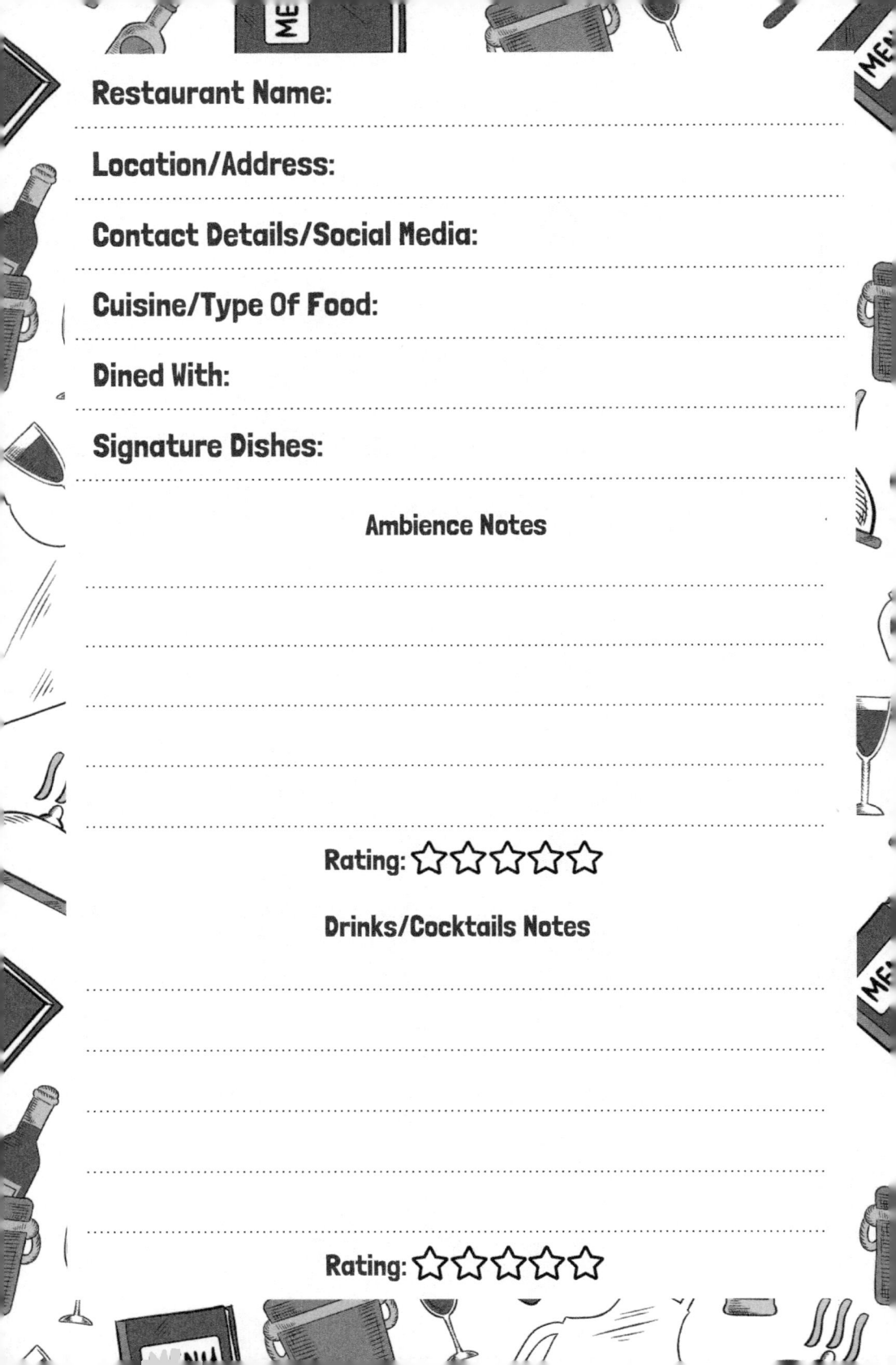

Location/Address:

Contact Details/Social Media:

Cuisine/Type Of Food:

Dined With:

Signature Dishes:

Ambience Notes

Rating: ☆☆☆☆☆

Drinks/Cocktails Notes

Rating: ☆☆☆☆☆

Appetizer Notes

....

....

....

....

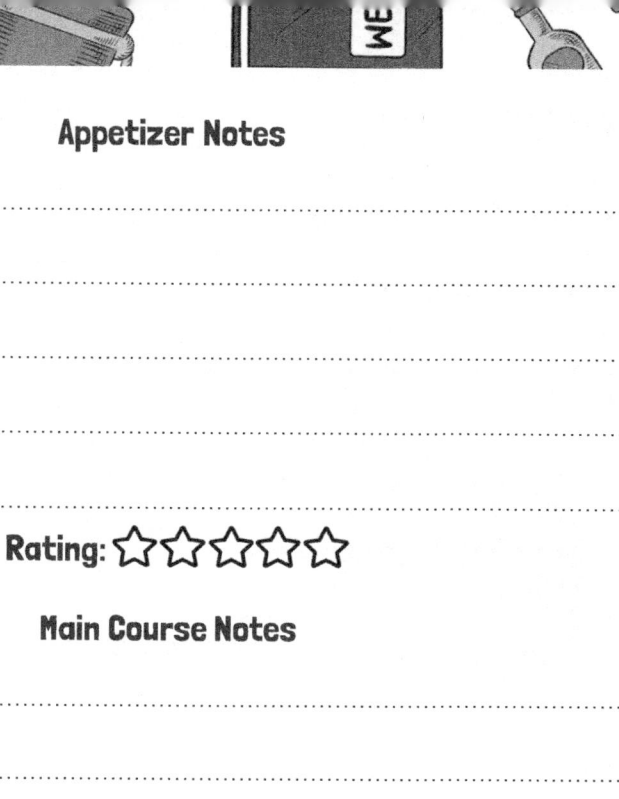

Rating: ☆☆☆☆☆

Main Course Notes

....

....

....

....

Rating: ☆☆☆☆☆

Desserts Note

....

....

....

....

Rating: ☆☆☆☆☆

Restaurant Name:

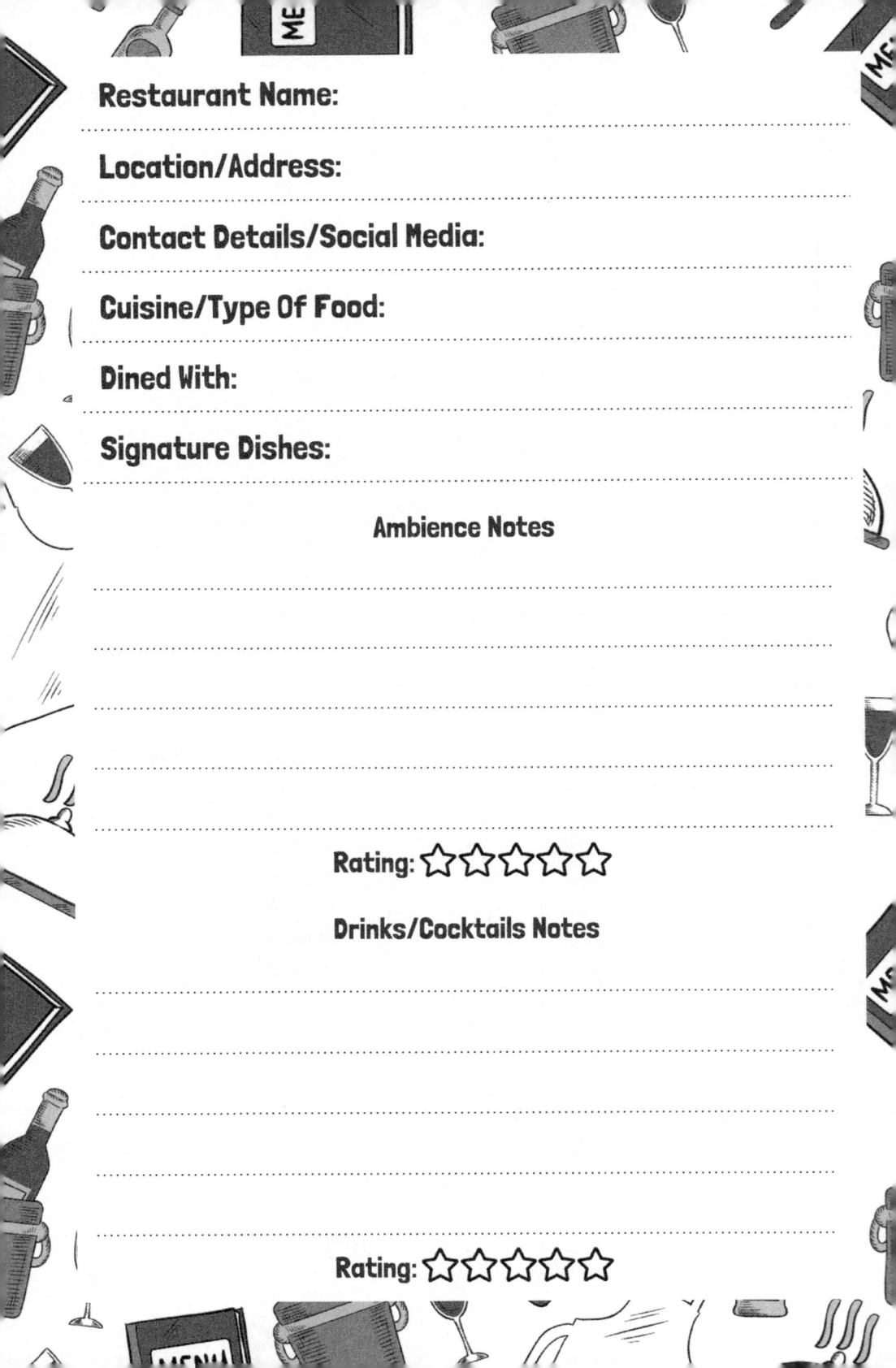

Location/Address:

Contact Details/Social Media:

Cuisine/Type Of Food:

Dined With:

Signature Dishes:

Ambience Notes

Rating: ☆☆☆☆☆

Drinks/Cocktails Notes

Rating: ☆☆☆☆☆

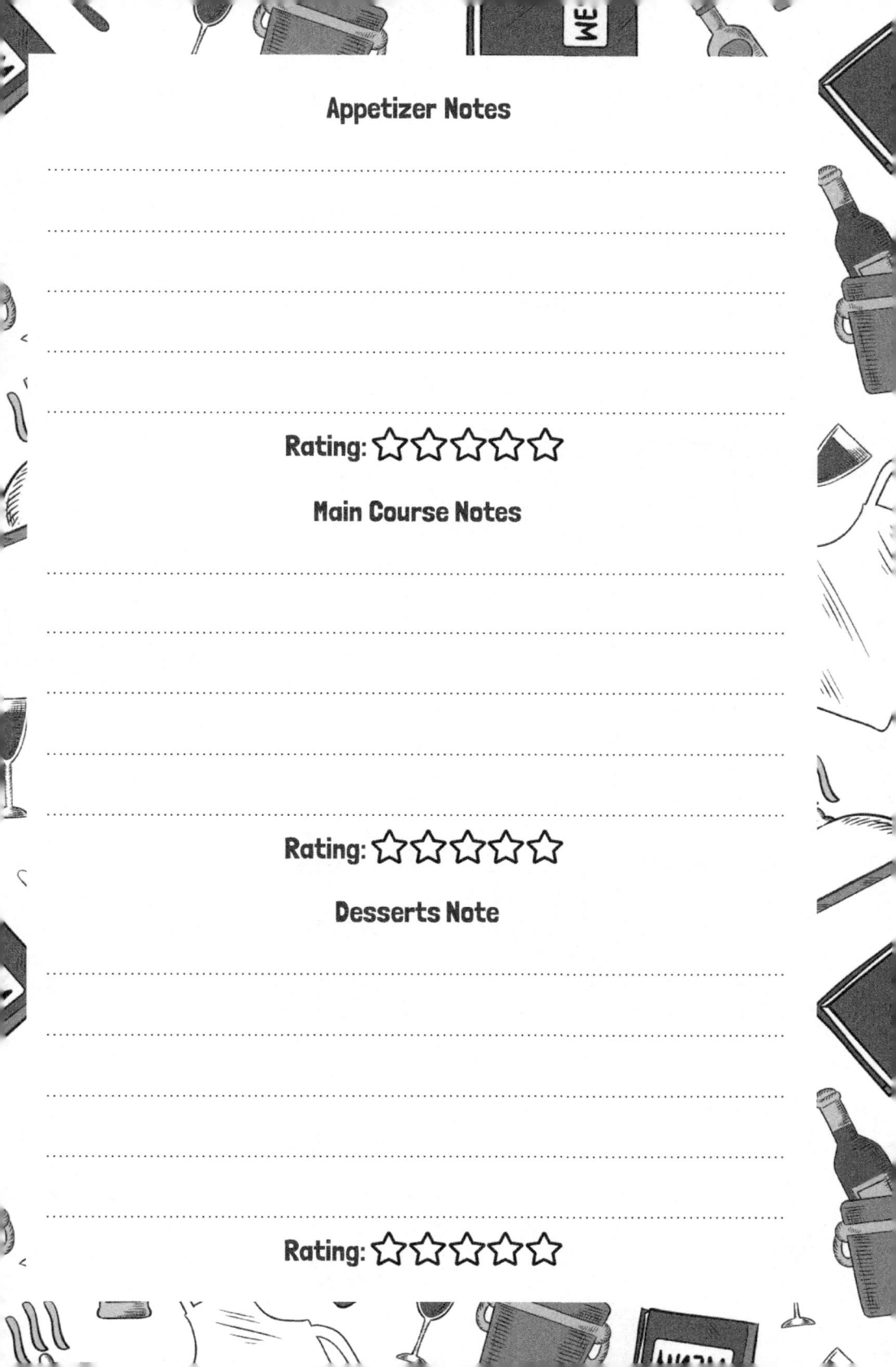

Appetizer Notes

....

....

....

....

Rating: ☆☆☆☆☆

Main Course Notes

....

....

....

....

Rating: ☆☆☆☆☆

Desserts Note

....

....

....

....

Rating: ☆☆☆☆☆

Restaurant Name:

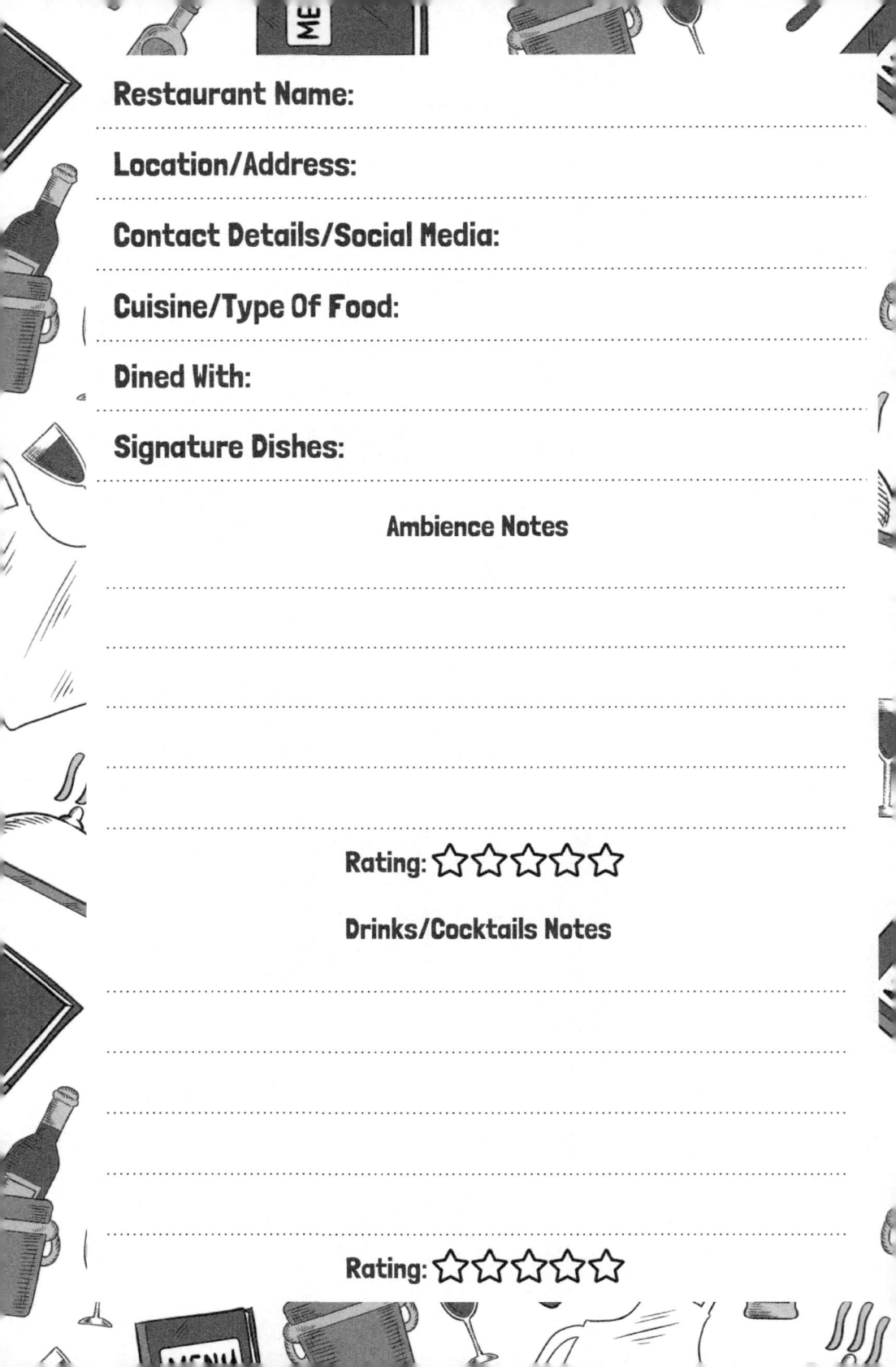

Location/Address:

Contact Details/Social Media:

Cuisine/Type Of Food:

Dined With:

Signature Dishes:

Ambience Notes

Rating: ☆☆☆☆☆

Drinks/Cocktails Notes

Rating: ☆☆☆☆☆

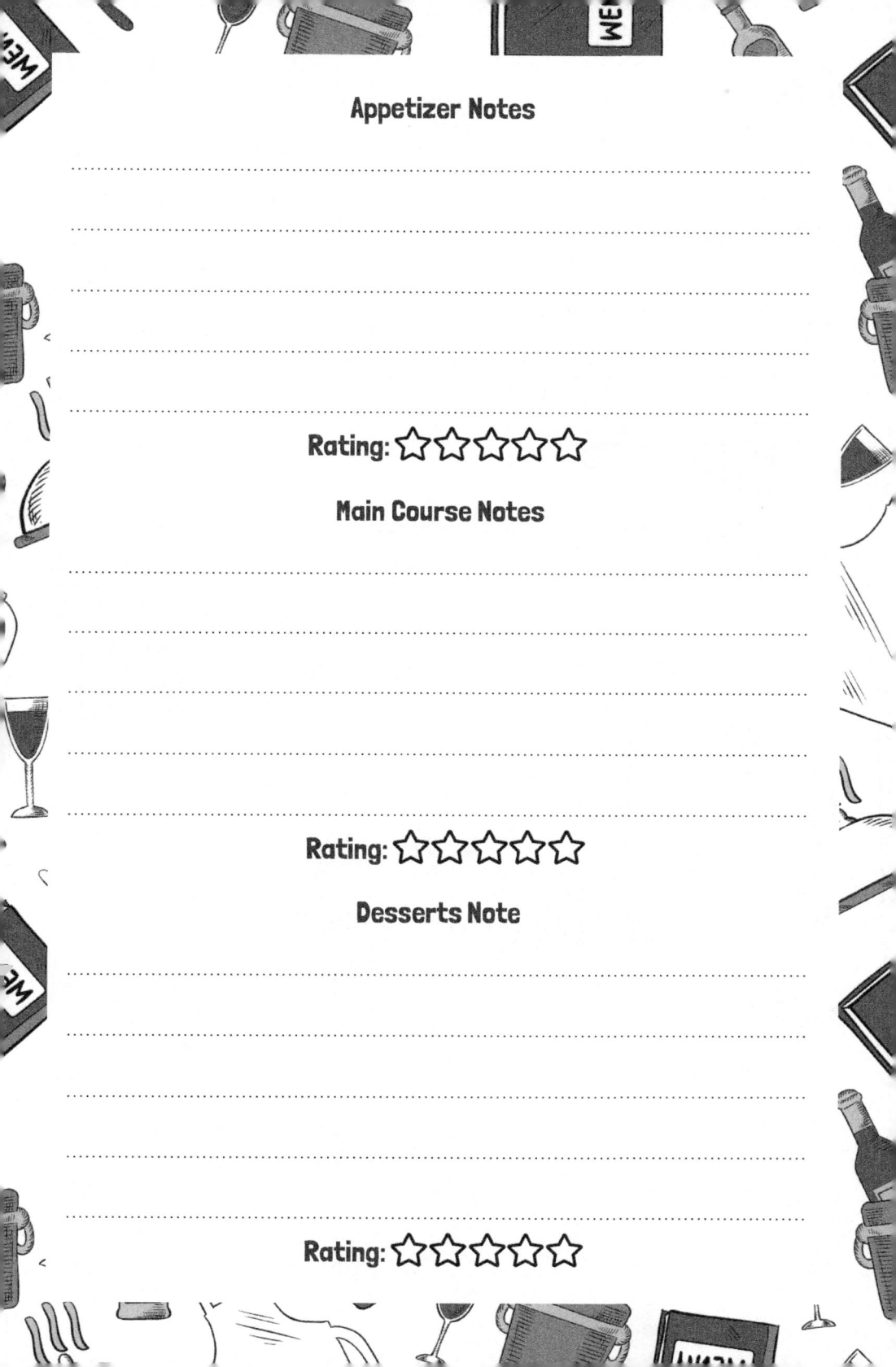

Appetizer Notes

....

....

....

....

Rating: ☆☆☆☆☆

Main Course Notes

....

....

....

....

Rating: ☆☆☆☆☆

Desserts Note

....

....

....

....

Rating: ☆☆☆☆☆

Restaurant Name:

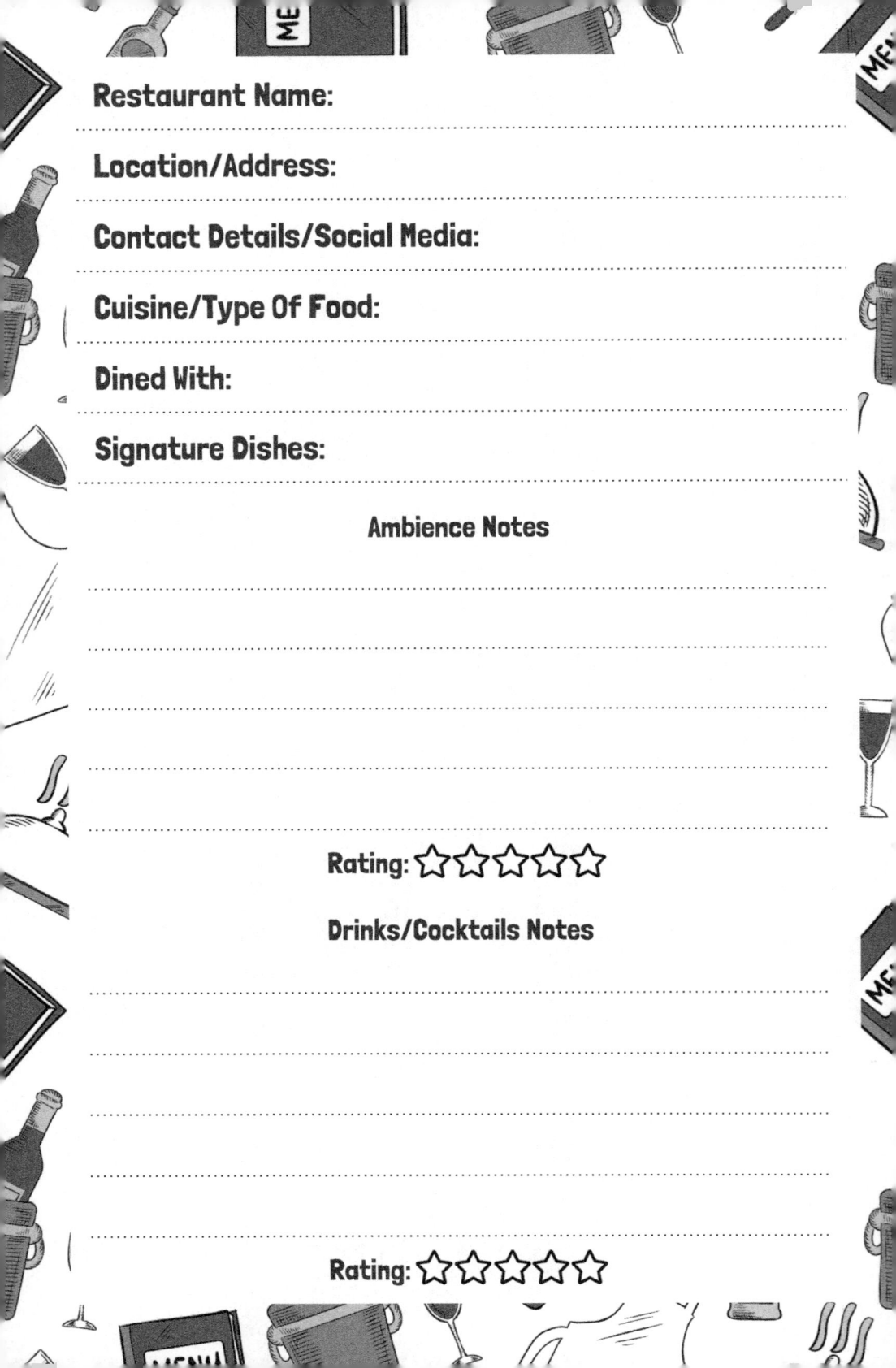

Location/Address:

Contact Details/Social Media:

Cuisine/Type Of Food:

Dined With:

Signature Dishes:

Ambience Notes

Rating: ☆☆☆☆☆

Drinks/Cocktails Notes

Rating: ☆☆☆☆☆

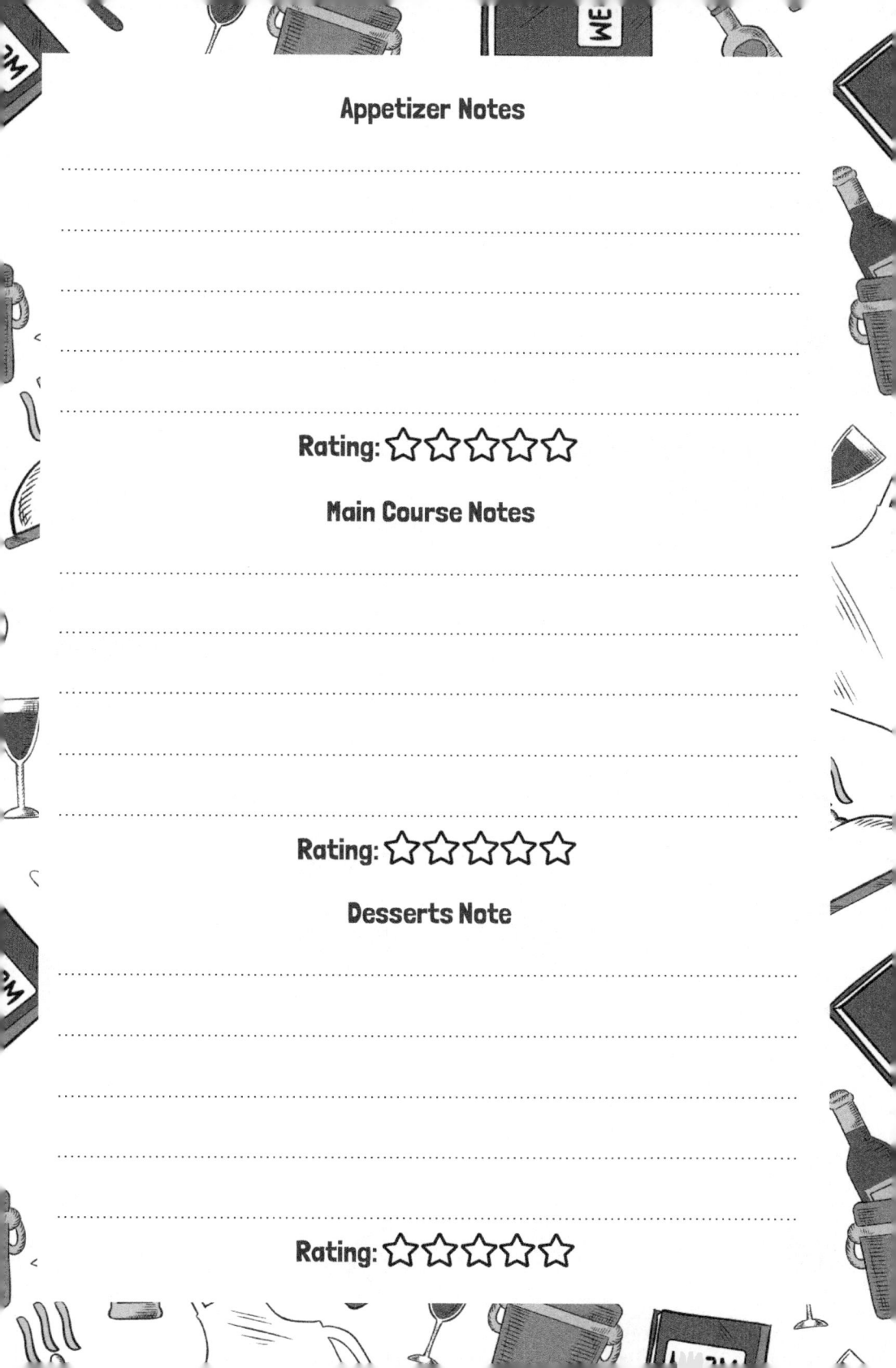

Appetizer Notes

....

....

....

....

Rating: ☆☆☆☆☆

Main Course Notes

....

....

....

....

Rating: ☆☆☆☆☆

Desserts Note

....

....

....

....

Rating: ☆☆☆☆☆

Restaurant Name:

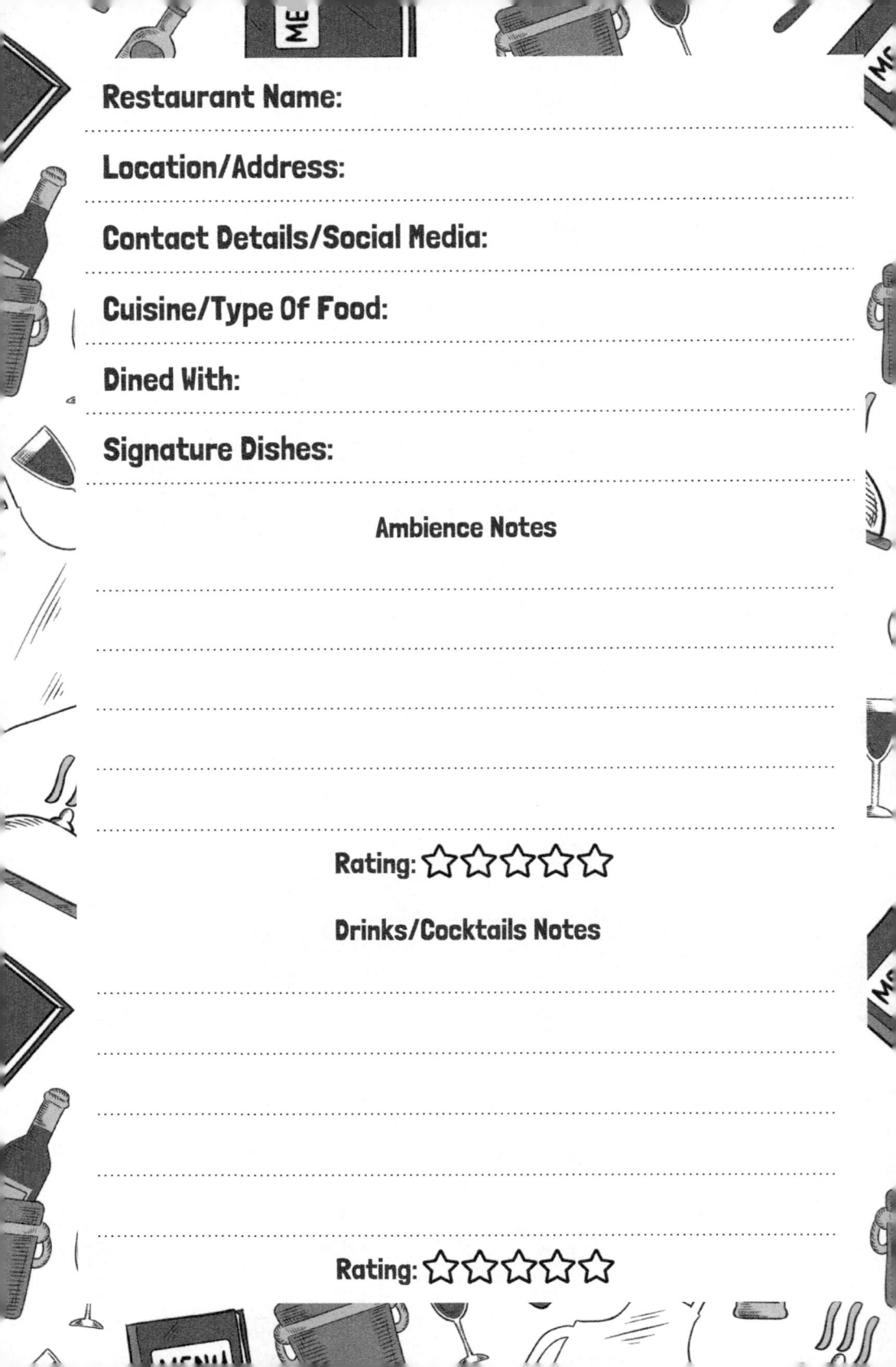

Location/Address:

Contact Details/Social Media:

Cuisine/Type Of Food:

Dined With:

Signature Dishes:

Ambience Notes

Rating: ☆☆☆☆☆

Drinks/Cocktails Notes

Rating: ☆☆☆☆☆

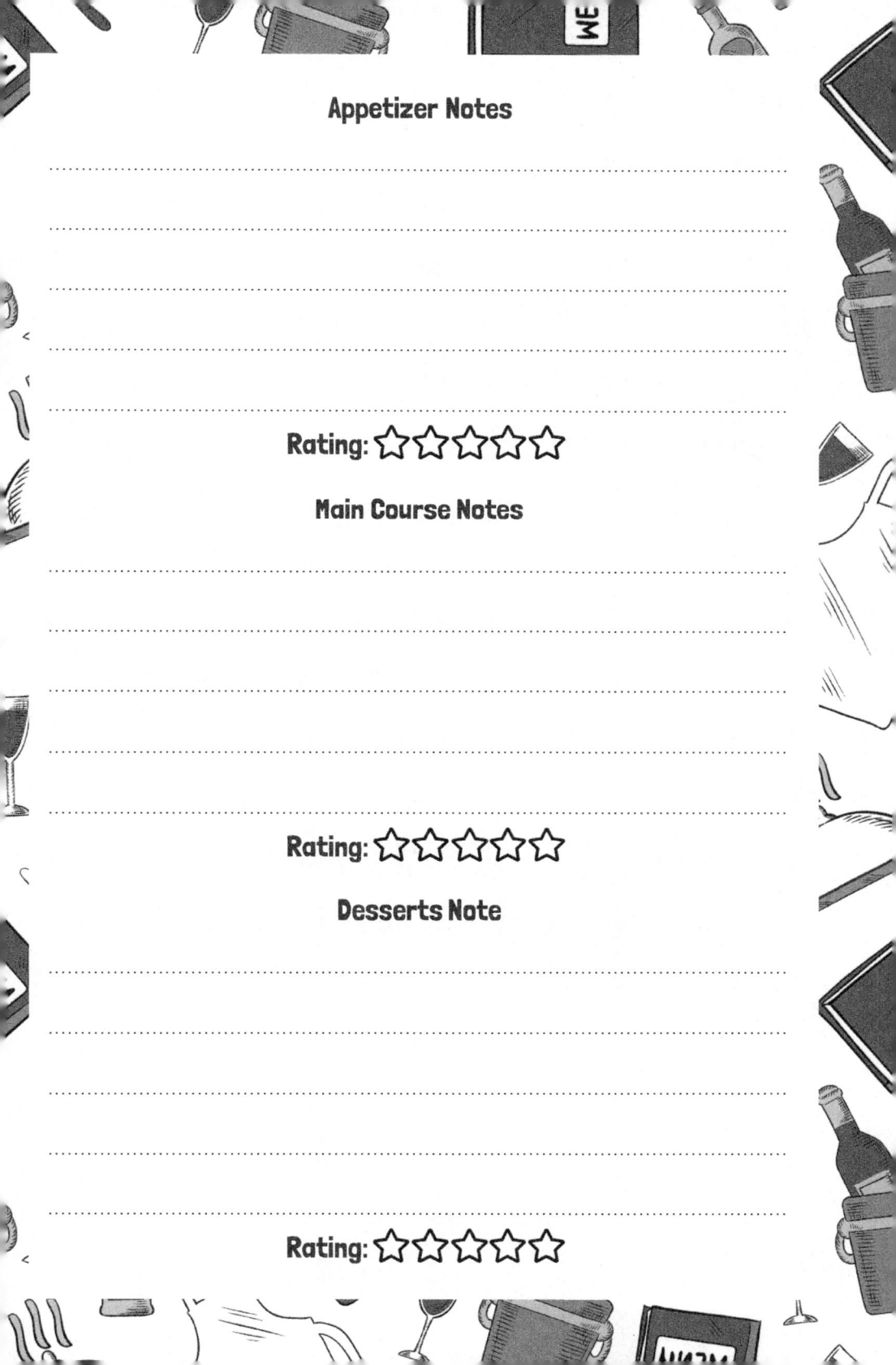

Appetizer Notes

....

....

....

....

Rating: ☆☆☆☆☆

Main Course Notes

....

....

....

....

Rating: ☆☆☆☆☆

Desserts Note

....

....

....

....

Rating: ☆☆☆☆☆

Restaurant Name:

Location/Address:

Contact Details/Social Media:

Cuisine/Type Of Food:

Dined With:

Signature Dishes:

Ambience Notes

Rating: ☆☆☆☆☆

Drinks/Cocktails Notes

Rating: ☆☆☆☆☆

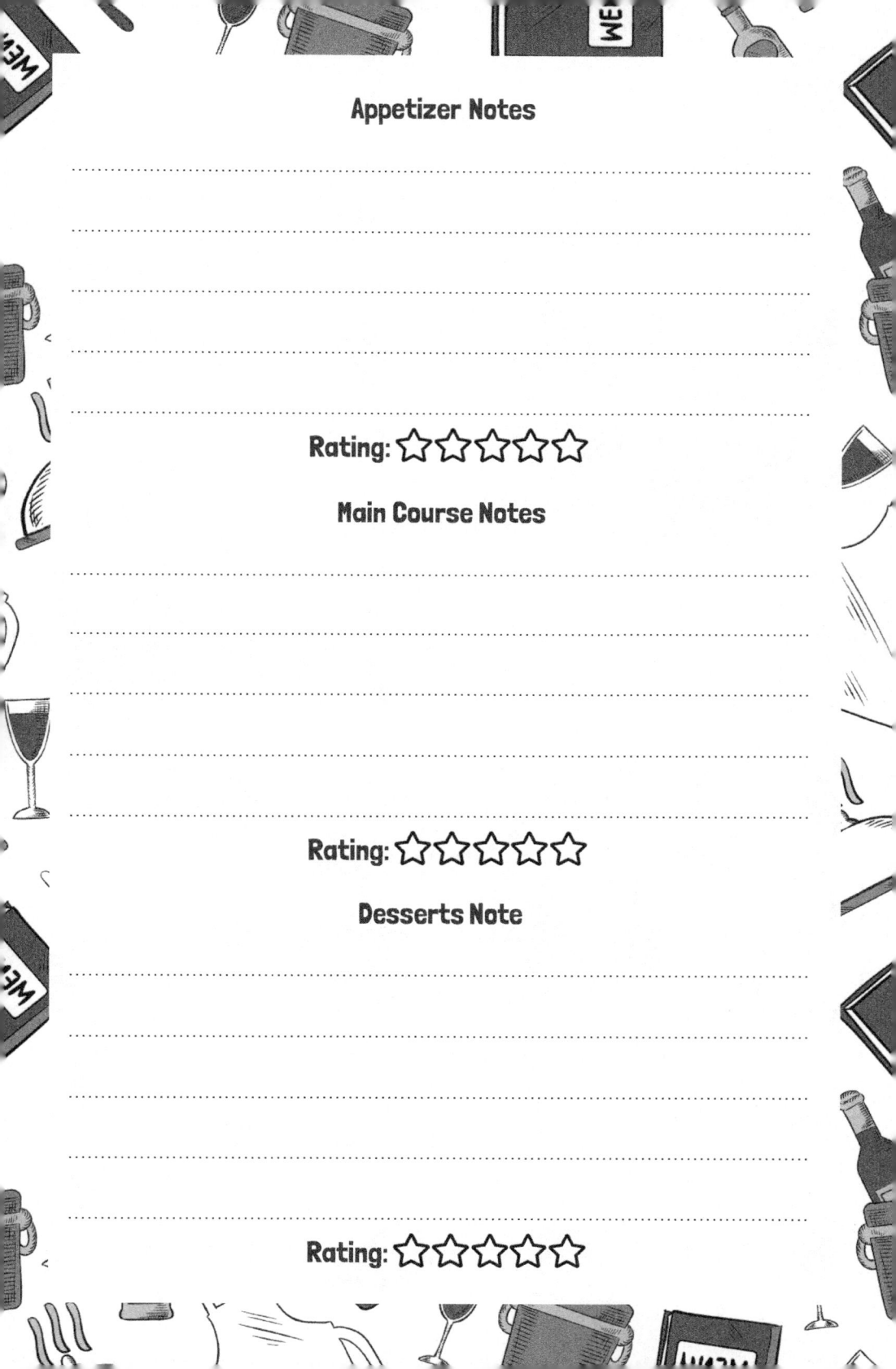

Appetizer Notes

....
....
....
....

Rating: ☆☆☆☆☆

Main Course Notes

....
....
....
....

Rating: ☆☆☆☆☆

Desserts Note

....
....
....
....

Rating: ☆☆☆☆☆

Restaurant Name:

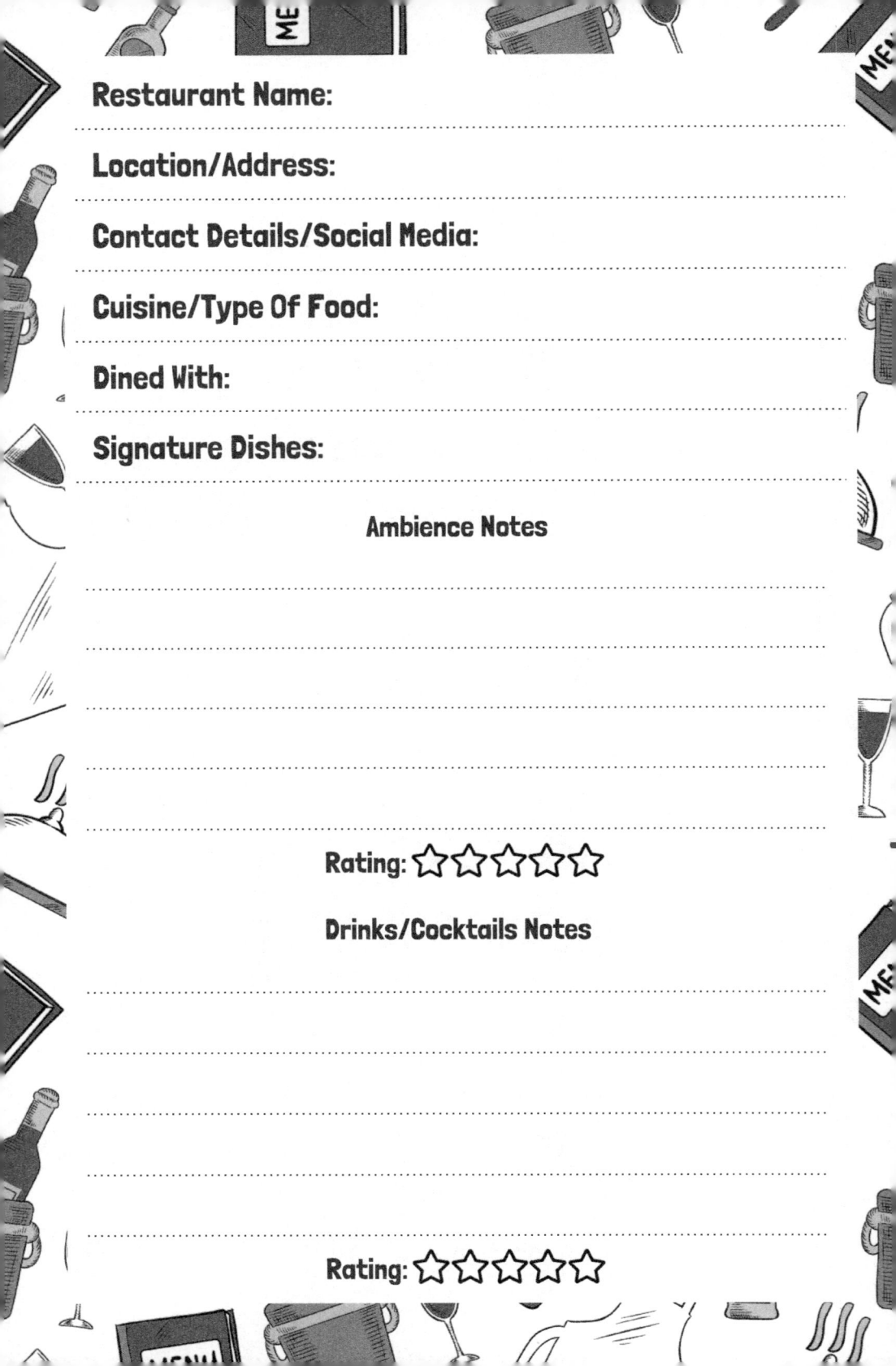

Location/Address:

Contact Details/Social Media:

Cuisine/Type Of Food:

Dined With:

Signature Dishes:

Ambience Notes

Rating: ☆☆☆☆☆

Drinks/Cocktails Notes

Rating: ☆☆☆☆☆

Appetizer Notes

....

....

....

....

Rating: ☆☆☆☆☆

Main Course Notes

....

....

....

....

Rating: ☆☆☆☆☆

Desserts Note

....

....

....

....

Rating: ☆☆☆☆☆

Restaurant Name:

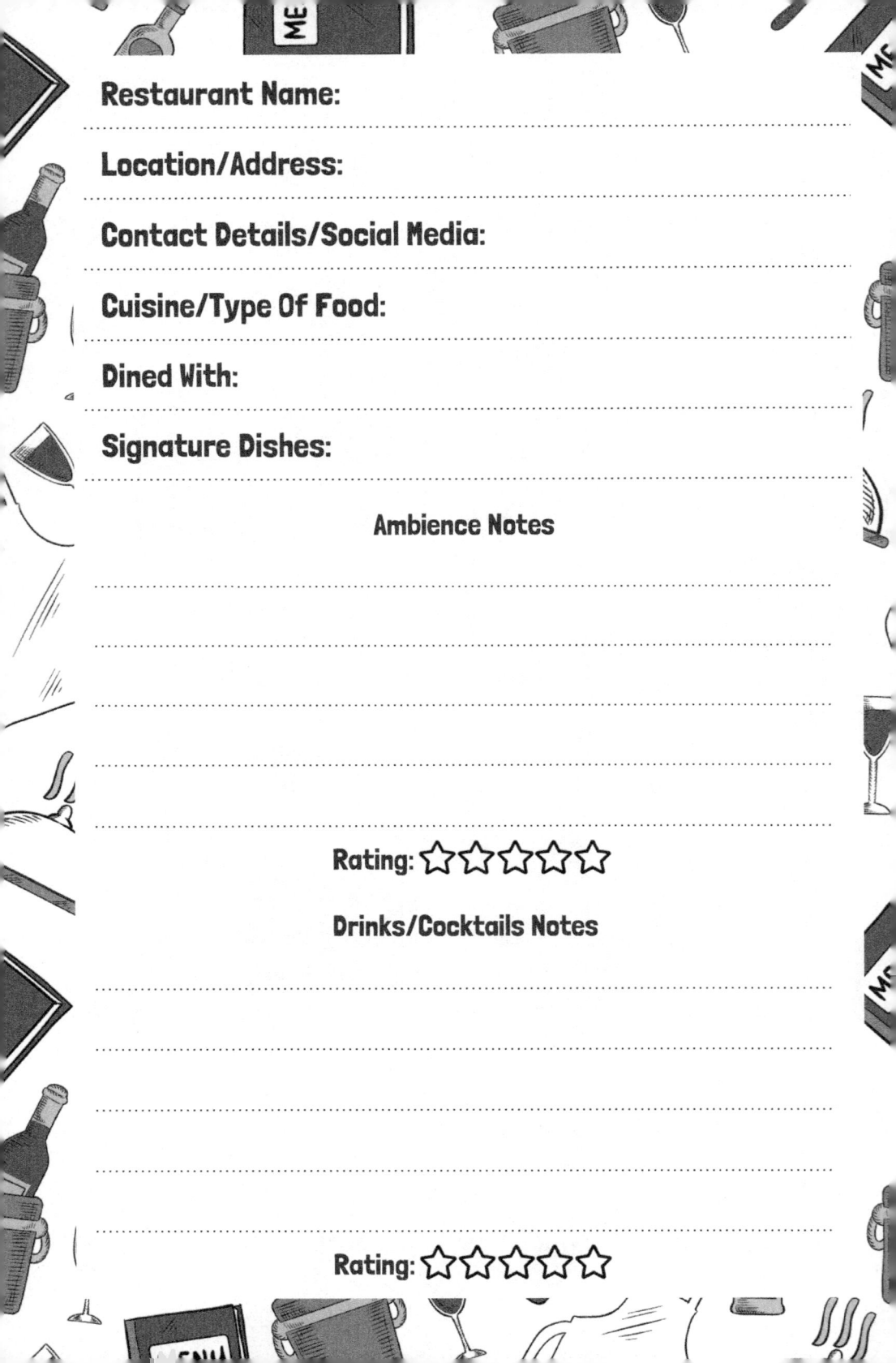

Location/Address:

Contact Details/Social Media:

Cuisine/Type Of Food:

Dined With:

Signature Dishes:

Ambience Notes

Rating: ☆☆☆☆☆

Drinks/Cocktails Notes

Rating: ☆☆☆☆☆

Appetizer Notes

....

....

....

....

Rating: ☆☆☆☆☆

Main Course Notes

....

....

....

....

Rating: ☆☆☆☆☆

Desserts Note

....

....

....

....

Rating: ☆☆☆☆☆

Restaurant Name:

Location/Address:

Contact Details/Social Media:

Cuisine/Type Of Food:

Dined With:

Signature Dishes:

Ambience Notes

Rating: ☆☆☆☆☆

Drinks/Cocktails Notes

Rating: ☆☆☆☆☆

Appetizer Notes

....

....

....

....

Rating: ☆☆☆☆☆

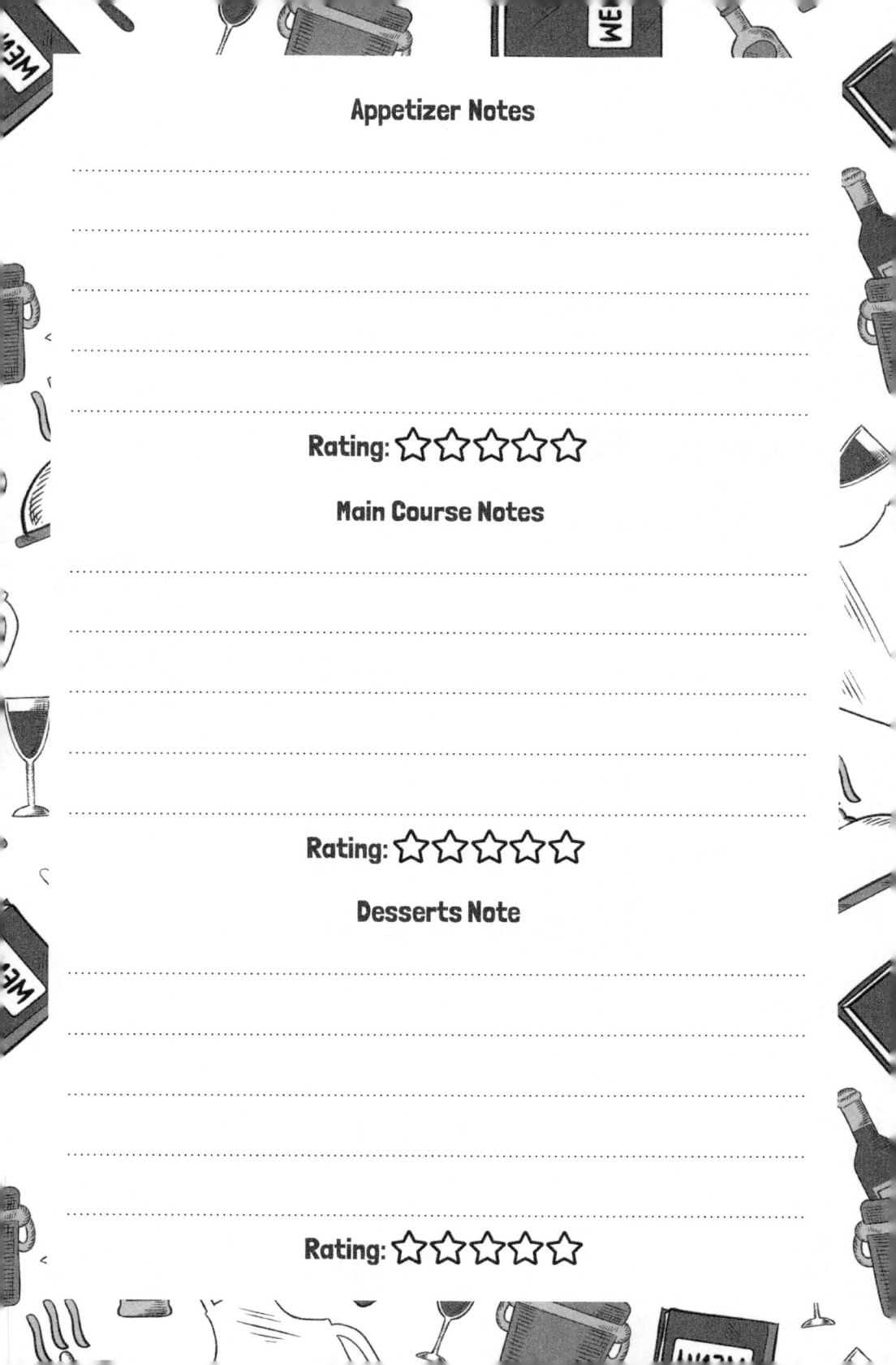

Main Course Notes

....

....

....

....

Rating: ☆☆☆☆☆

Desserts Note

....

....

....

....

Rating: ☆☆☆☆☆

Restaurant Name:

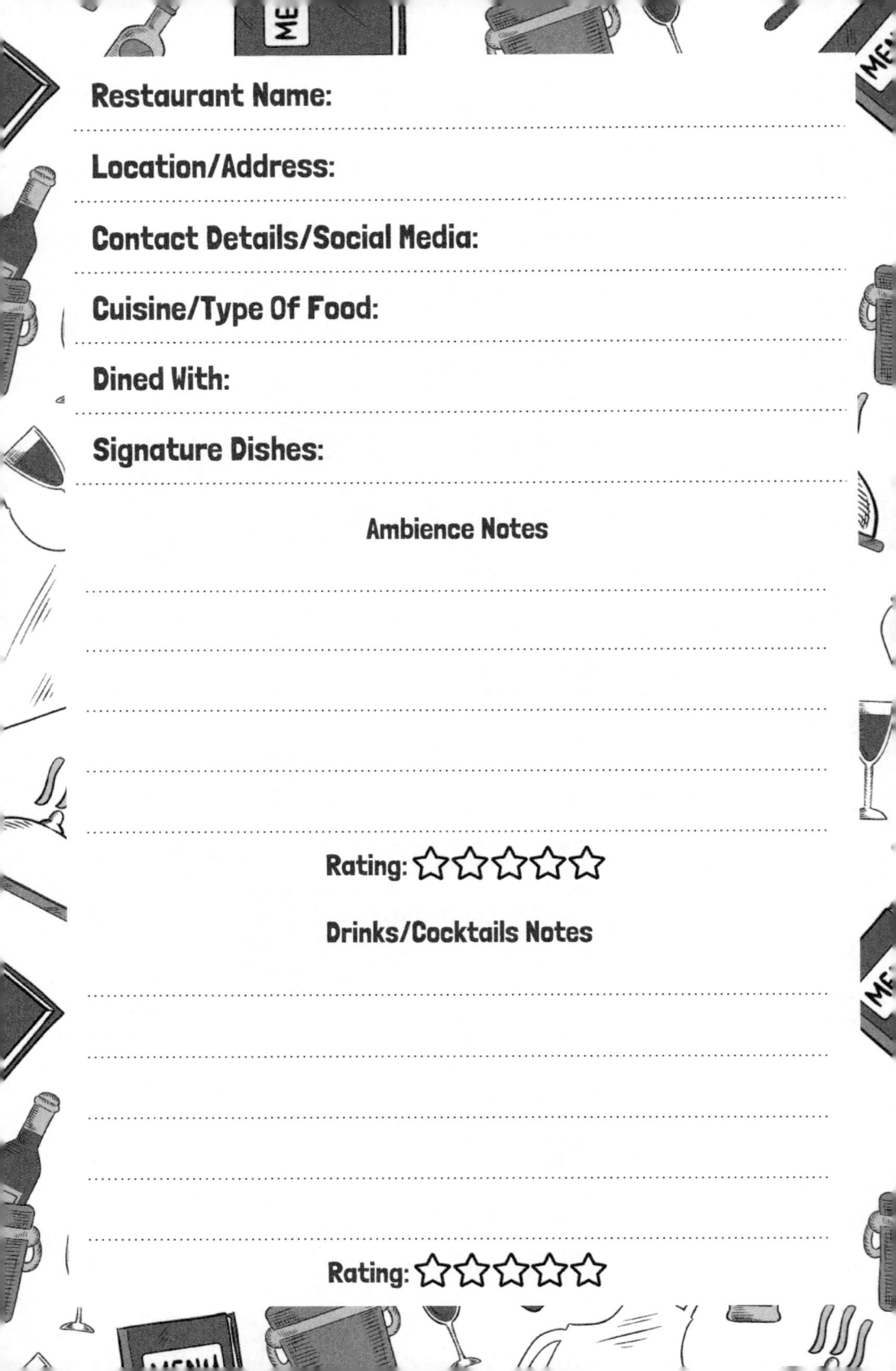

Location/Address:

Contact Details/Social Media:

Cuisine/Type Of Food:

Dined With:

Signature Dishes:

Ambience Notes

Rating: ☆☆☆☆☆

Drinks/Cocktails Notes

Rating: ☆☆☆☆☆

Appetizer Notes

....

....

....

....

Rating: ☆☆☆☆☆

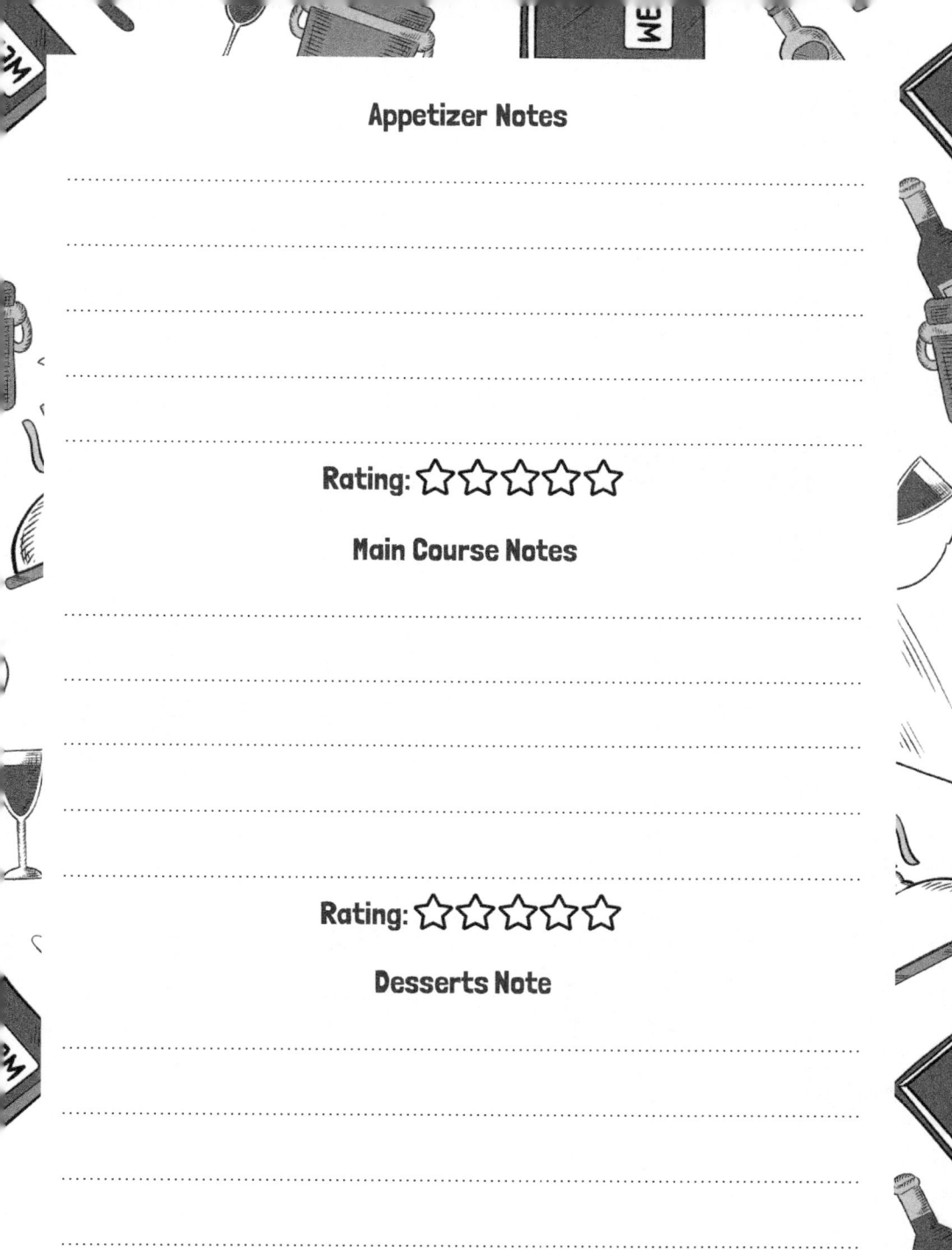

Main Course Notes

....

....

....

....

Rating: ☆☆☆☆☆

Desserts Note

....

....

....

....

Rating: ☆☆☆☆☆

Restaurant Name:

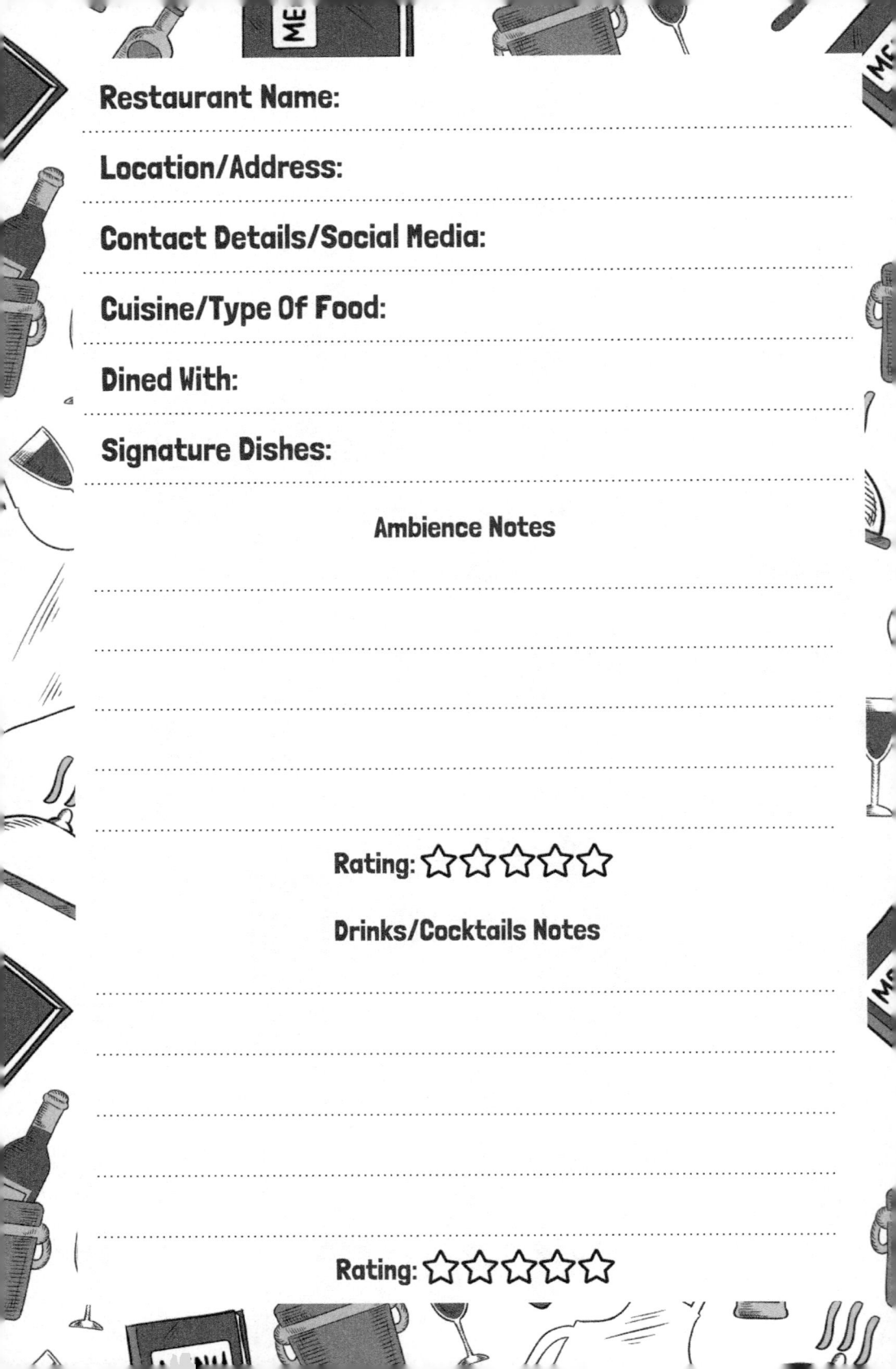

Location/Address:

Contact Details/Social Media:

Cuisine/Type Of Food:

Dined With:

Signature Dishes:

Ambience Notes

Rating: ☆☆☆☆☆

Drinks/Cocktails Notes

Rating: ☆☆☆☆☆

Appetizer Notes

....
....
....
....

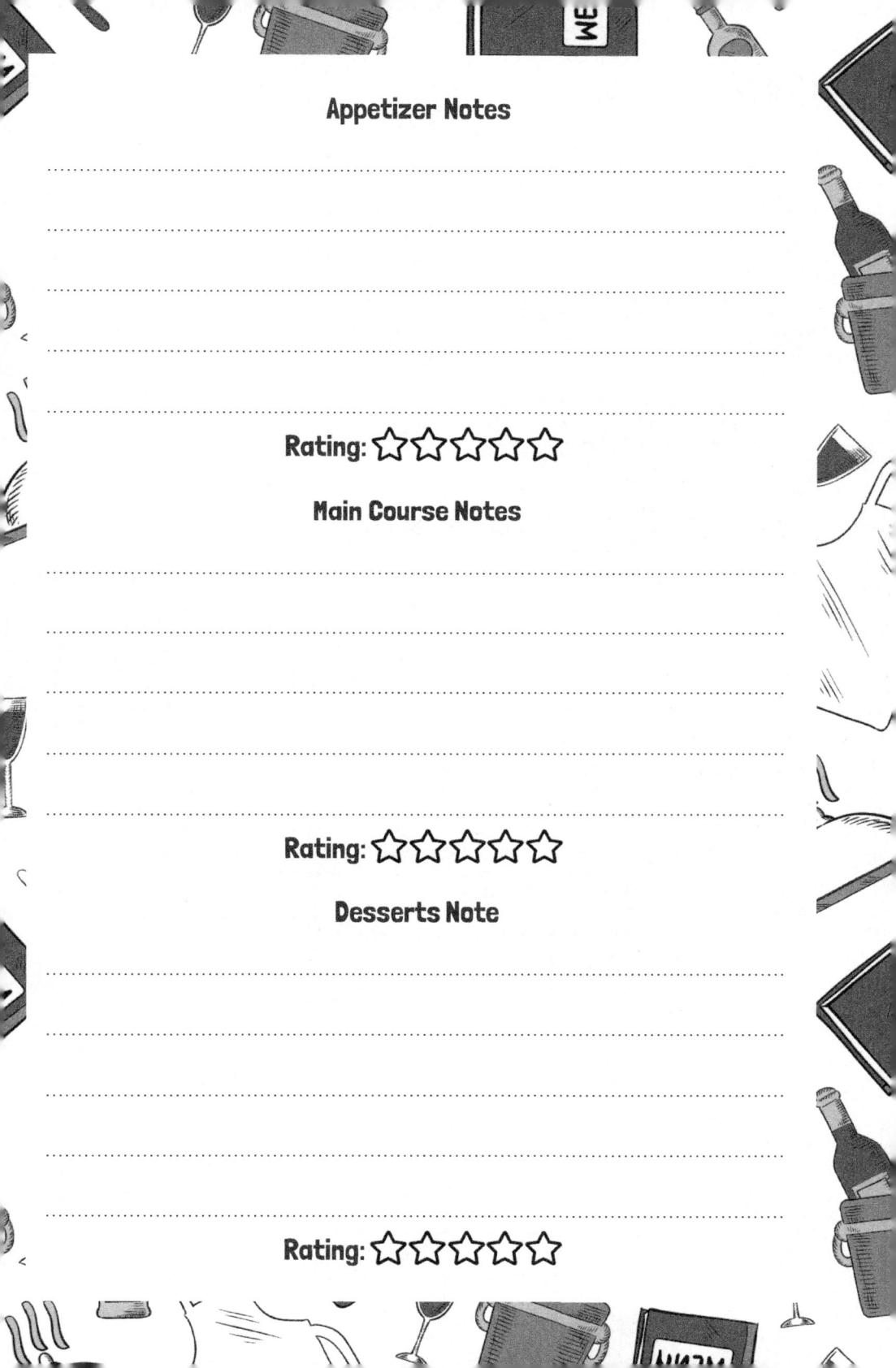

Rating: ☆☆☆☆☆

Main Course Notes

....
....
....
....

Rating: ☆☆☆☆☆

Desserts Note

....
....
....
....

Rating: ☆☆☆☆☆

Restaurant Name: ....

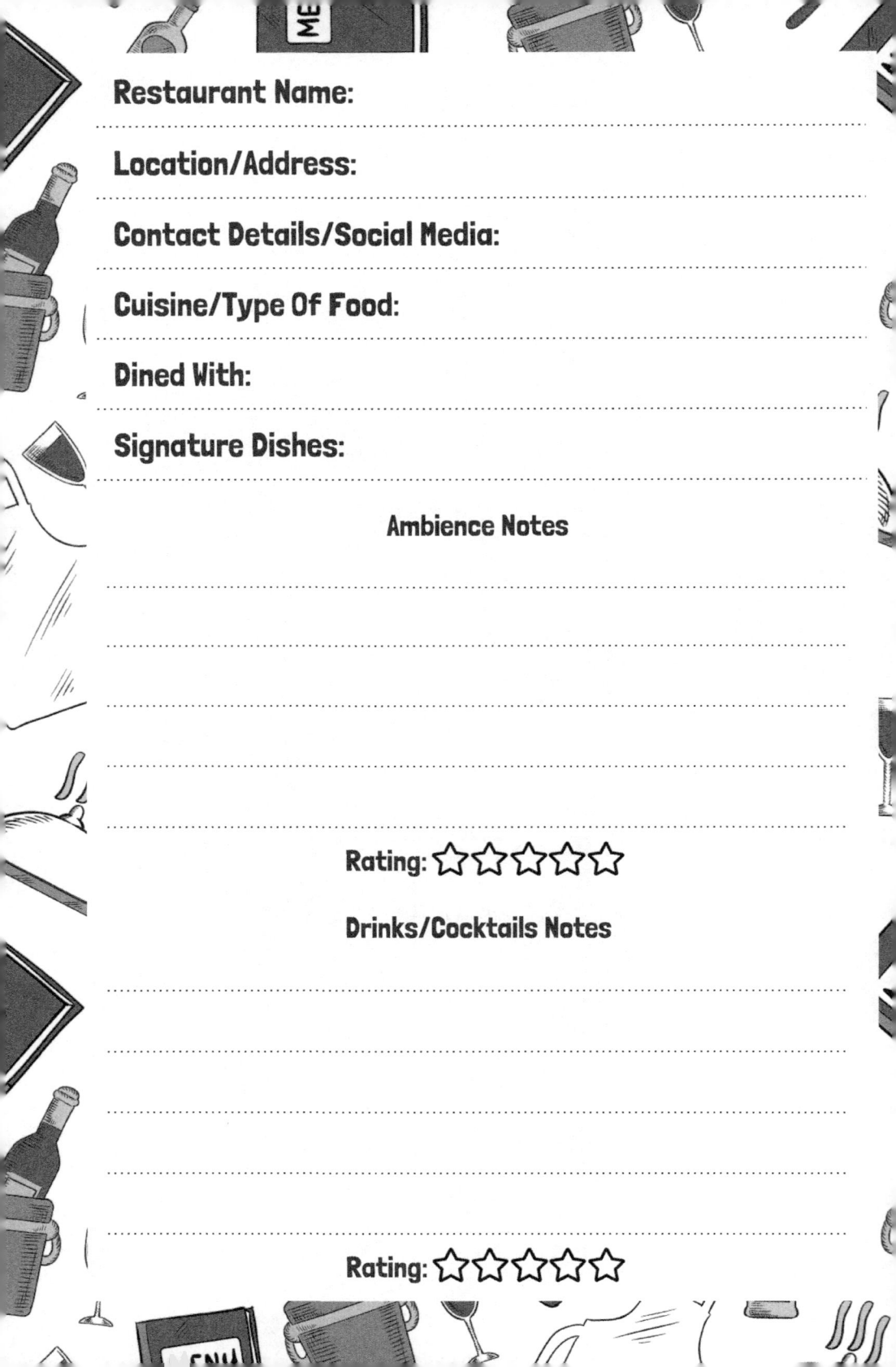

Location/Address: ....

Contact Details/Social Media: ....

Cuisine/Type Of Food: ....

Dined With: ....

Signature Dishes: ....

Ambience Notes

....

....

....

....

Rating: ☆☆☆☆☆

Drinks/Cocktails Notes

....

....

....

....

Rating: ☆☆☆☆☆

Appetizer Notes

....
....
....
....

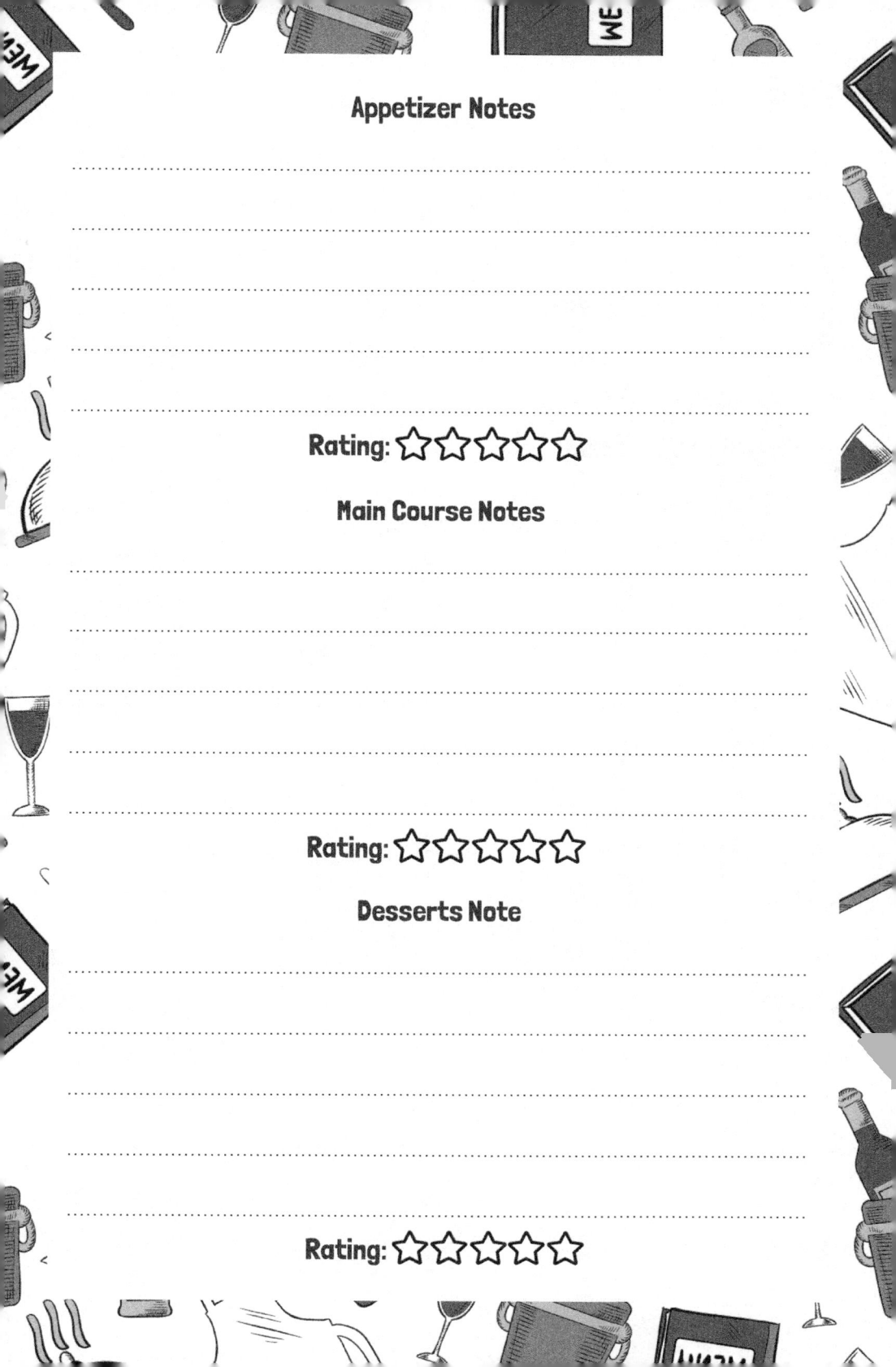

Rating: ☆☆☆☆☆

Main Course Notes

....
....
....
....

Rating: ☆☆☆☆☆

Desserts Note

....
....
....
....

Rating: ☆☆☆☆☆

Restaurant Name:

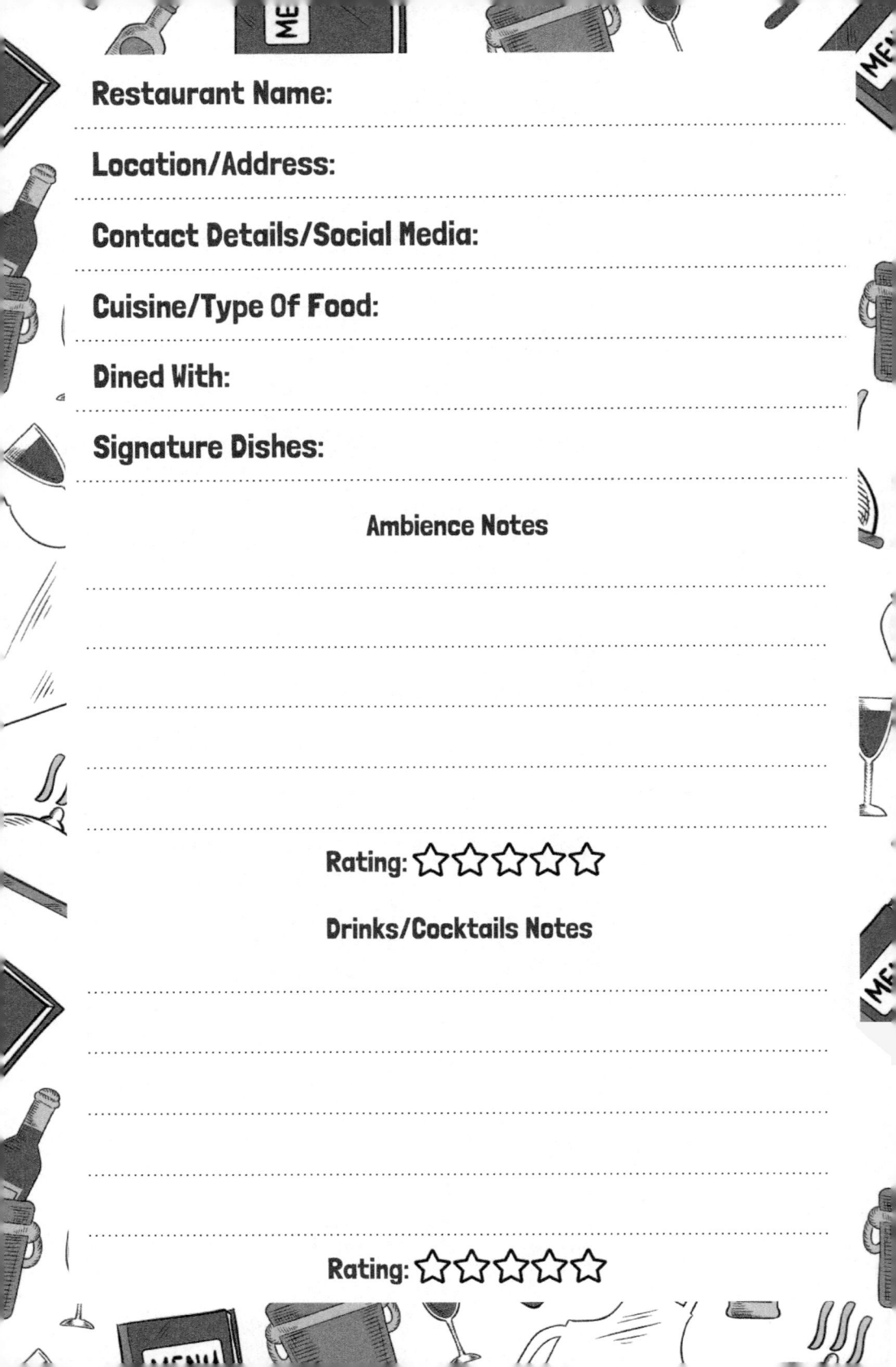

Location/Address:

Contact Details/Social Media:

Cuisine/Type Of Food:

Dined With:

Signature Dishes:

Ambience Notes

Rating: ☆☆☆☆☆

Drinks/Cocktails Notes

Rating: ☆☆☆☆☆

Appetizer Notes

....

....

....

....

....

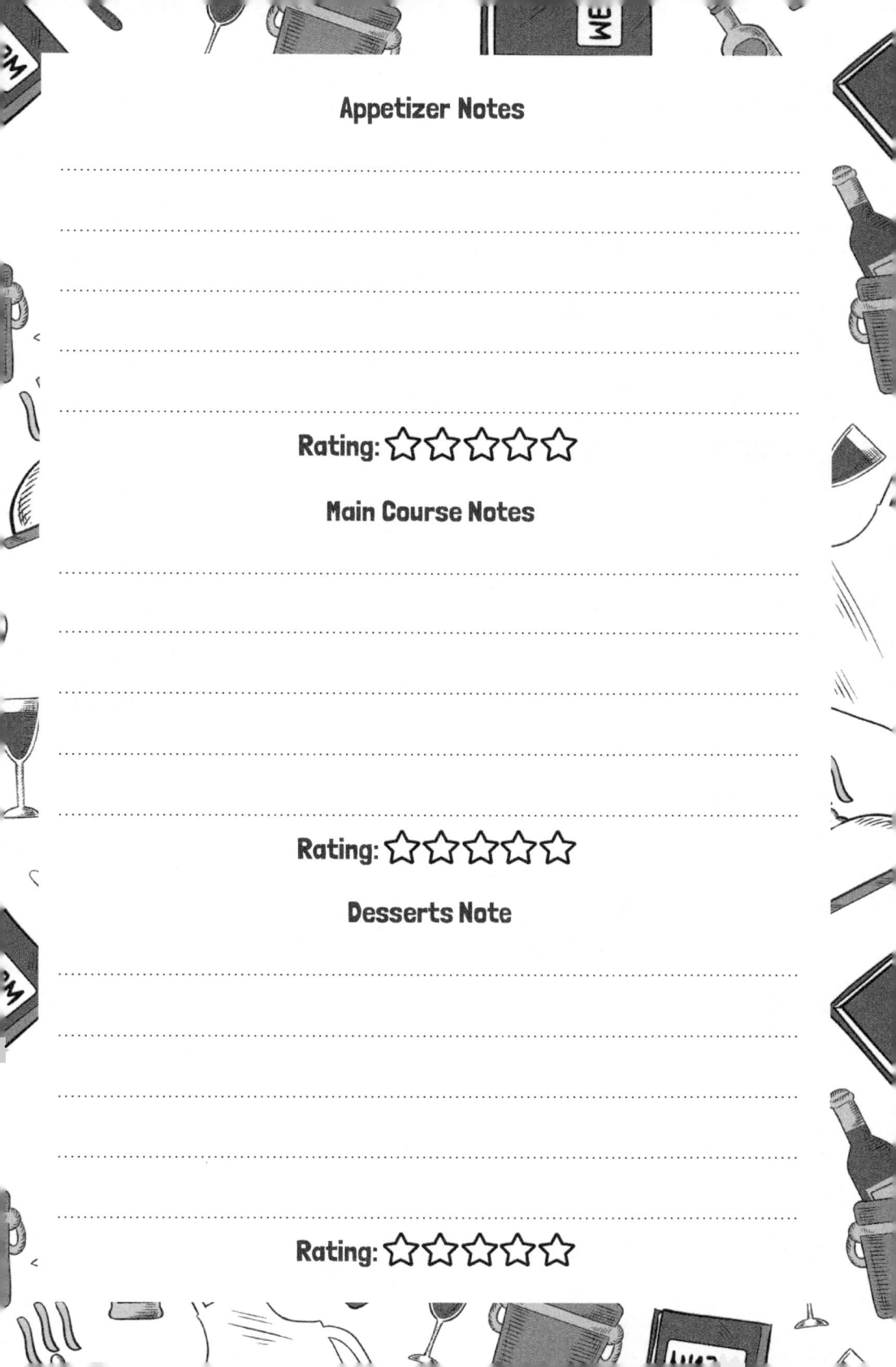

Rating: ☆☆☆☆☆

Main Course Notes

....

....

....

....

....

Rating: ☆☆☆☆☆

Desserts Note

....

....

....

....

....

Rating: ☆☆☆☆☆

Restaurant Name:

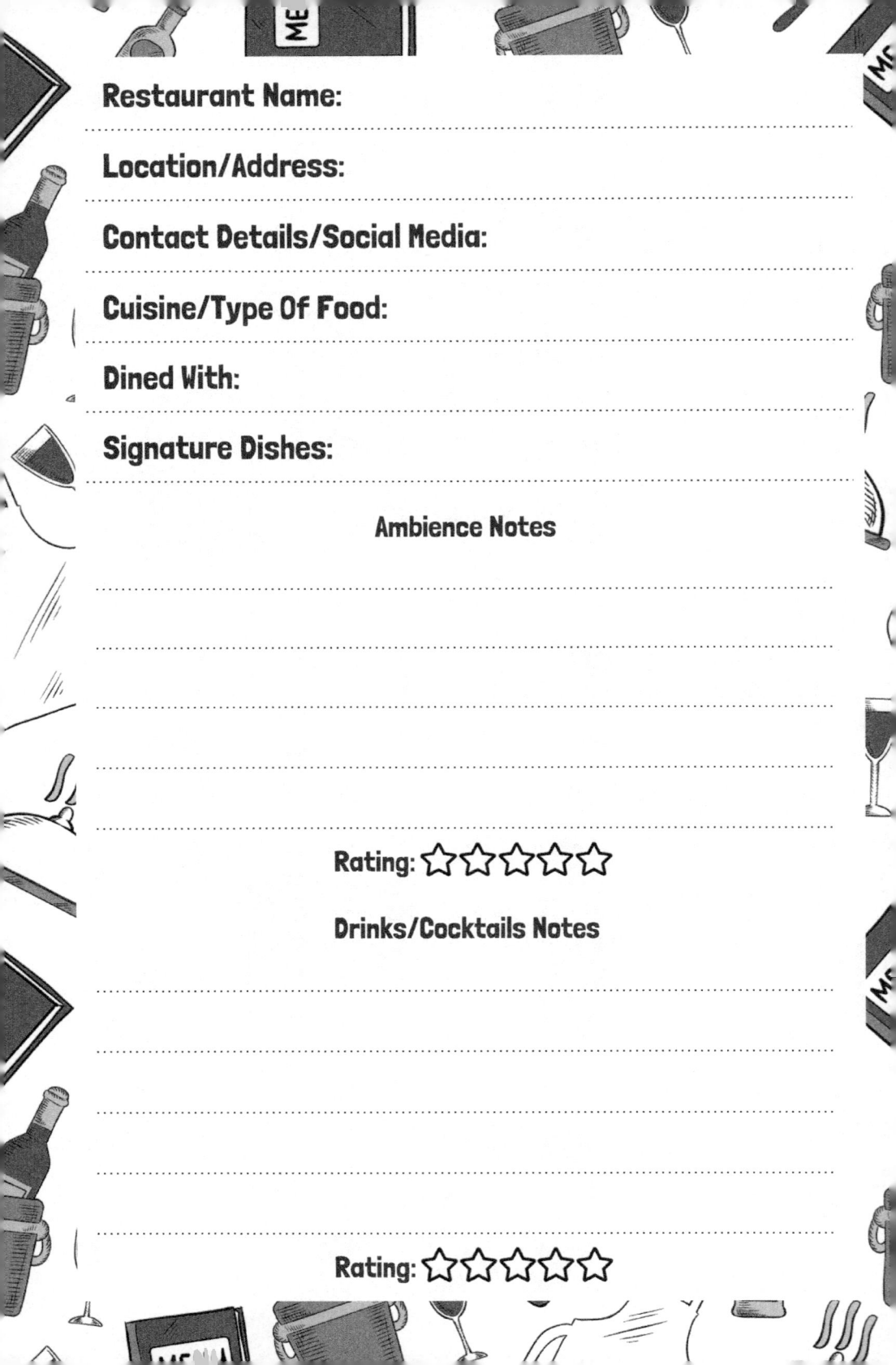

Location/Address:

Contact Details/Social Media:

Cuisine/Type Of Food:

Dined With:

Signature Dishes:

Ambience Notes

Rating: ☆☆☆☆☆

Drinks/Cocktails Notes

Rating: ☆☆☆☆☆

Appetizer Notes

....
....
....
....

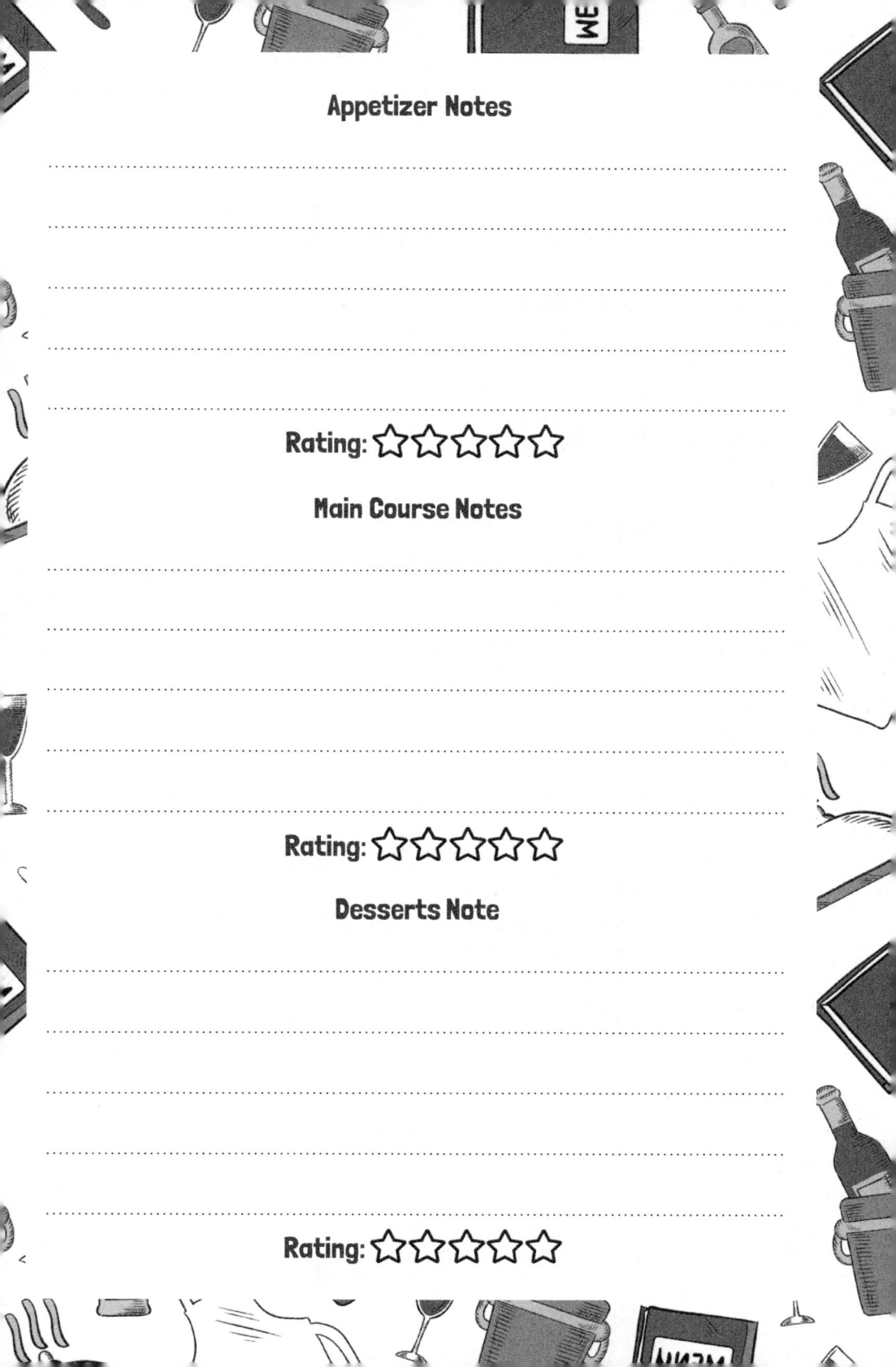

Rating: ☆☆☆☆☆

Main Course Notes

....
....
....
....

Rating: ☆☆☆☆☆

Desserts Note

....
....
....
....

Rating: ☆☆☆☆☆

Restaurant Name:

Location/Address:

Contact Details/Social Media:

Cuisine/Type Of Food:

Dined With:

Signature Dishes:

Ambience Notes

Rating: ☆☆☆☆☆

Drinks/Cocktails Notes

Rating: ☆☆☆☆☆

Appetizer Notes

....

....

....

....

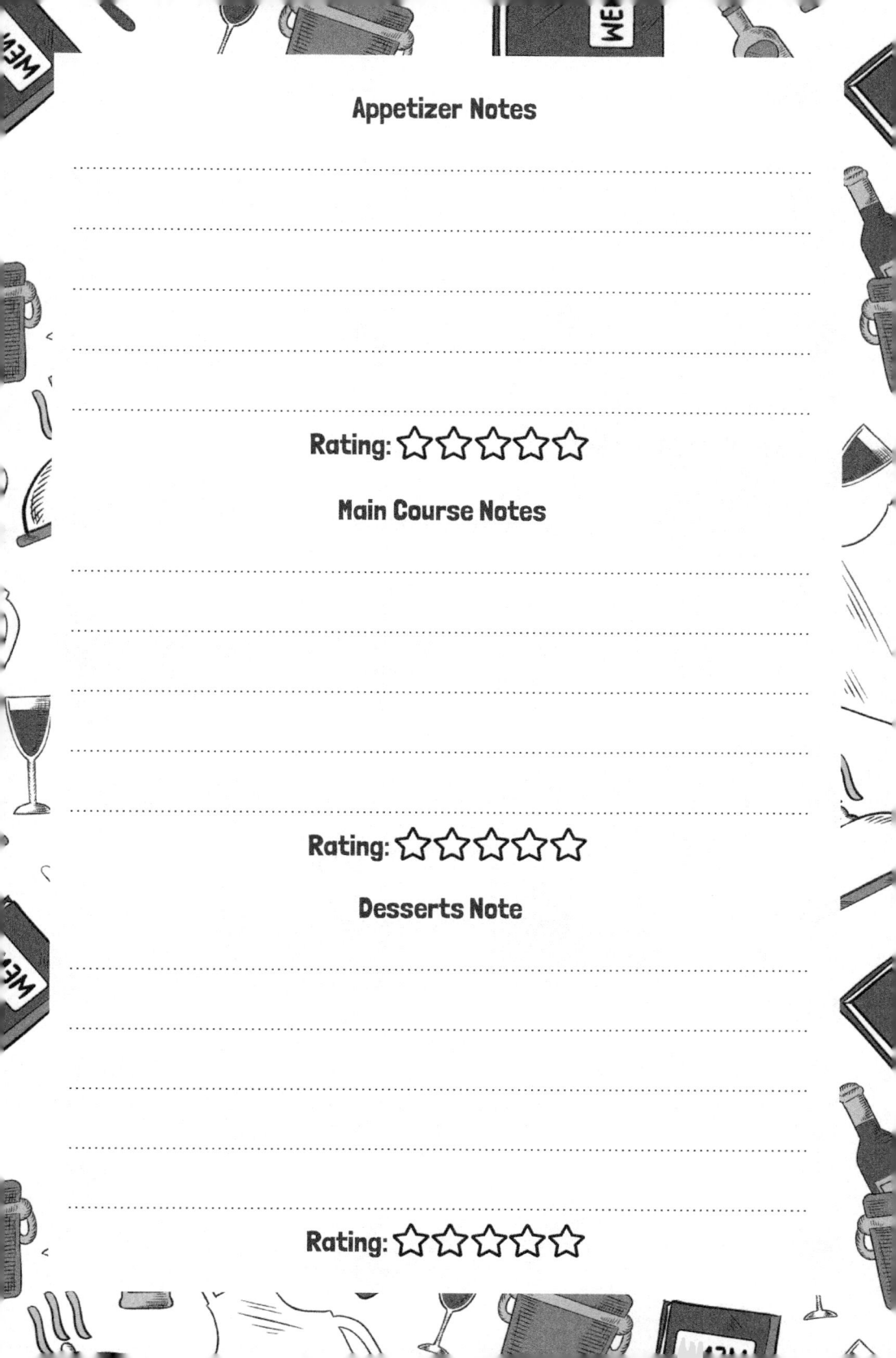

Rating: ☆☆☆☆☆

Main Course Notes

....

....

....

....

Rating: ☆☆☆☆☆

Desserts Note

....

....

....

....

Rating: ☆☆☆☆☆

Restaurant Name:

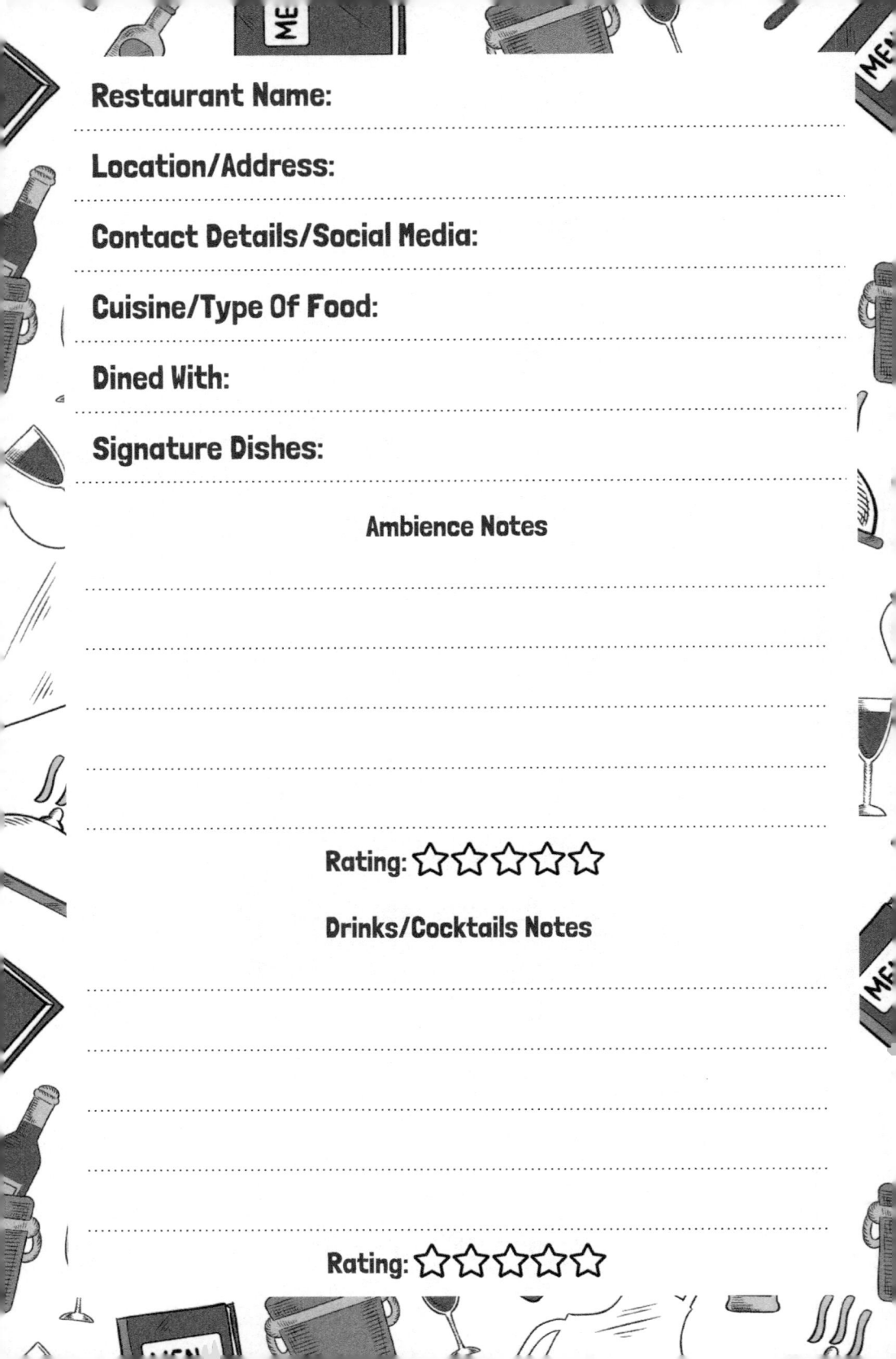

Location/Address:

Contact Details/Social Media:

Cuisine/Type Of Food:

Dined With:

Signature Dishes:

Ambience Notes

Rating: ☆☆☆☆☆

Drinks/Cocktails Notes

Rating: ☆☆☆☆☆

Appetizer Notes

....

....

....

....

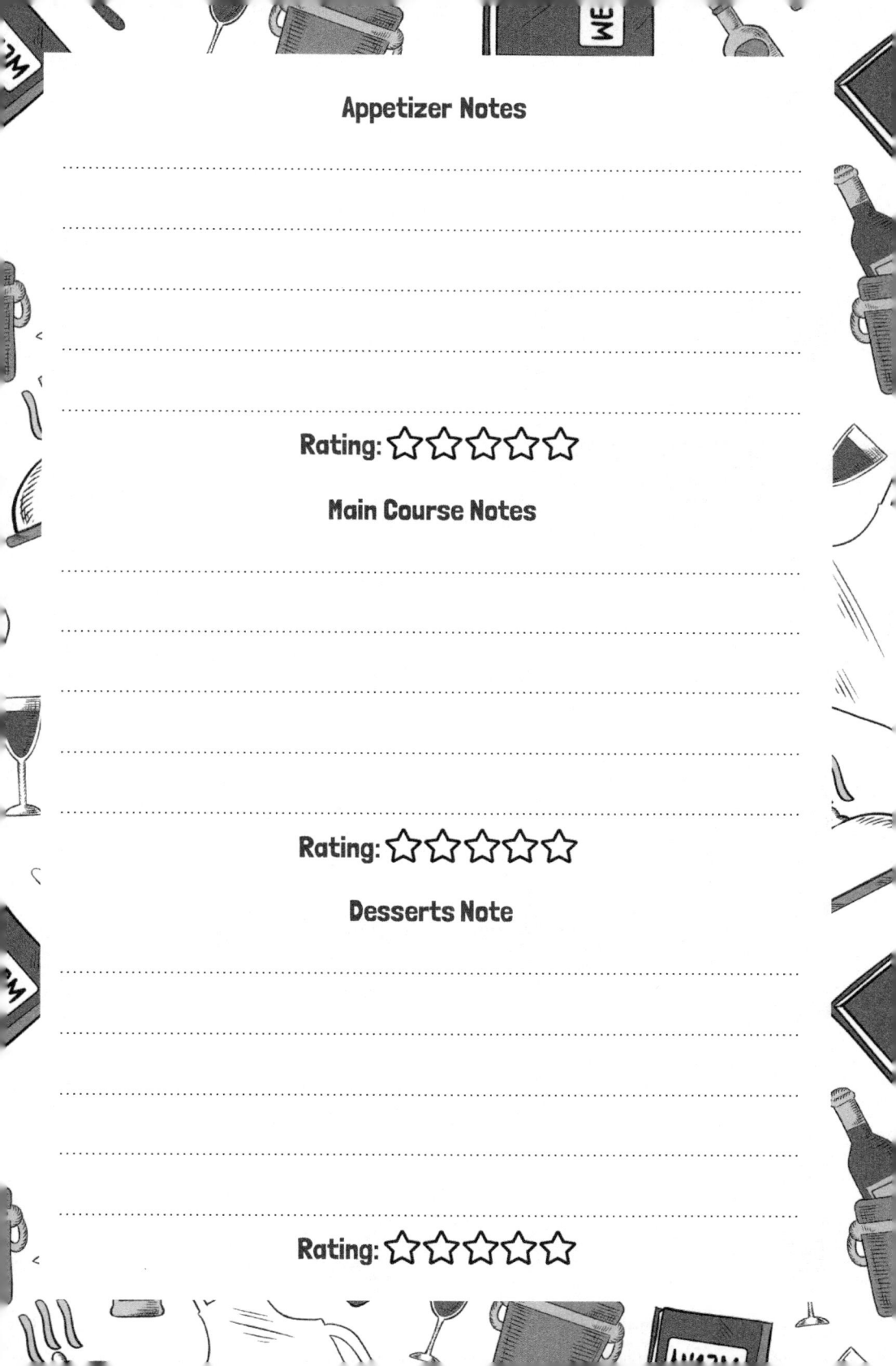

Rating: ☆☆☆☆☆

Main Course Notes

....

....

....

....

Rating: ☆☆☆☆☆

Desserts Note

....

....

....

....

Rating: ☆☆☆☆☆

Restaurant Name:

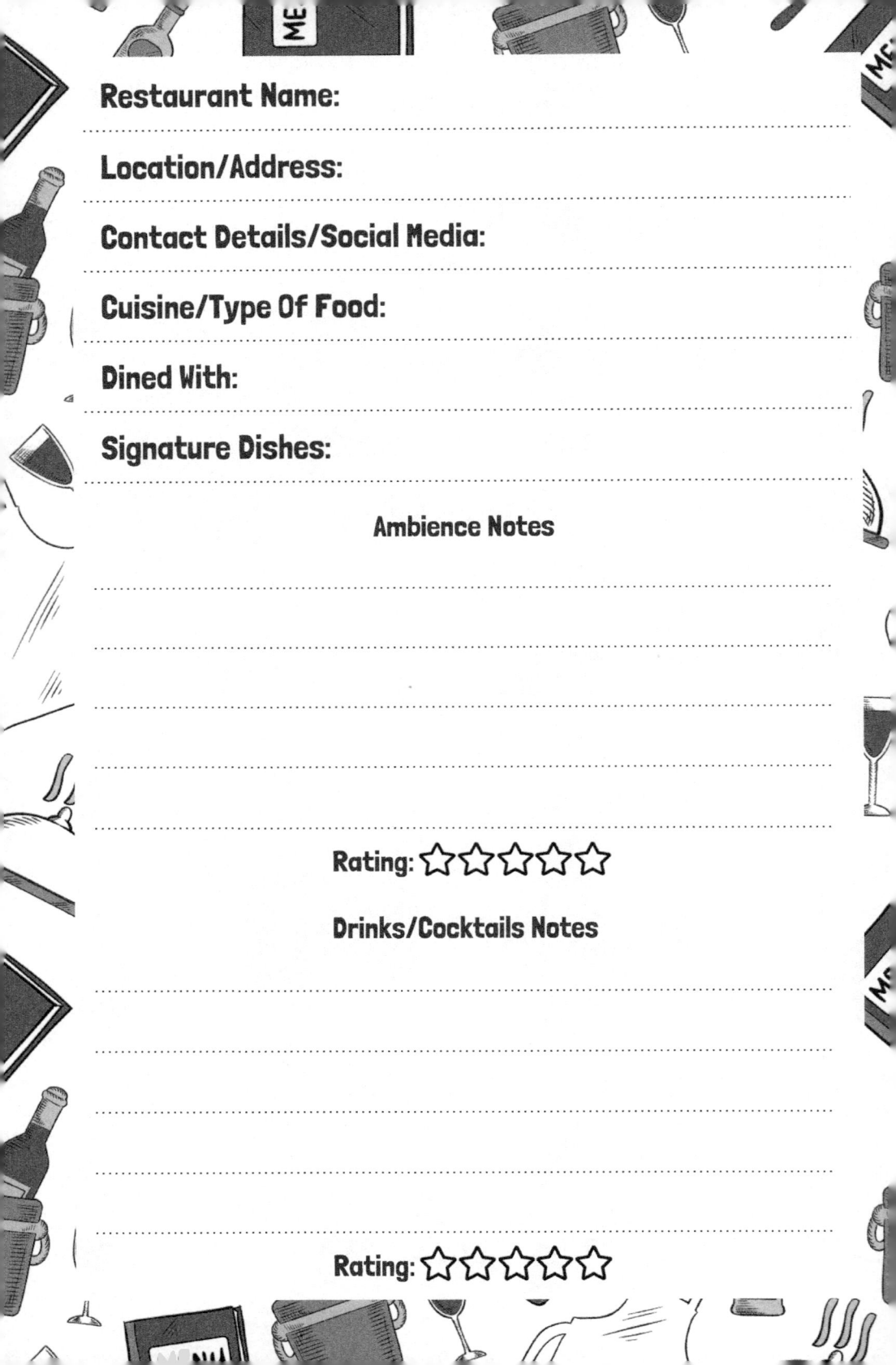

Location/Address:

Contact Details/Social Media:

Cuisine/Type Of Food:

Dined With:

Signature Dishes:

Ambience Notes

Rating: ☆☆☆☆☆

Drinks/Cocktails Notes

Rating: ☆☆☆☆☆

Appetizer Notes

....

....

....

....

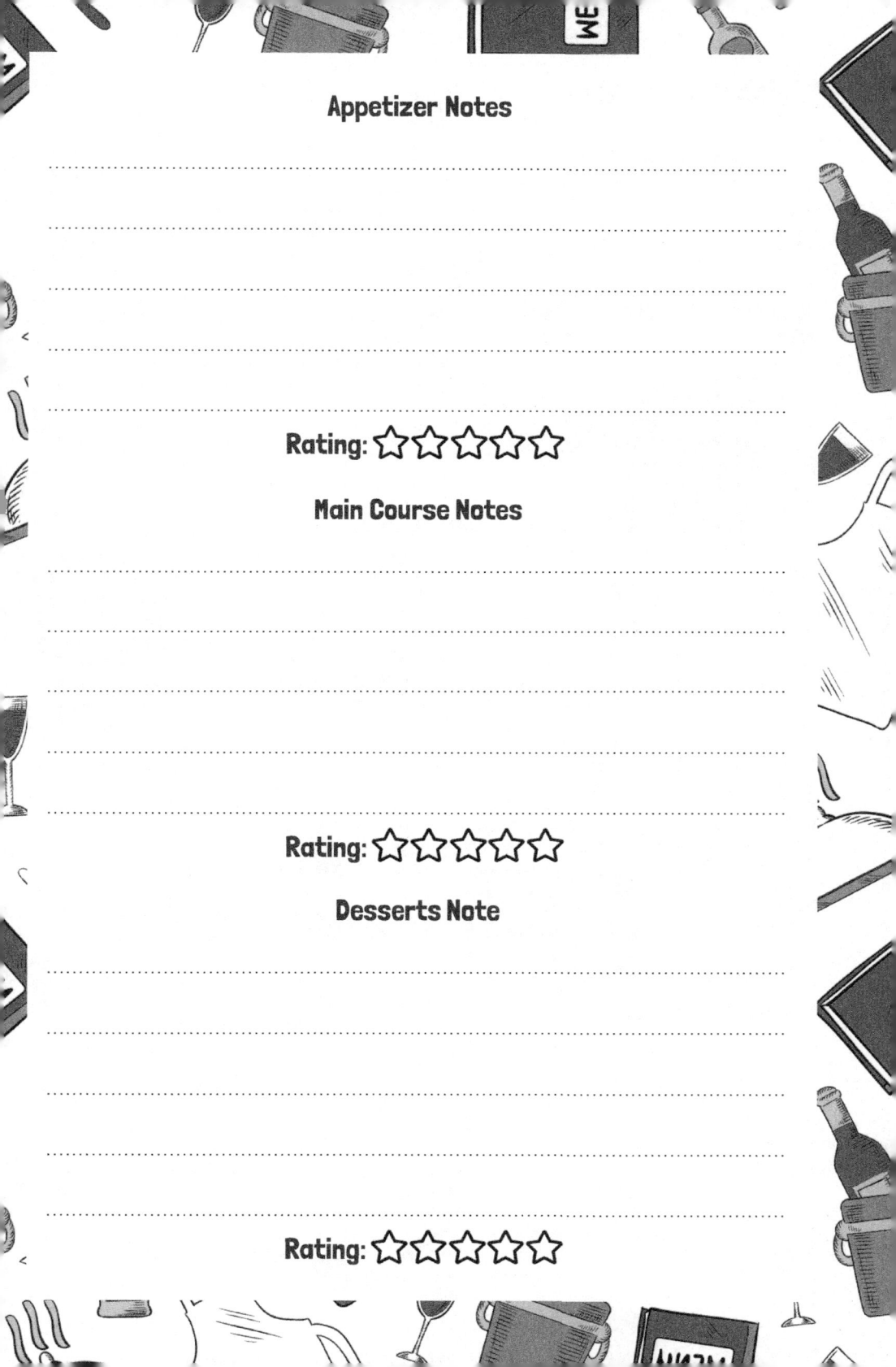

Rating: ☆☆☆☆☆

Main Course Notes

....

....

....

....

Rating: ☆☆☆☆☆

Desserts Note

....

....

....

....

Rating: ☆☆☆☆☆

Restaurant Name:

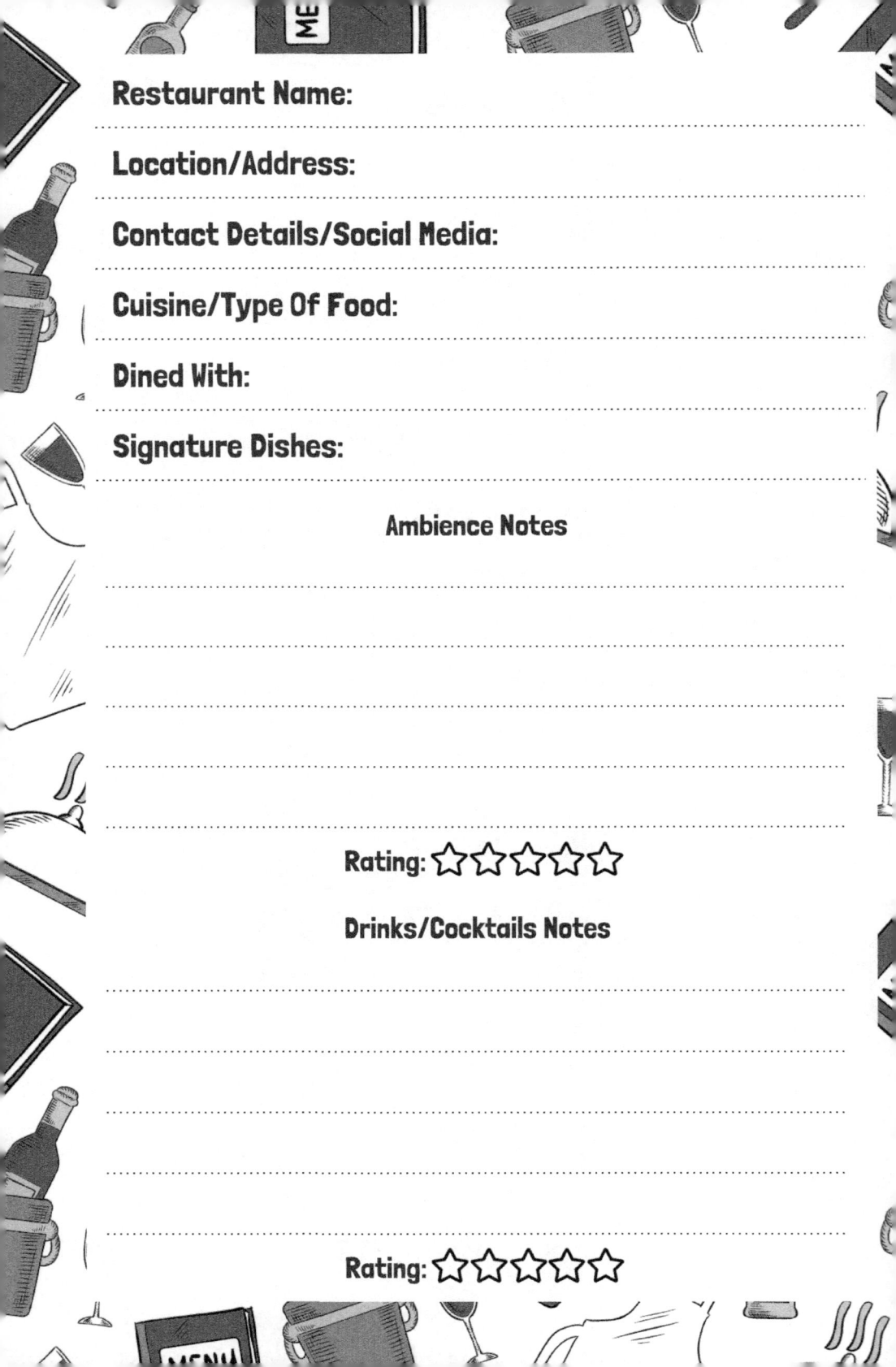

Location/Address:

Contact Details/Social Media:

Cuisine/Type Of Food:

Dined With:

Signature Dishes:

Ambience Notes

Rating: ☆☆☆☆☆

Drinks/Cocktails Notes

Rating: ☆☆☆☆☆

Appetizer Notes

....

....

....

....

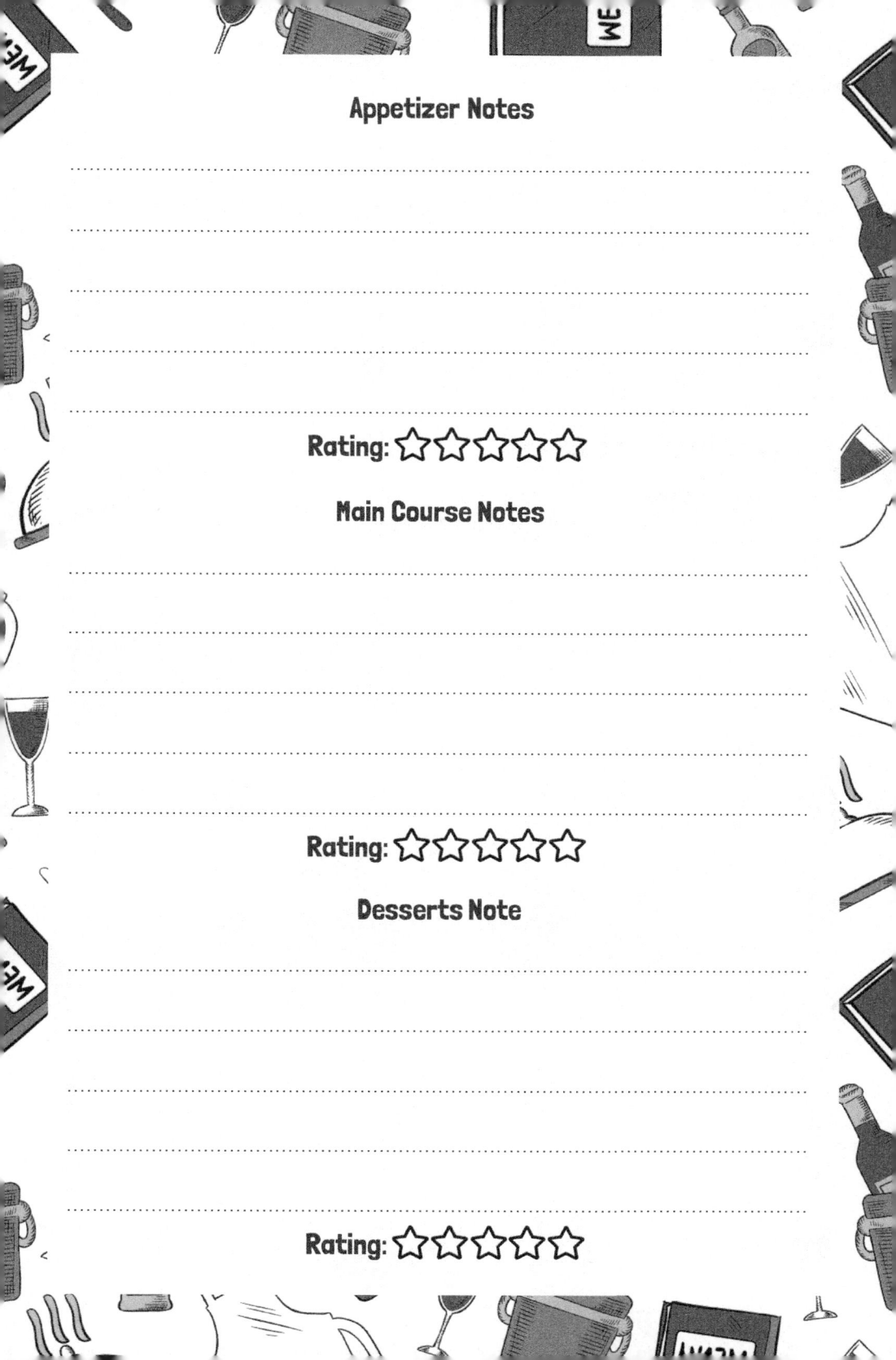

Rating: ☆☆☆☆☆

Main Course Notes

....

....

....

....

Rating: ☆☆☆☆☆

Desserts Note

....

....

....

....

Rating: ☆☆☆☆☆

Restaurant Name:

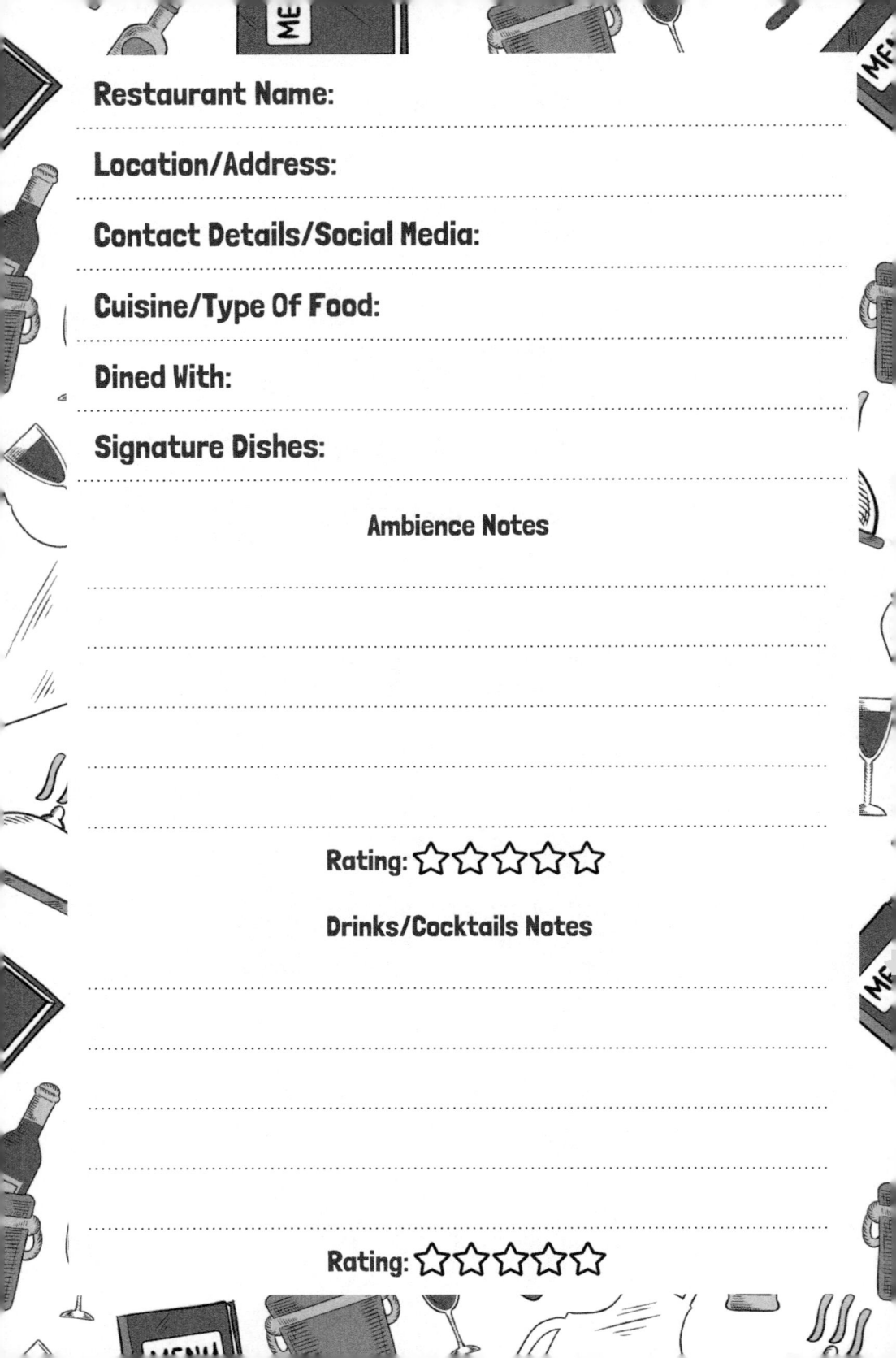

Location/Address:

Contact Details/Social Media:

Cuisine/Type Of Food:

Dined With:

Signature Dishes:

Ambience Notes

Rating: ☆☆☆☆☆

Drinks/Cocktails Notes

Rating: ☆☆☆☆☆

Appetizer Notes

....

....

....

....

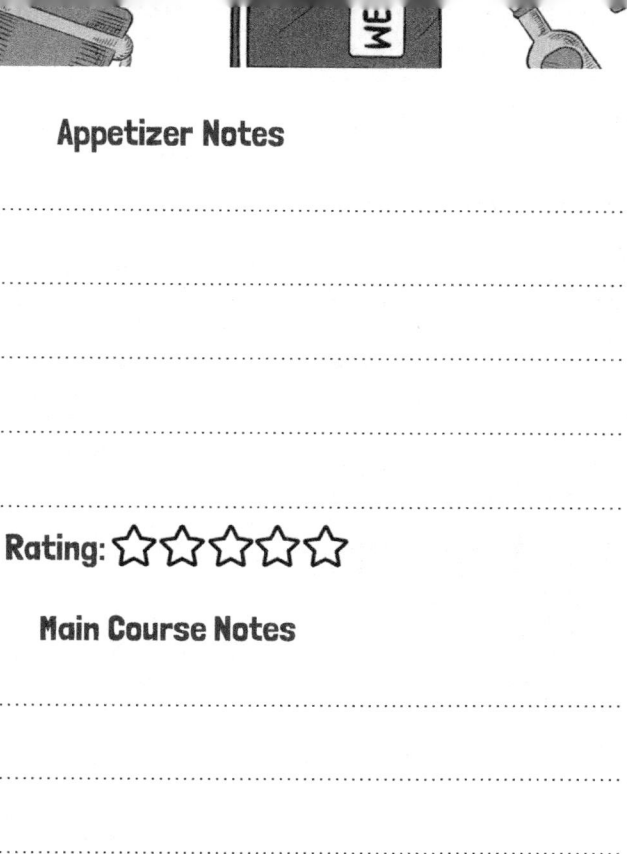

Rating: ☆☆☆☆☆

Main Course Notes

....

....

....

....

Rating: ☆☆☆☆☆

Desserts Note

....

....

....

....

Rating: ☆☆☆☆☆

Restaurant Name:

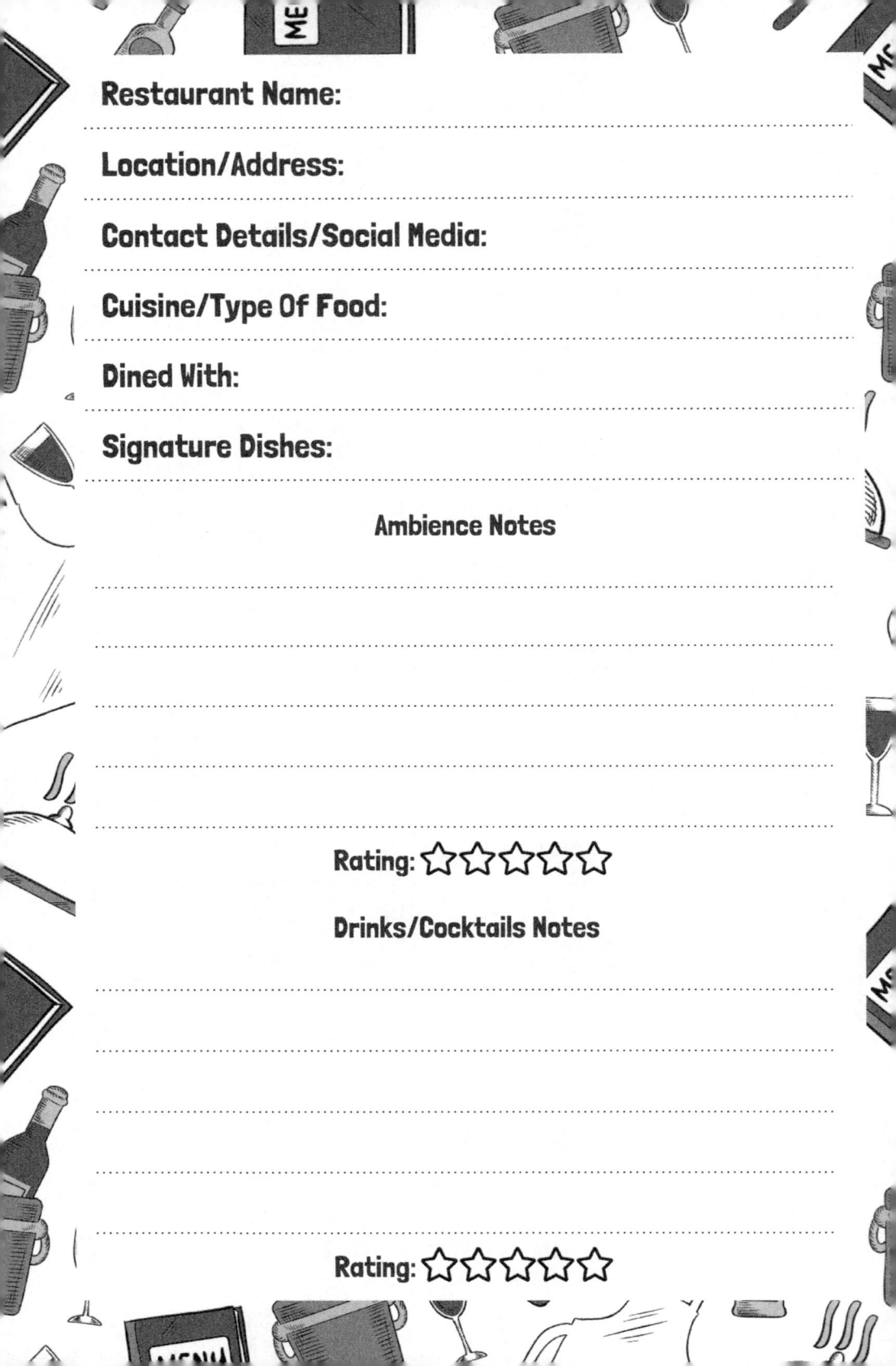

Location/Address:

Contact Details/Social Media:

Cuisine/Type Of Food:

Dined With:

Signature Dishes:

Ambience Notes

Rating: ☆☆☆☆☆

Drinks/Cocktails Notes

Rating: ☆☆☆☆☆

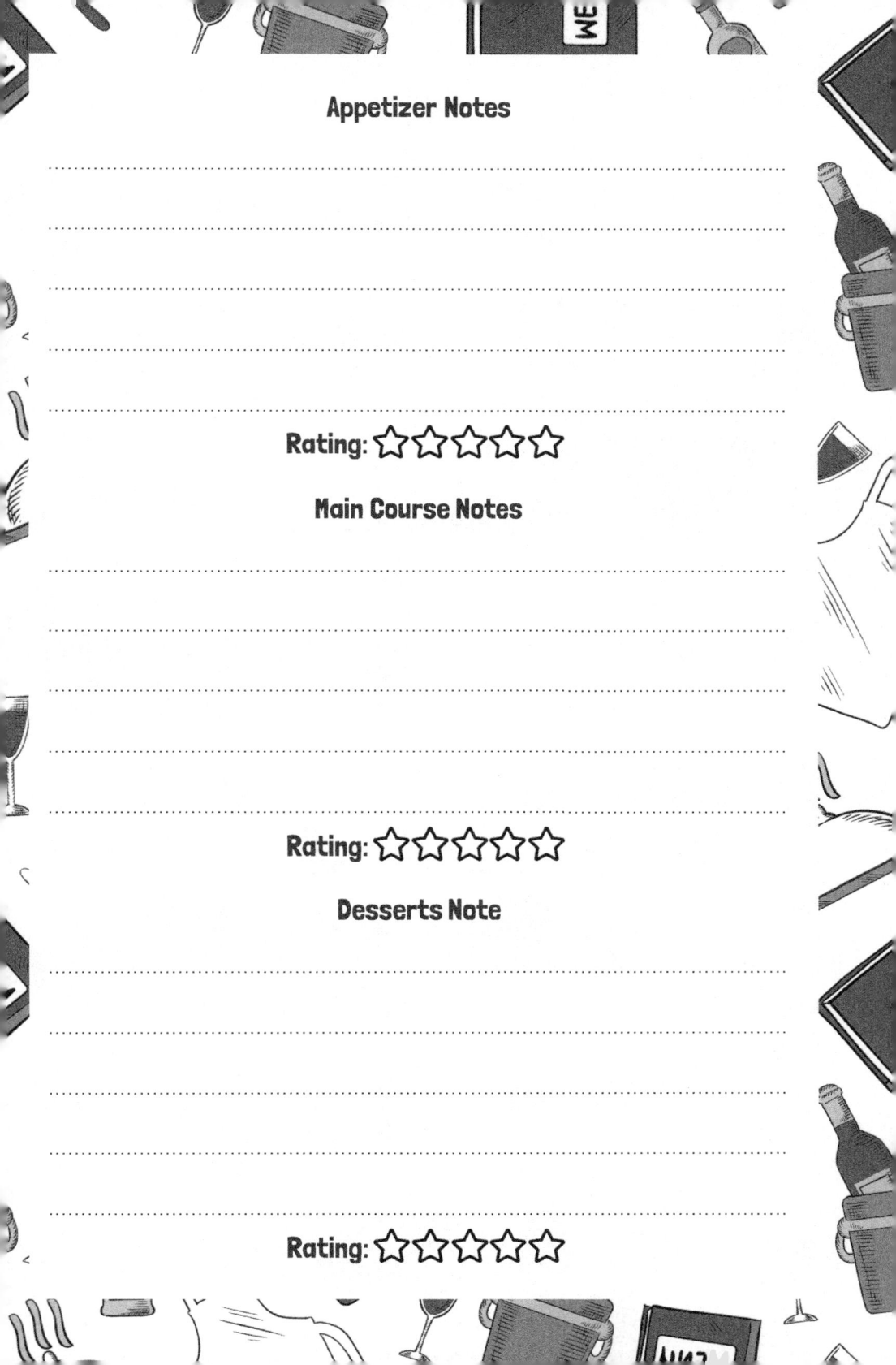

Appetizer Notes

....

....

....

....

Rating: ☆☆☆☆☆

Main Course Notes

....

....

....

....

Rating: ☆☆☆☆☆

Desserts Note

....

....

....

....

Rating: ☆☆☆☆☆

Restaurant Name:

Location/Address:

Contact Details/Social Media:

Cuisine/Type Of Food:

Dined With:

Signature Dishes:

Ambience Notes

Rating: ☆☆☆☆☆

Drinks/Cocktails Notes

Rating: ☆☆☆☆☆

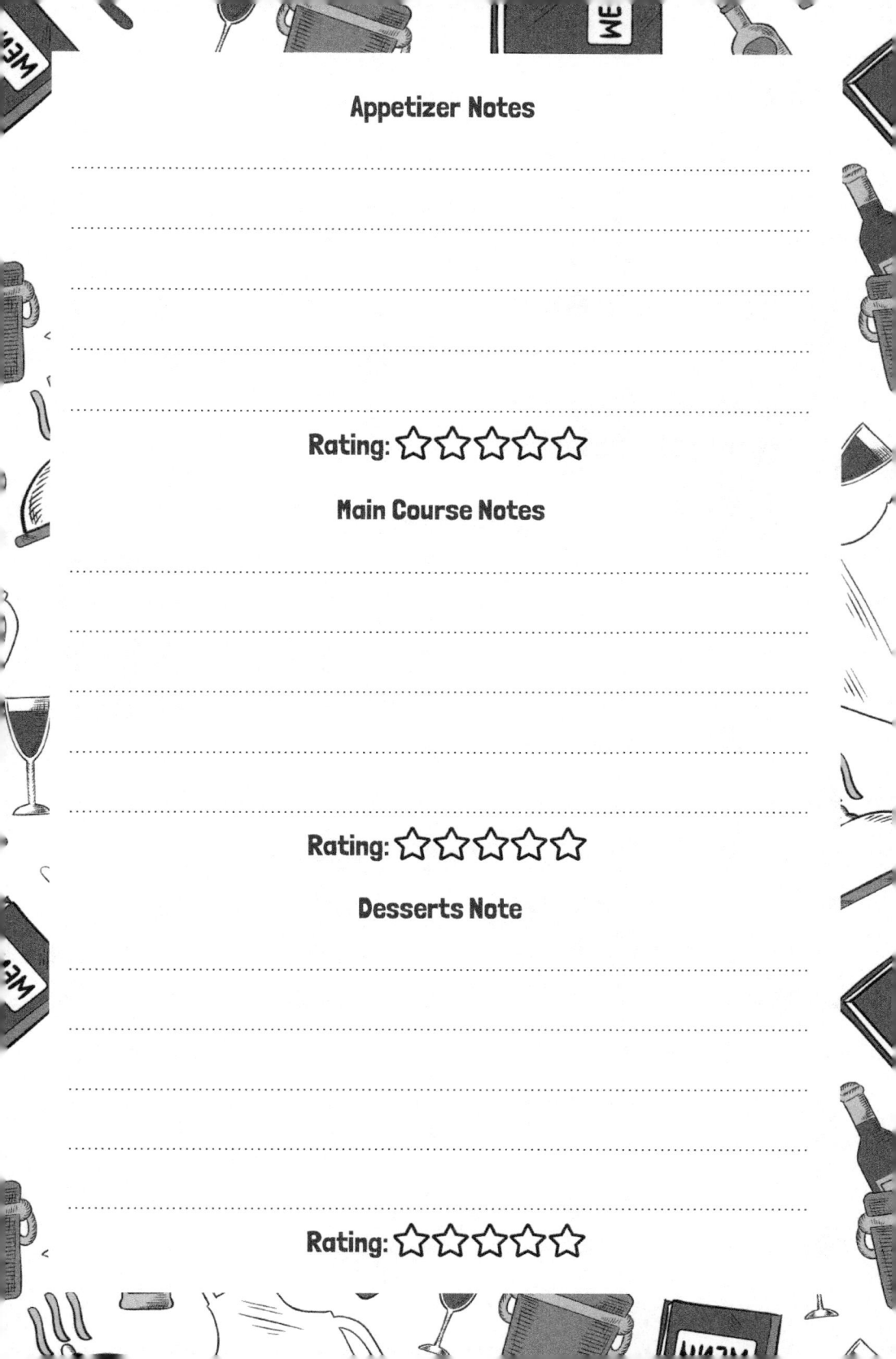

Appetizer Notes

....

....

....

....

Rating: ☆☆☆☆☆

Main Course Notes

....

....

....

....

Rating: ☆☆☆☆☆

Desserts Note

....

....

....

....

Rating: ☆☆☆☆☆

Restaurant Name:

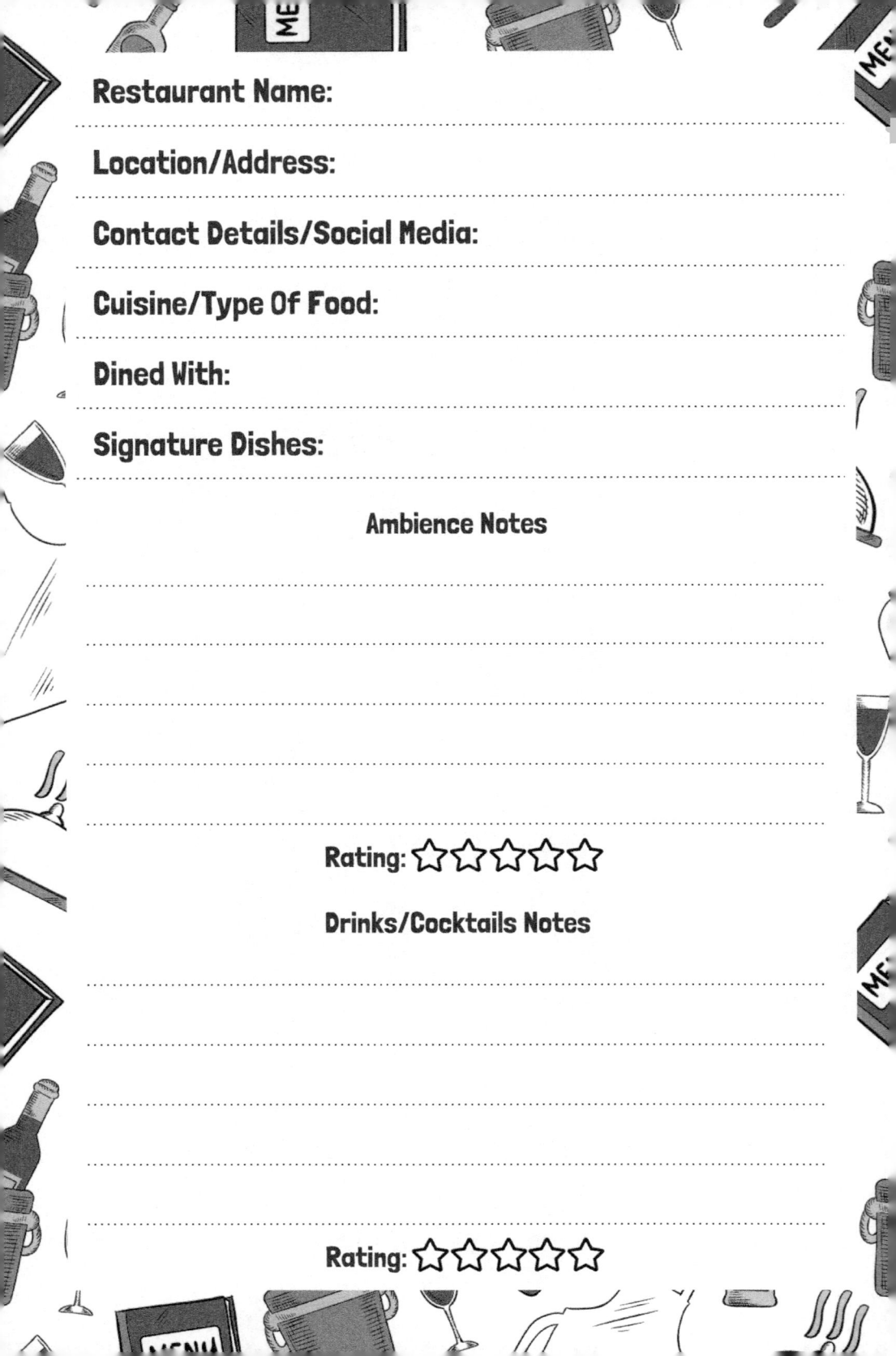

Location/Address:

Contact Details/Social Media:

Cuisine/Type Of Food:

Dined With:

Signature Dishes:

Ambience Notes

Rating: ☆☆☆☆☆

Drinks/Cocktails Notes

Rating: ☆☆☆☆☆

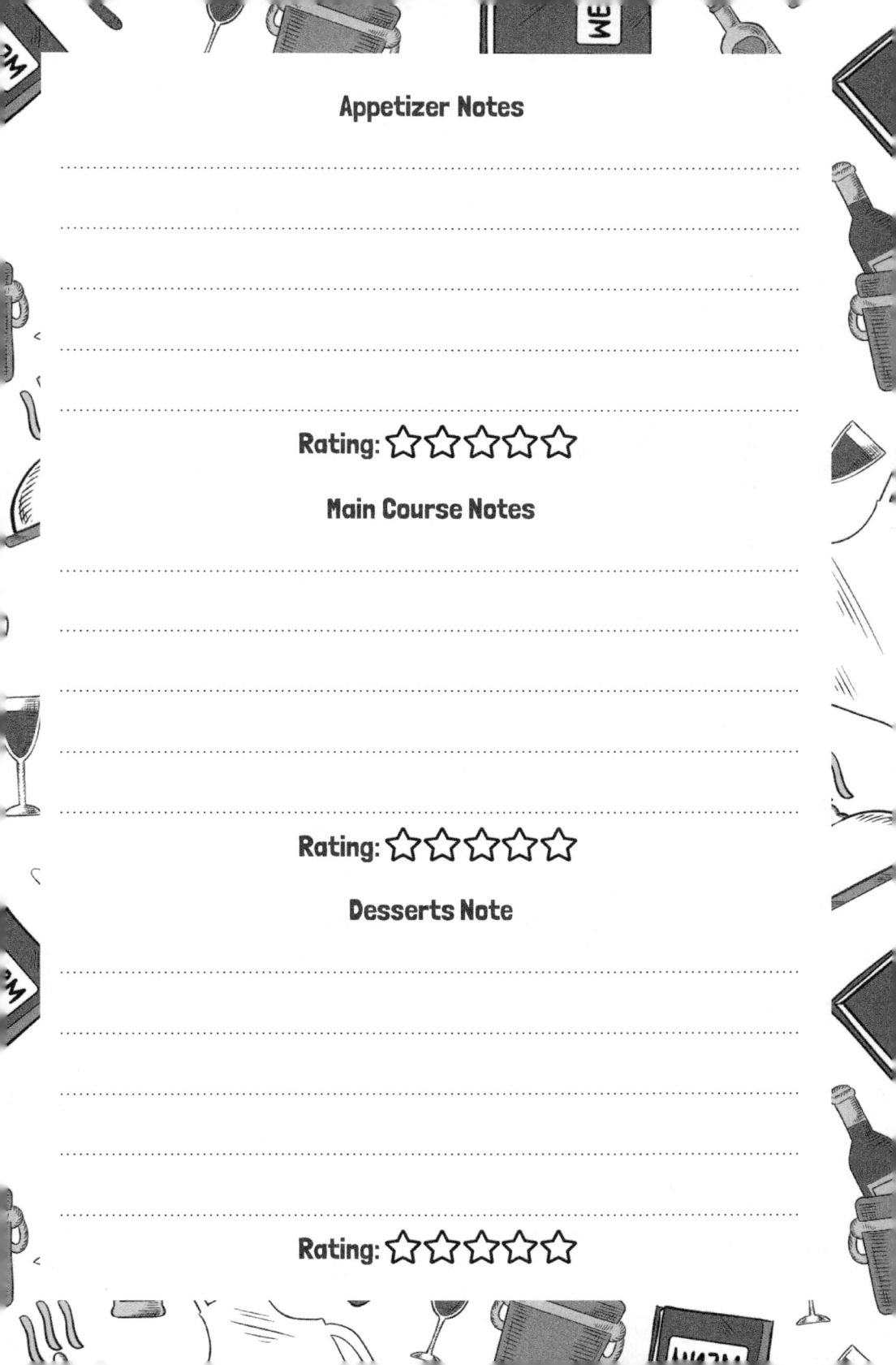

Appetizer Notes

....

....

....

....

Rating: ☆☆☆☆☆

Main Course Notes

....

....

....

....

Rating: ☆☆☆☆☆

Desserts Note

....

....

....

....

Rating: ☆☆☆☆☆

Restaurant Name:

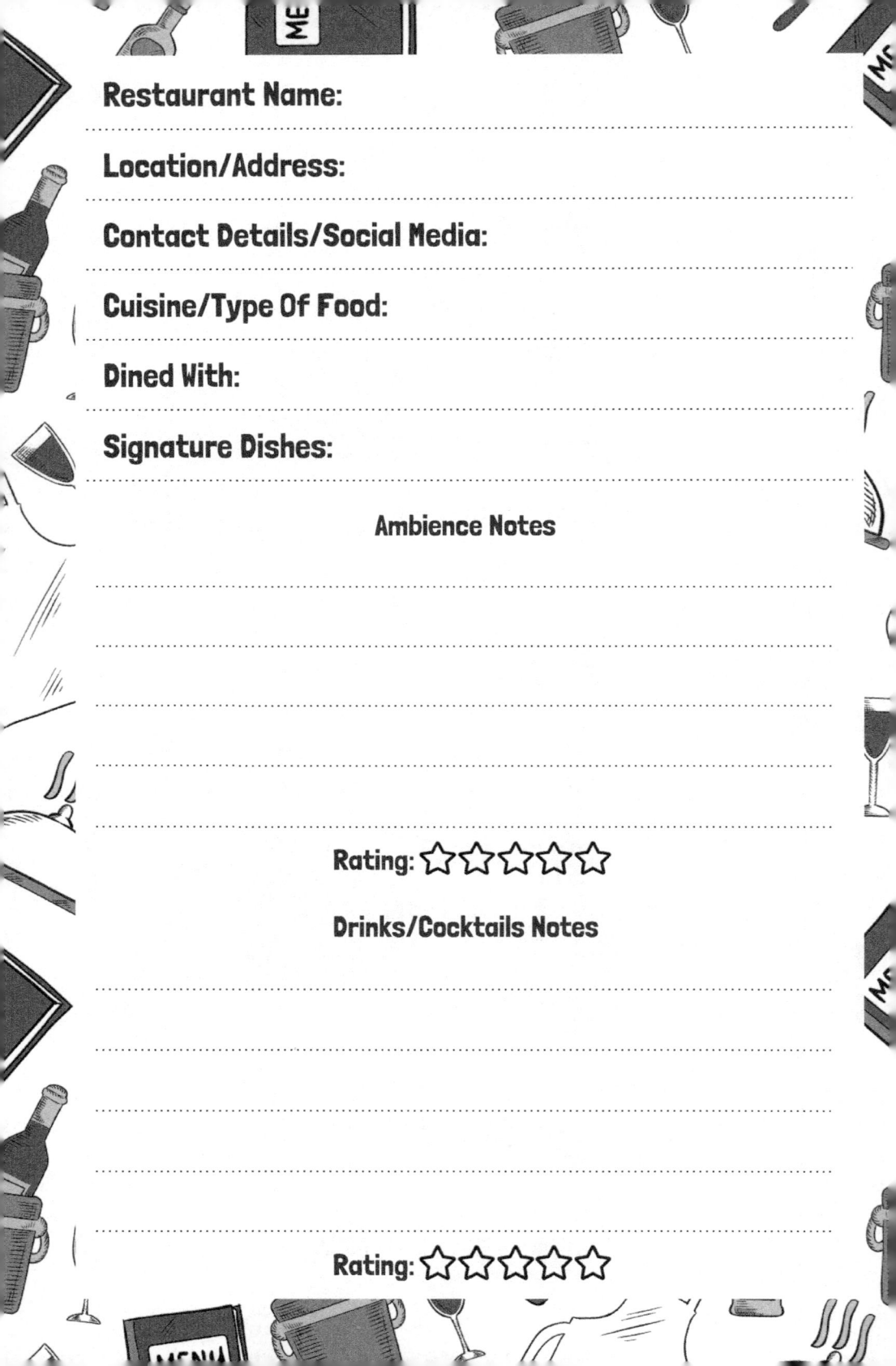

Location/Address:

Contact Details/Social Media:

Cuisine/Type Of Food:

Dined With:

Signature Dishes:

Ambience Notes

Rating: ☆☆☆☆☆

Drinks/Cocktails Notes

Rating: ☆☆☆☆☆

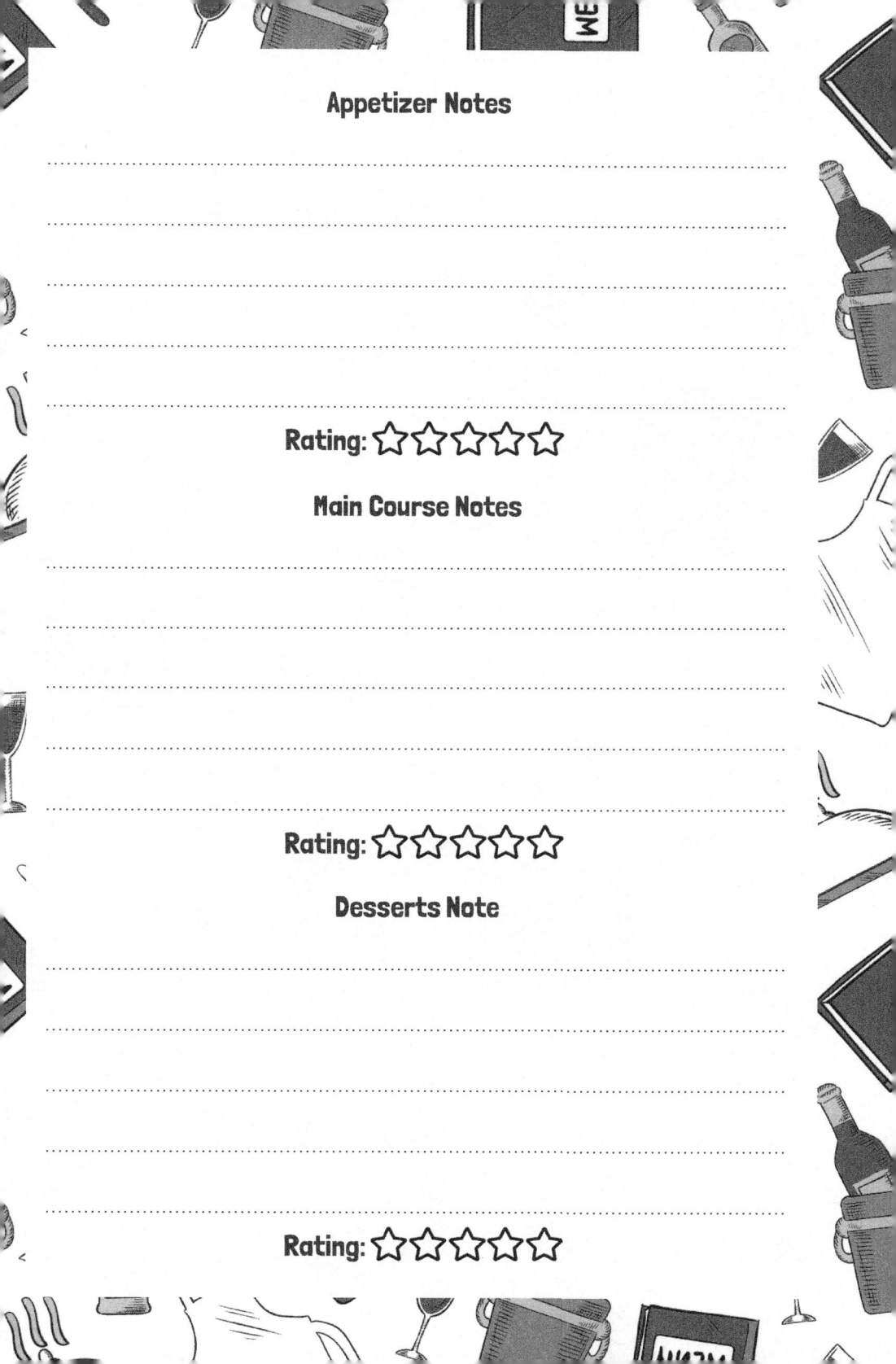

Appetizer Notes

....
....
....
....
....

Rating: ☆☆☆☆☆

Main Course Notes

....
....
....
....
....

Rating: ☆☆☆☆☆

Desserts Note

....
....
....
....
....

Rating: ☆☆☆☆☆

Restaurant Name:

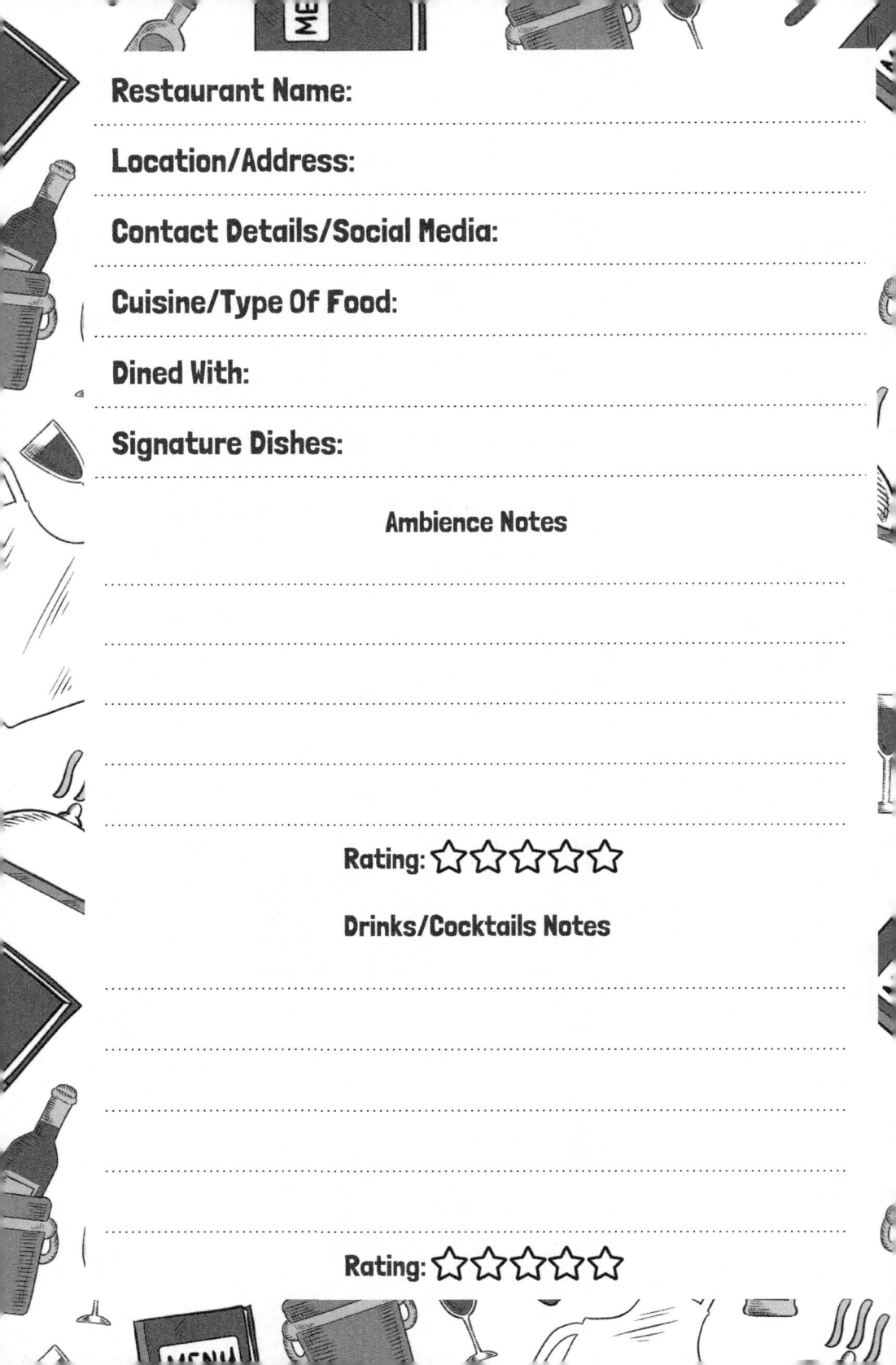

Location/Address:

Contact Details/Social Media:

Cuisine/Type Of Food:

Dined With:

Signature Dishes:

Ambience Notes

Rating: ☆☆☆☆☆

Drinks/Cocktails Notes

Rating: ☆☆☆☆☆

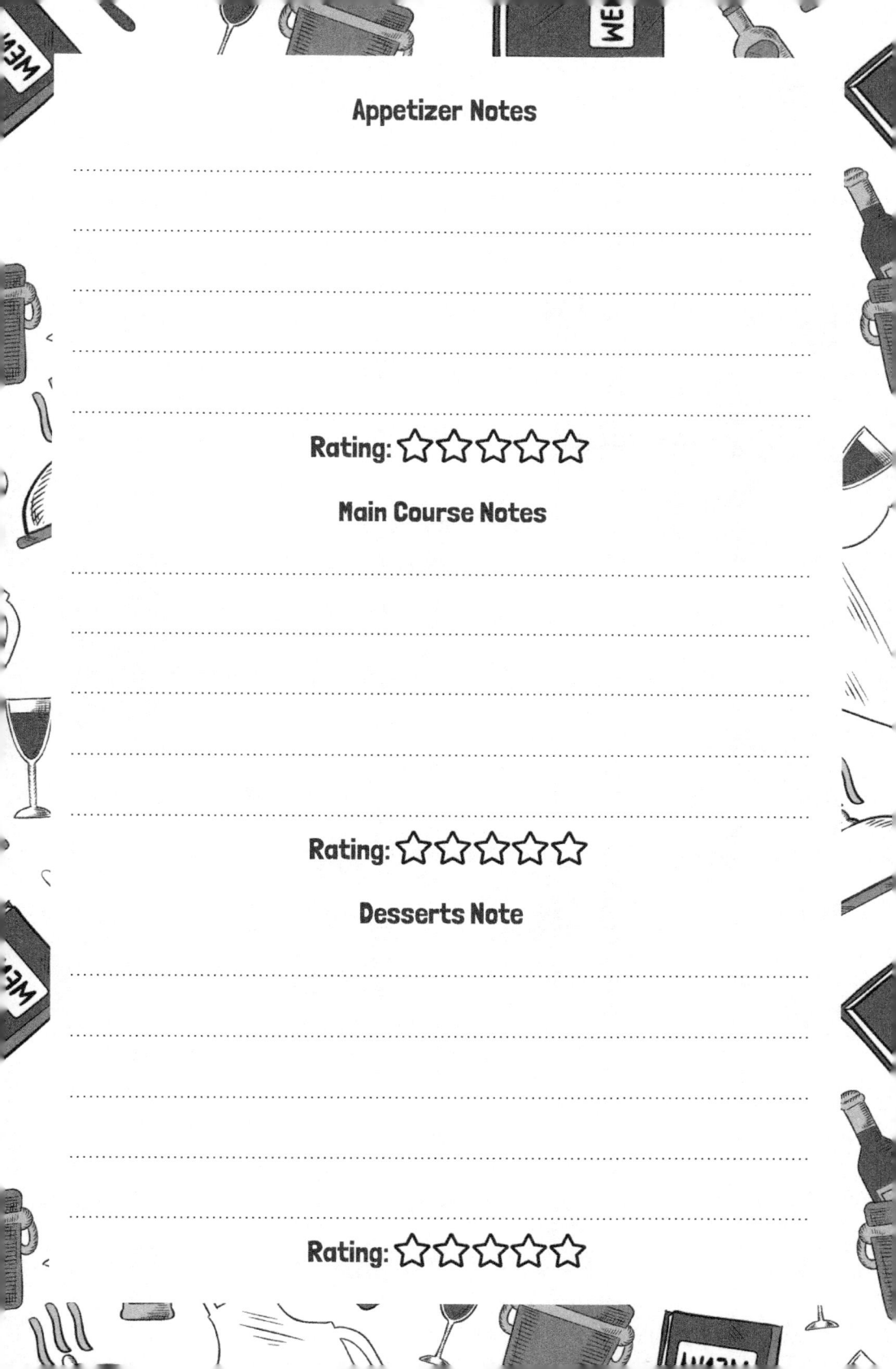

Appetizer Notes

....

....

....

....

....

Rating: ☆☆☆☆☆

Main Course Notes

....

....

....

....

....

Rating: ☆☆☆☆☆

Desserts Note

....

....

....

....

....

Rating: ☆☆☆☆☆

Restaurant Name:

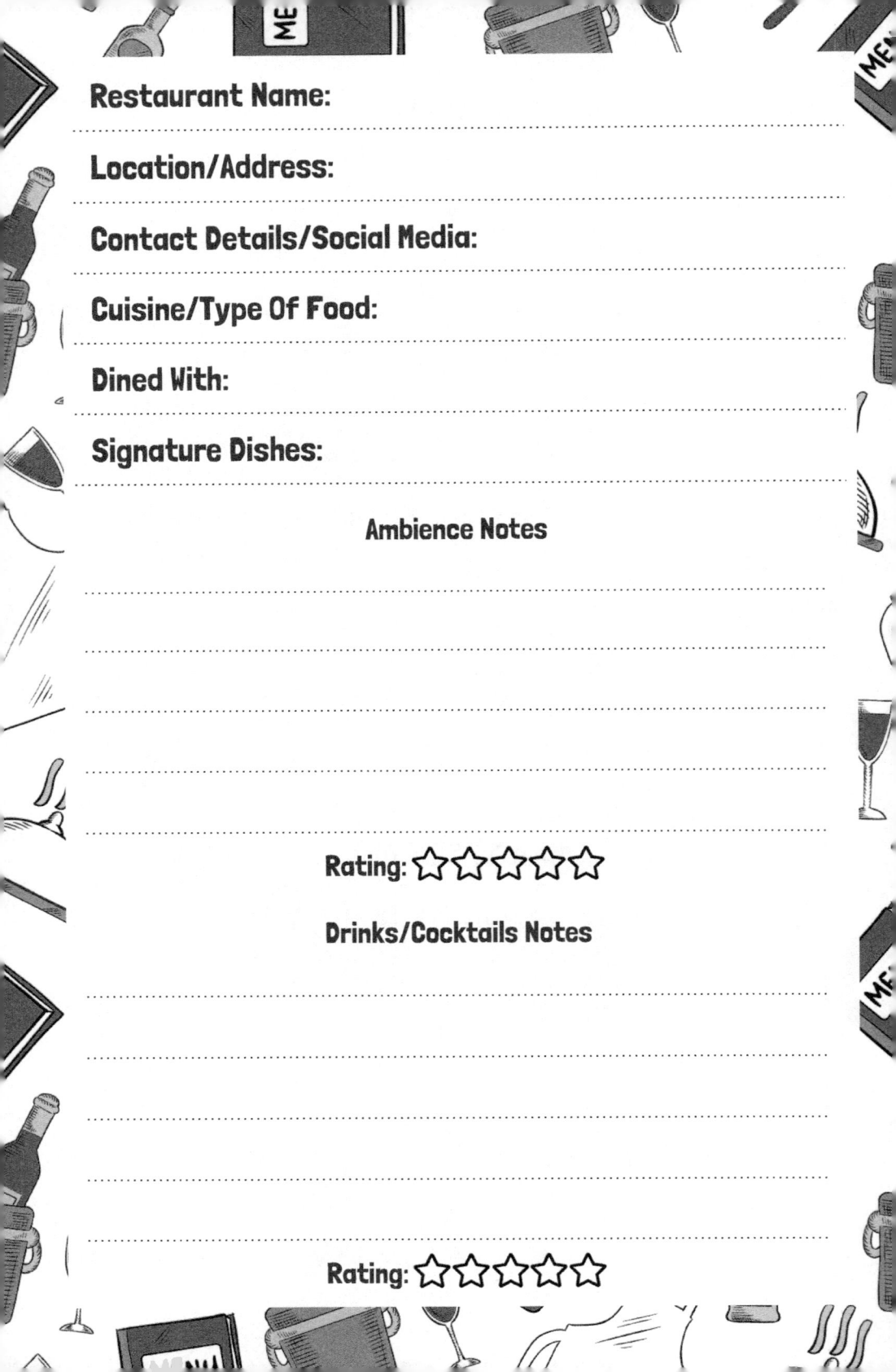

Location/Address:

Contact Details/Social Media:

Cuisine/Type Of Food:

Dined With:

Signature Dishes:

Ambience Notes

Rating: ☆☆☆☆☆

Drinks/Cocktails Notes

Rating: ☆☆☆☆☆

Appetizer Notes

....

....

....

....

Rating: ☆☆☆☆☆

Main Course Notes

....

....

....

....

Rating: ☆☆☆☆☆

Desserts Note

....

....

....

....

Rating: ☆☆☆☆☆

Restaurant Name:

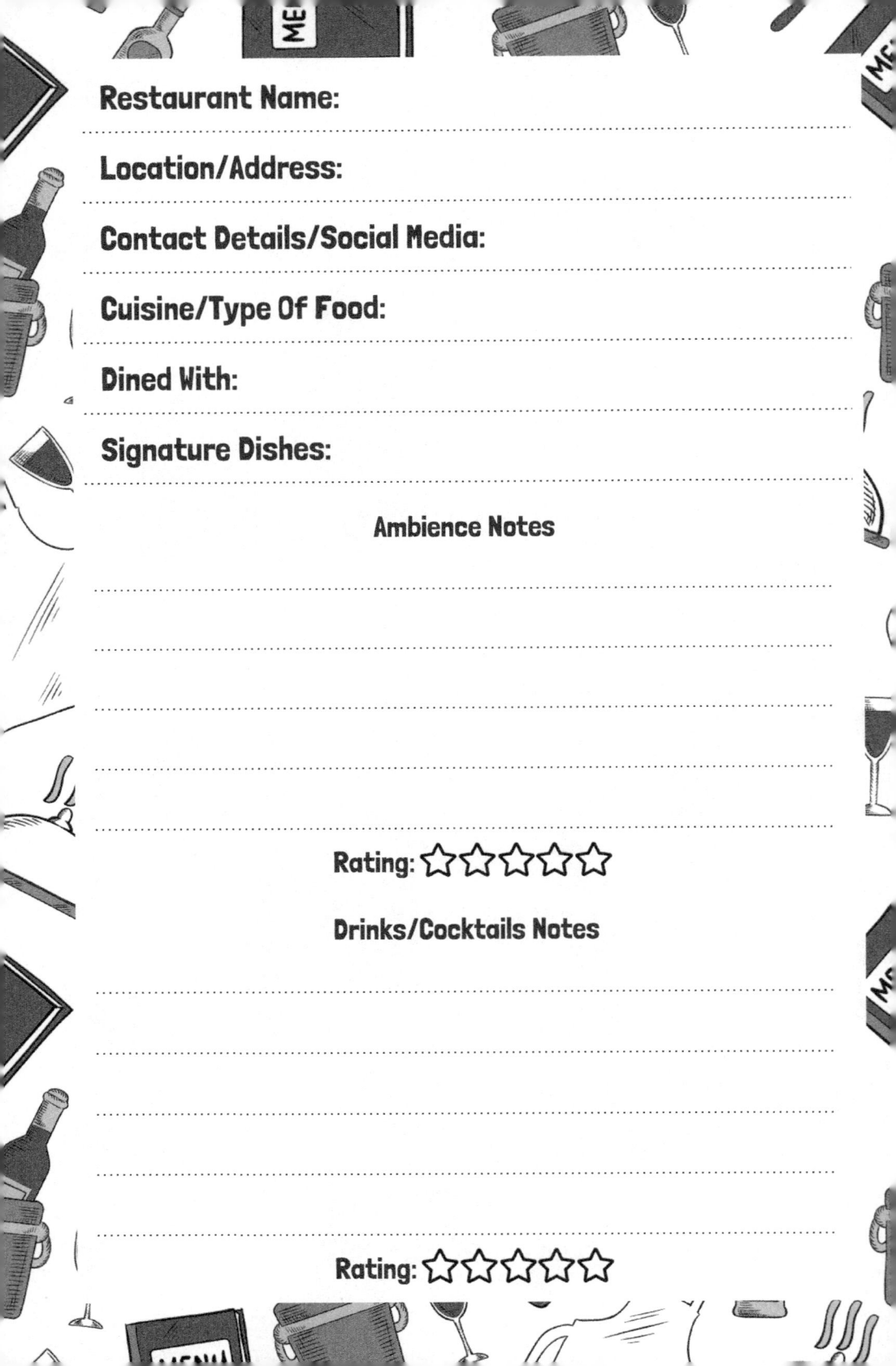

Location/Address:

Contact Details/Social Media:

Cuisine/Type Of Food:

Dined With:

Signature Dishes:

Ambience Notes

Rating: ☆☆☆☆☆

Drinks/Cocktails Notes

Rating: ☆☆☆☆☆

Appetizer Notes

....

....

....

....

Rating: ☆☆☆☆☆

Main Course Notes

....

....

....

....

Rating: ☆☆☆☆☆

Desserts Note

....

....

....

....

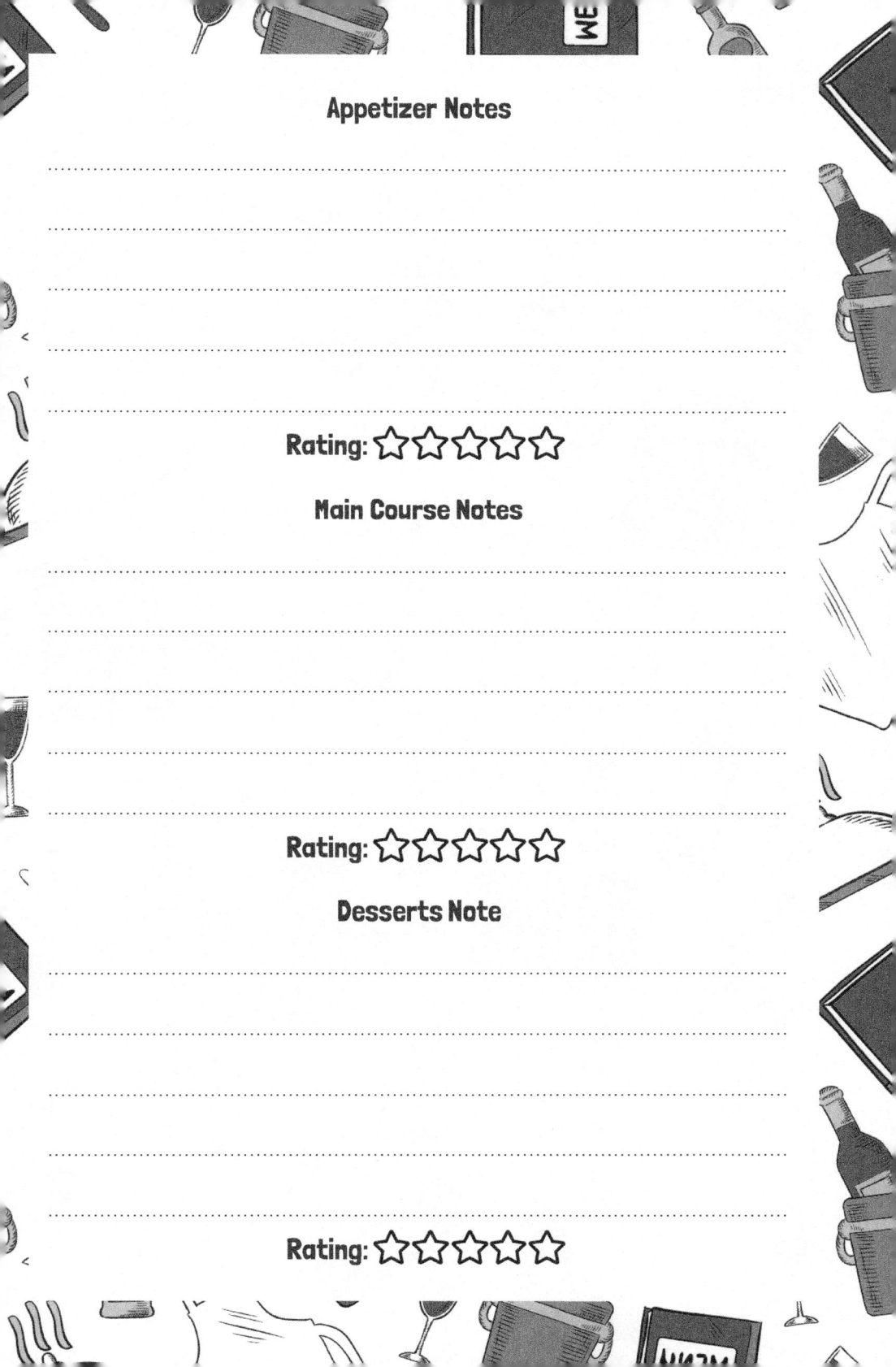

Rating: ☆☆☆☆☆

Restaurant Name:

Location/Address:

Contact Details/Social Media:

Cuisine/Type Of Food:

Dined With:

Signature Dishes:

Ambience Notes

Rating: ☆☆☆☆☆

Drinks/Cocktails Notes

Rating: ☆☆☆☆☆

Appetizer Notes

....

....

....

....

Rating: ☆☆☆☆☆

Main Course Notes

....

....

....

....

Rating: ☆☆☆☆☆

Desserts Note

....

....

....

....

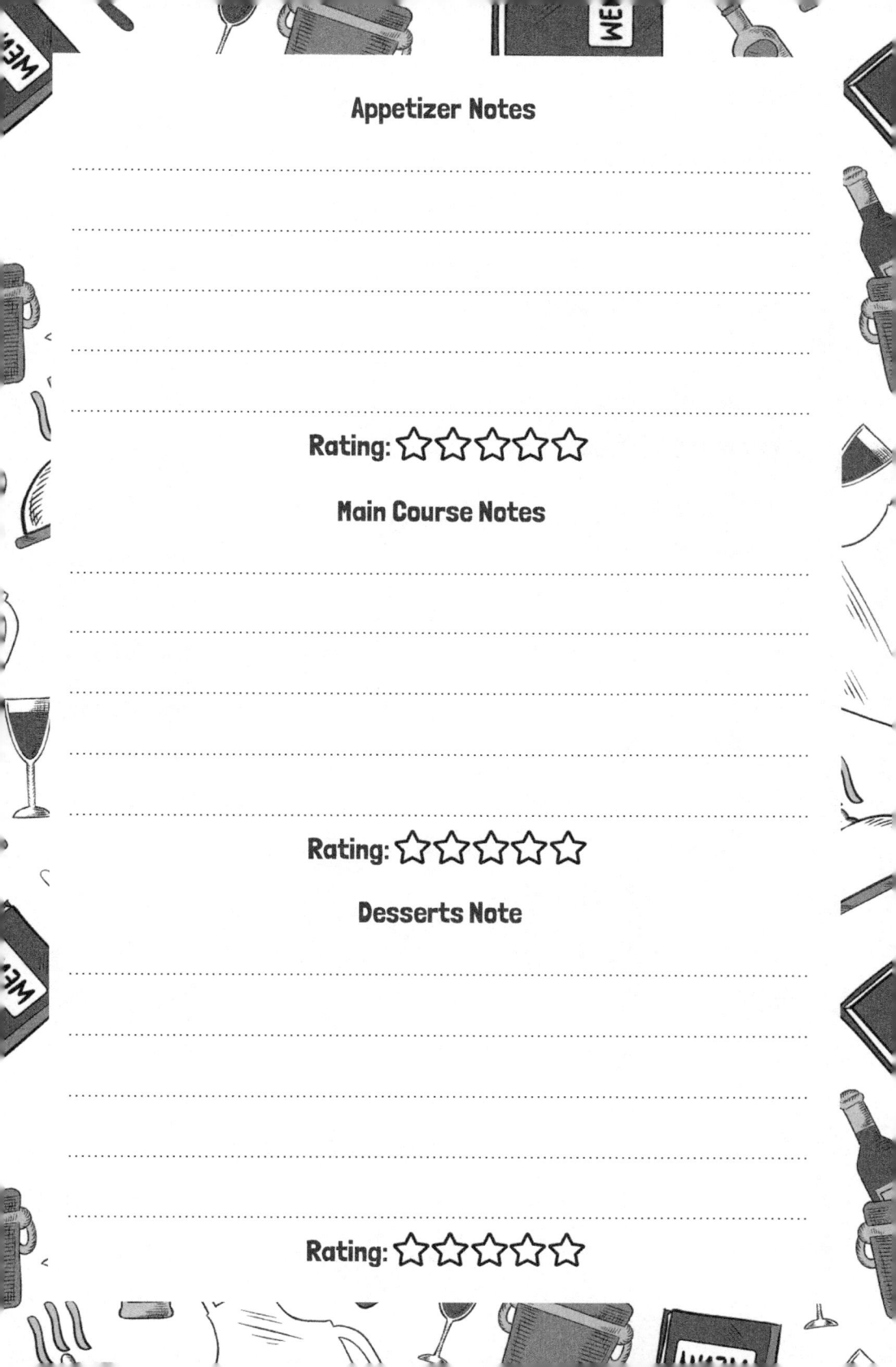

Rating: ☆☆☆☆☆

Restaurant Name:

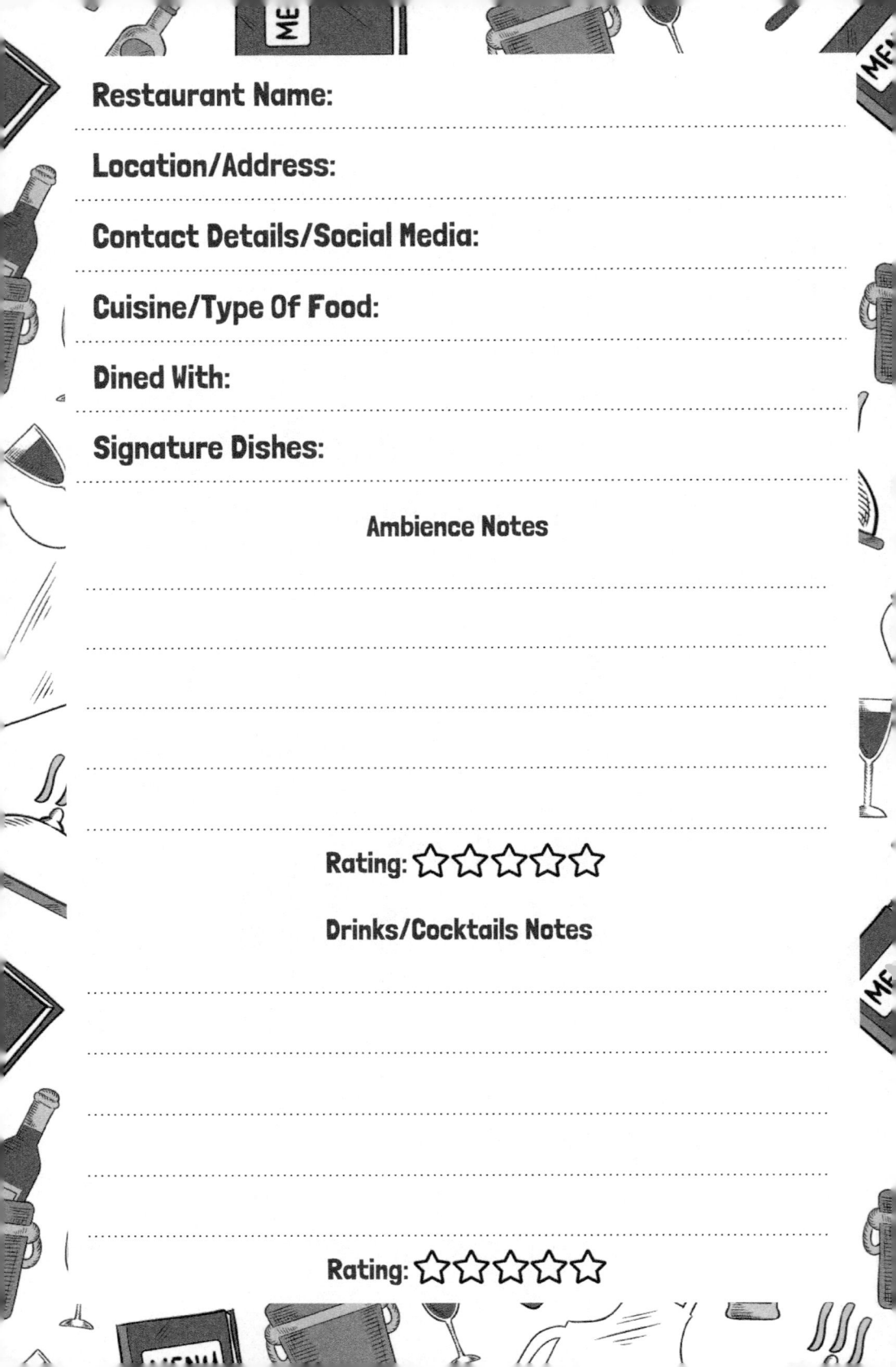

Location/Address:

Contact Details/Social Media:

Cuisine/Type Of Food:

Dined With:

Signature Dishes:

Ambience Notes

Rating: ☆☆☆☆☆

Drinks/Cocktails Notes

Rating: ☆☆☆☆☆

Appetizer Notes

....

....

....

....

Rating: ☆☆☆☆☆

Main Course Notes

....

....

....

....

Rating: ☆☆☆☆☆

Desserts Note

....

....

....

....

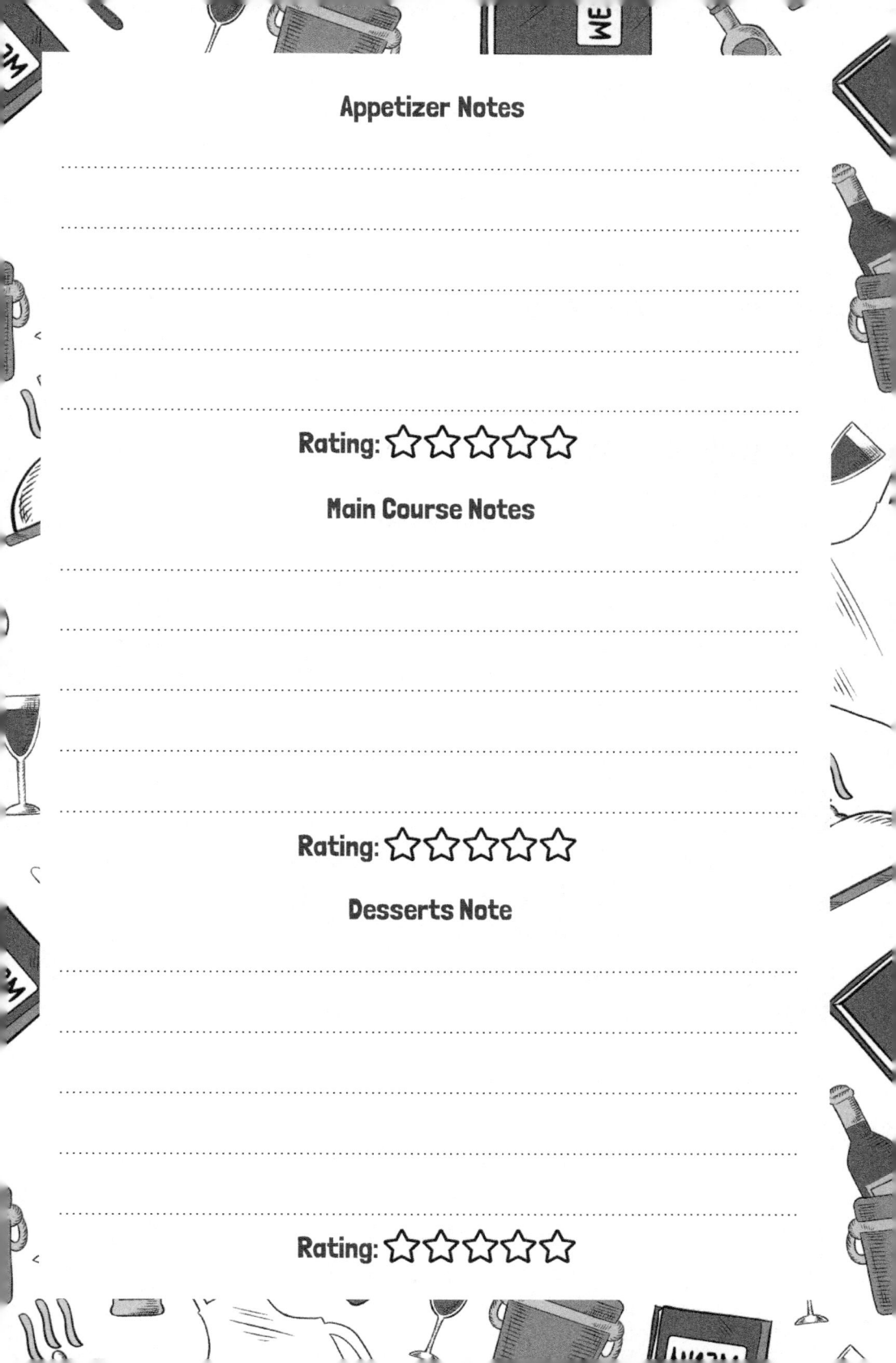

Rating: ☆☆☆☆☆

Restaurant Name:

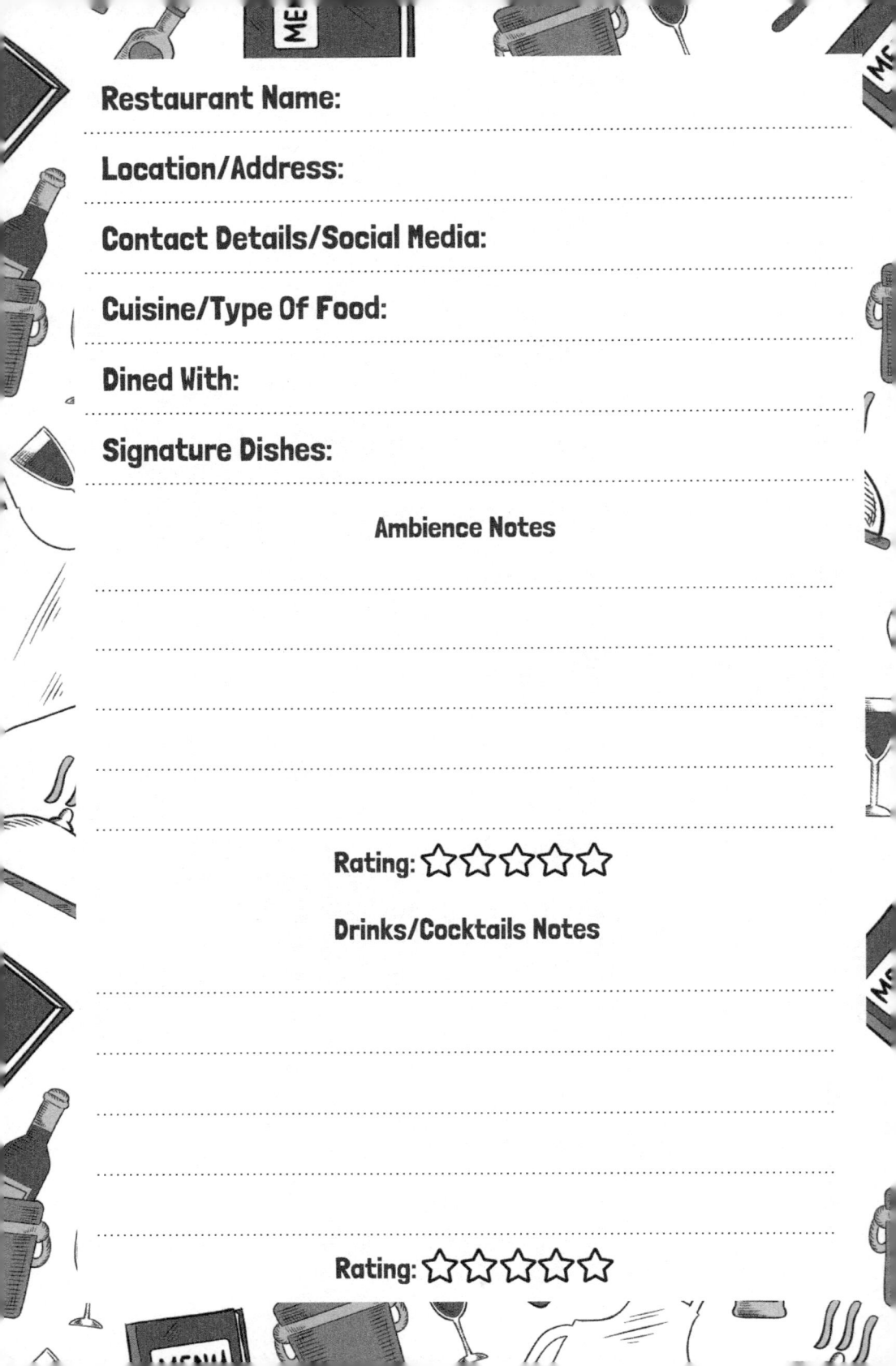

Location/Address:

Contact Details/Social Media:

Cuisine/Type Of Food:

Dined With:

Signature Dishes:

Ambience Notes

Rating: ☆☆☆☆☆

Drinks/Cocktails Notes

Rating: ☆☆☆☆☆

Appetizer Notes

....
....
....
....

Rating: ☆☆☆☆☆

Main Course Notes

....
....
....
....

Rating: ☆☆☆☆☆

Desserts Note

....
....
....
....
....

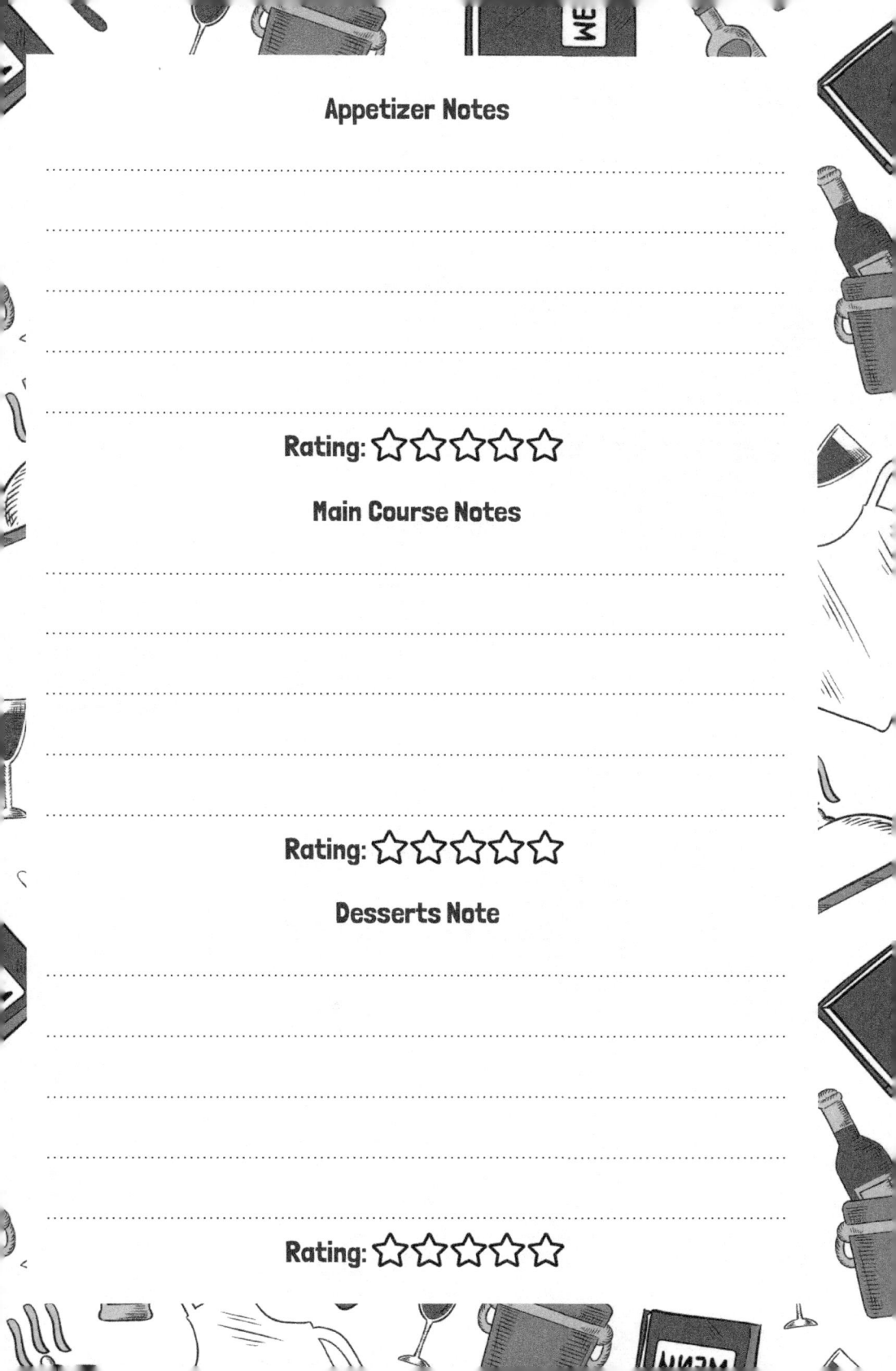

Rating: ☆☆☆☆☆

Restaurant Name:

Location/Address:

Contact Details/Social Media:

Cuisine/Type Of Food:

Dined With:

Signature Dishes:

Ambience Notes

Rating: ☆☆☆☆☆

Drinks/Cocktails Notes

Rating: ☆☆☆☆☆

Appetizer Notes

....
....
....
....

Rating: ☆☆☆☆☆

Main Course Notes

....
....
....
....

Rating: ☆☆☆☆☆

Desserts Note

....
....
....
....

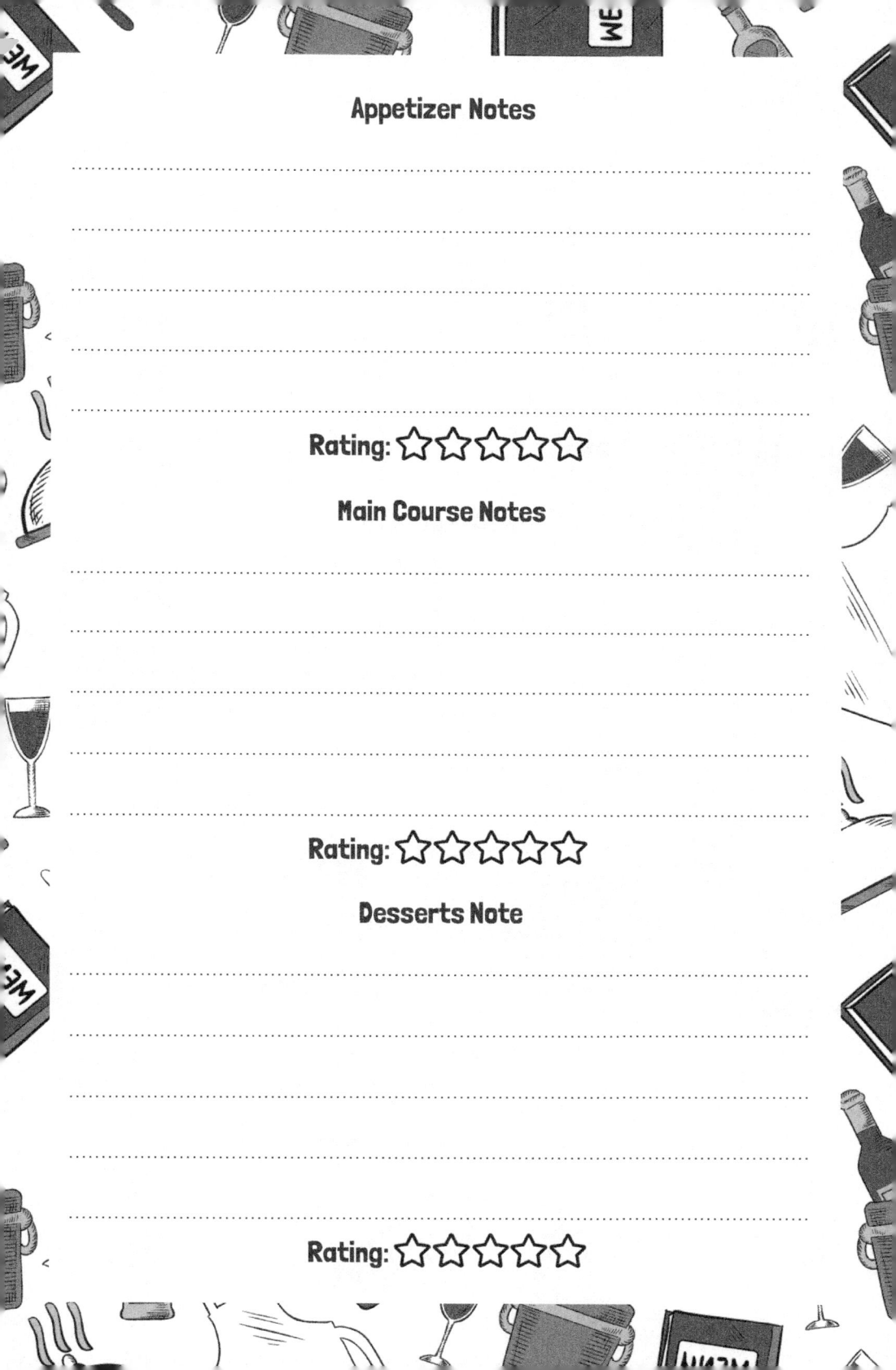

Rating: ☆☆☆☆☆

Restaurant Name:

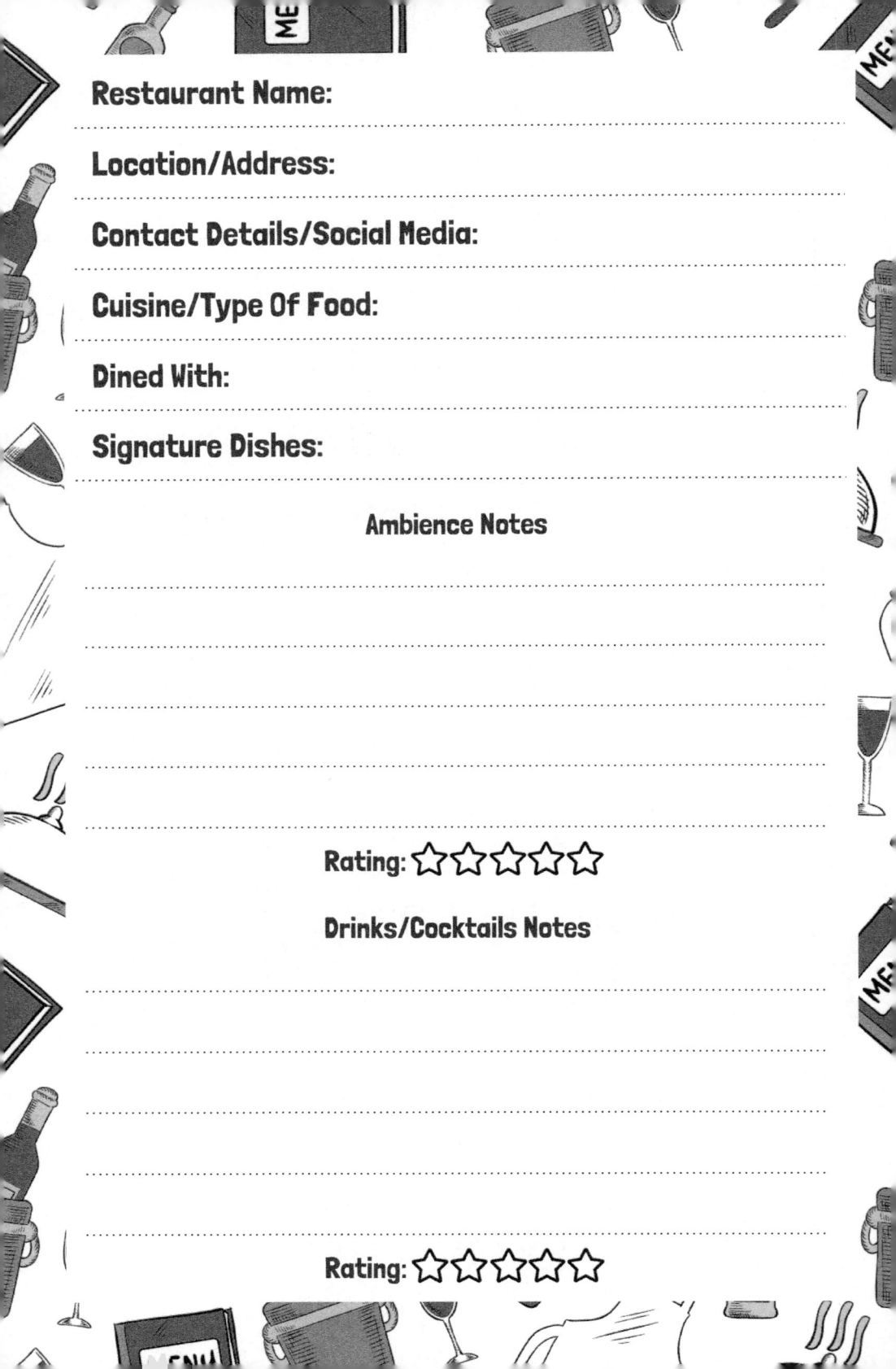

Location/Address:

Contact Details/Social Media:

Cuisine/Type Of Food:

Dined With:

Signature Dishes:

Ambience Notes

Rating: ☆☆☆☆☆

Drinks/Cocktails Notes

Rating: ☆☆☆☆☆

Appetizer Notes

....

....

....

....

Rating: ☆☆☆☆☆

Main Course Notes

....

....

....

....

Rating: ☆☆☆☆☆

Desserts Note

....

....

....

....

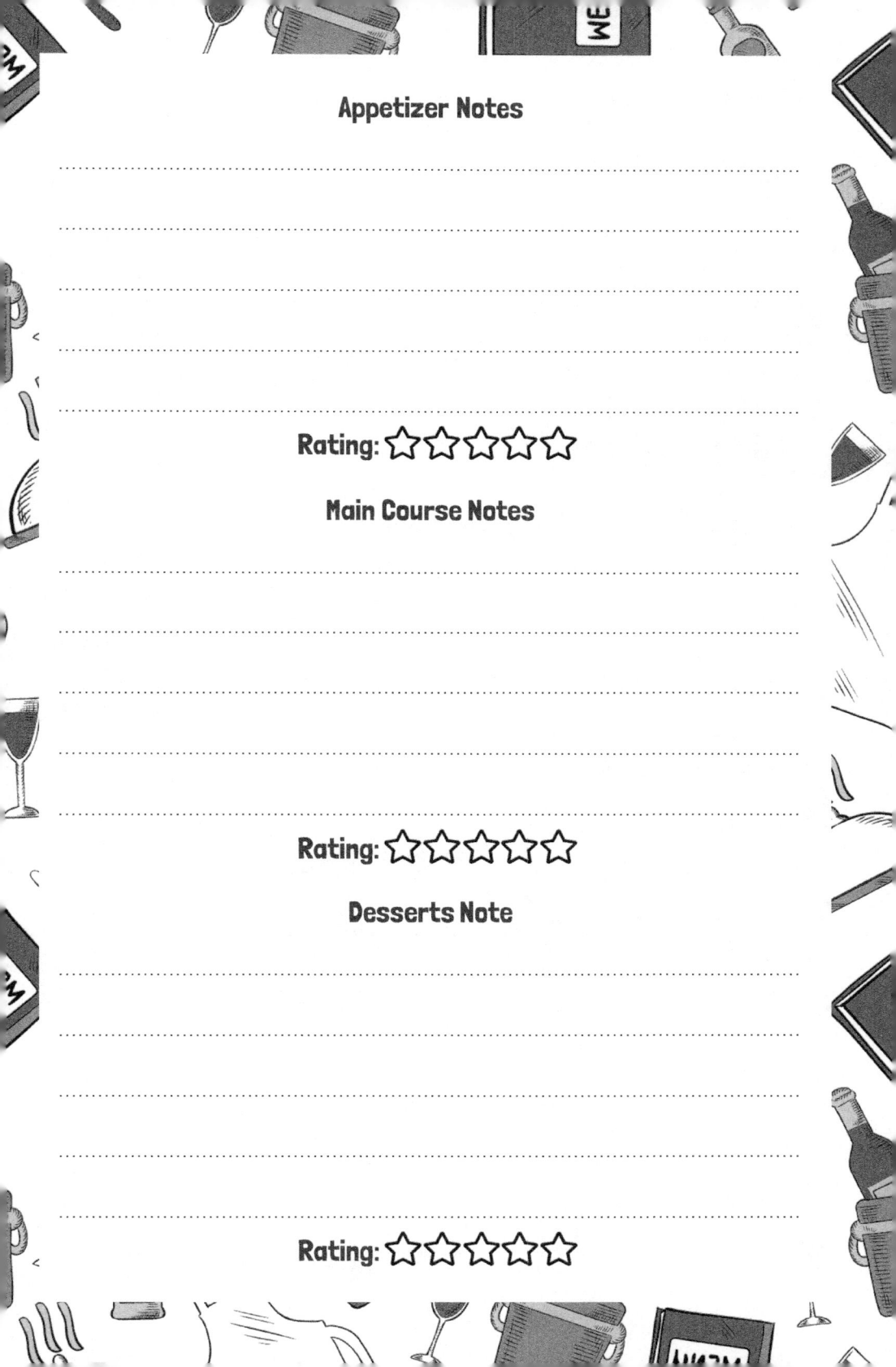

Rating: ☆☆☆☆☆

Restaurant Name:

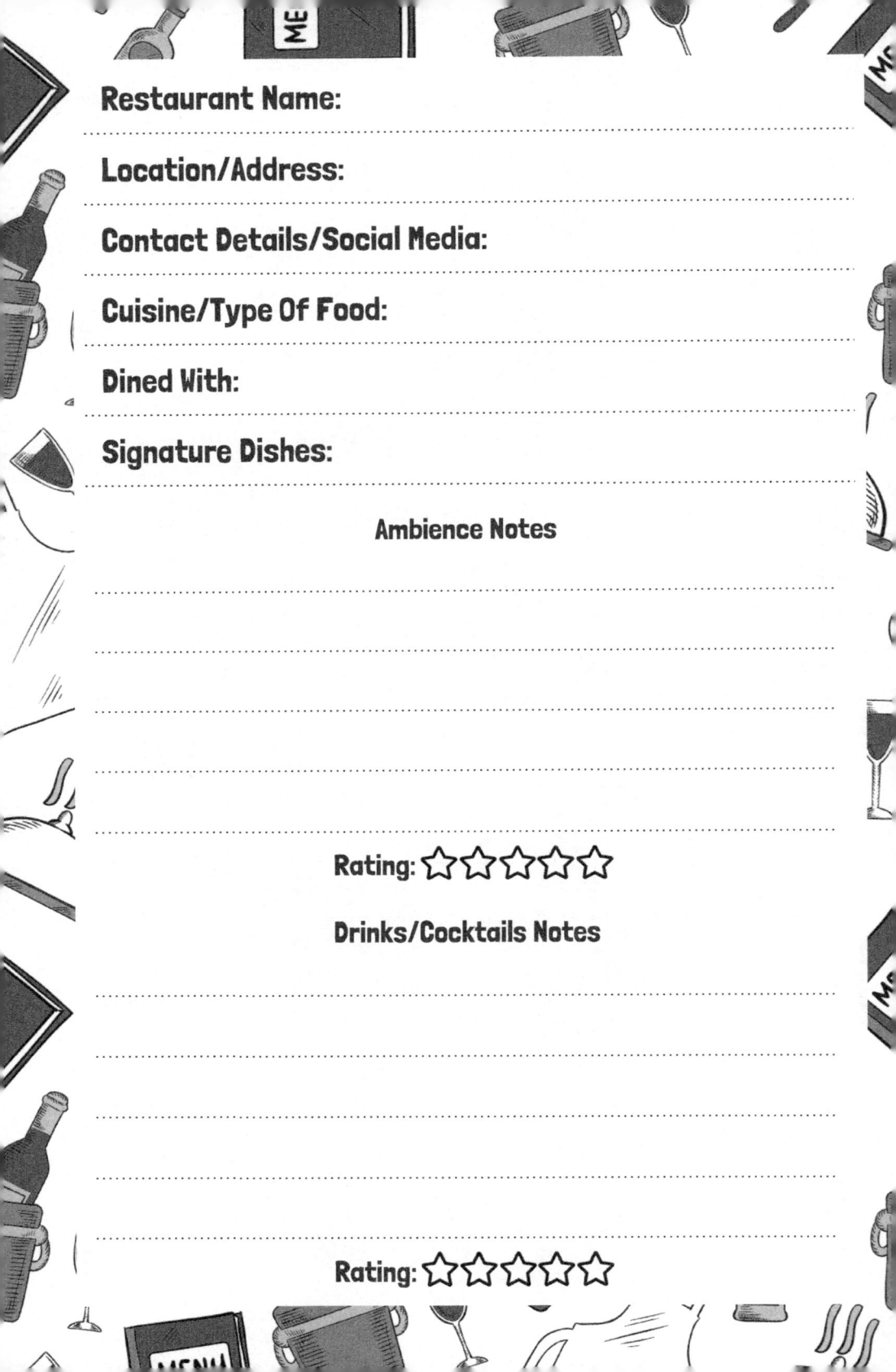

Location/Address:

Contact Details/Social Media:

Cuisine/Type Of Food:

Dined With:

Signature Dishes:

Ambience Notes

Rating: ☆☆☆☆☆

Drinks/Cocktails Notes

Rating: ☆☆☆☆☆

Appetizer Notes

....
....
....
....

Rating: ☆☆☆☆☆

Main Course Notes

....
....
....
....

Rating: ☆☆☆☆☆

Desserts Note

....
....
....
....

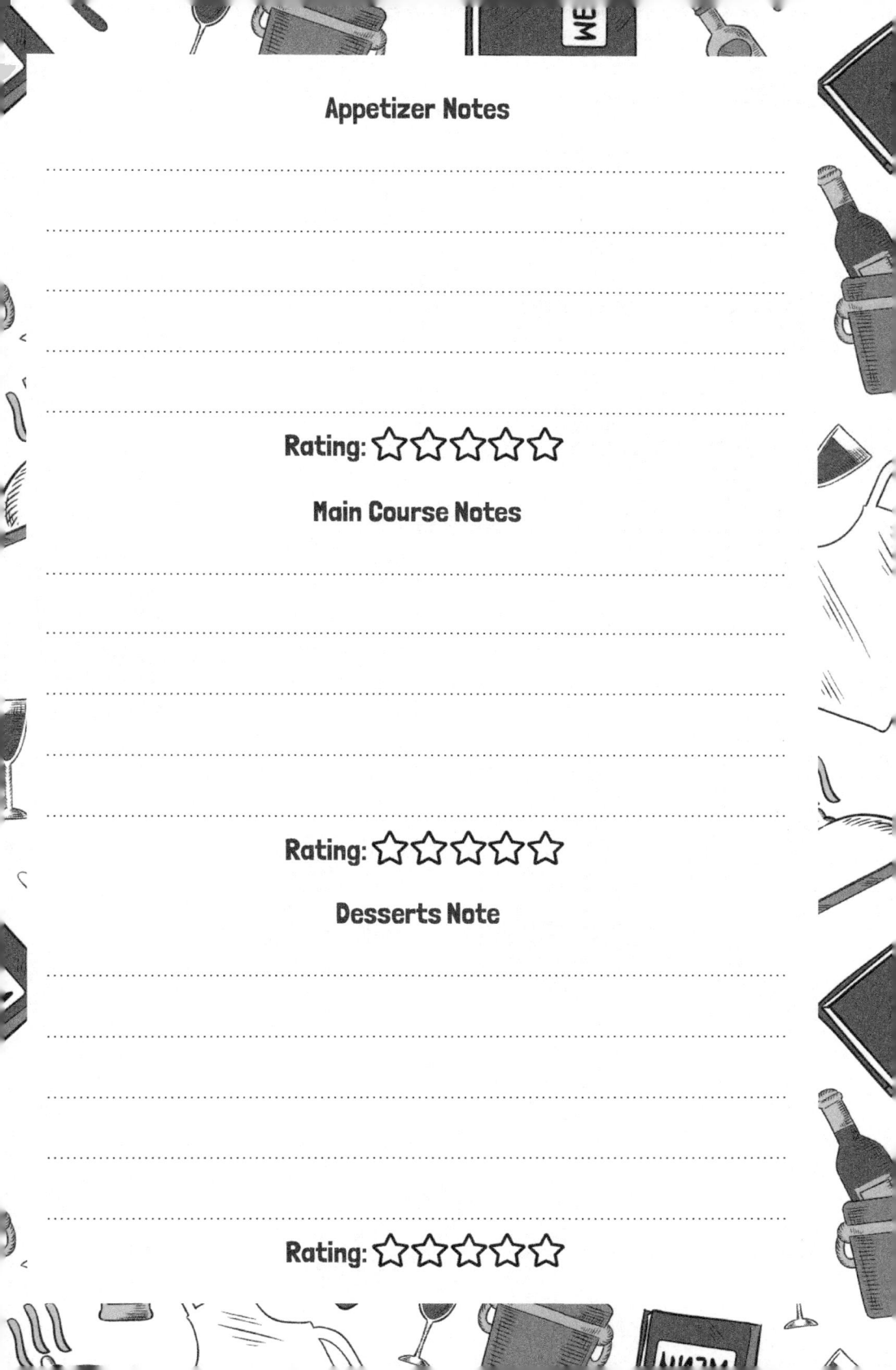

Rating: ☆☆☆☆☆

Restaurant Name:

Location/Address:

Contact Details/Social Media:

Cuisine/Type Of Food:

Dined With:

Signature Dishes:

Ambience Notes

Rating: ☆☆☆☆☆

Drinks/Cocktails Notes

Rating: ☆☆☆☆☆

Appetizer Notes

....

....

....

....

Rating: ☆☆☆☆☆

Main Course Notes

....

....

....

....

Rating: ☆☆☆☆☆

Desserts Note

....

....

....

....

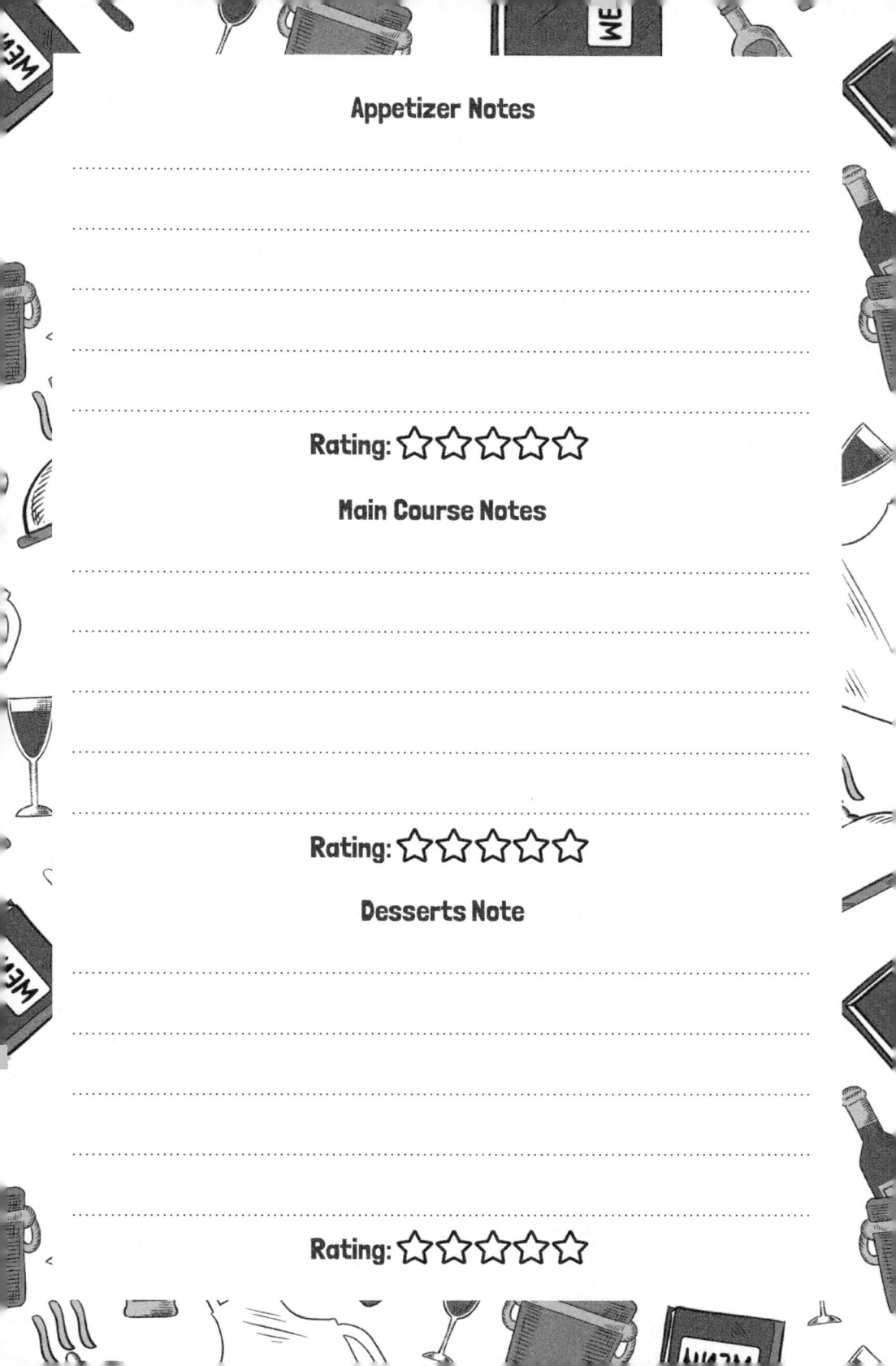

Rating: ☆☆☆☆☆

Printed in Great Britain
by Amazon